CONFLICT & CONNECTION
Baptist Identity in New Zealand

Baptist identity is constantly reconstructing. In New Zealand this has been a difficult, contested process. This book examines both cases of conflict and the strategies for connection which New Zealand Baptists have employed in their short history. Baptists wrestled with each other, wriggled to find space among the denominations and regarded wider colonial society with suspicion. Conflict was endemic in colonial Baptist life and would not be far from the surface for much of the twentieth century. Gradually, the more profound impulse for connection prevailed but the integrity of the emerging Baptist edifice faced severe tests. Mid-century conflicts were survived and a remarkably confident denomination emerged. However, the relative peace and success of the 'fifties meant Baptists were poorly equipped for the upheavals to come. As churches took up the emphases of the renewal movement and other global trends the sense of being Baptist diminished. Institutions which had been a focus of unity declined or were devolved. By century's end conflict over the Baptist way was muted but so was a sense of shared identity. A picture emerges of a dynamic Christian community which finds creative development out of tensions but which begins to drift when potentially divisive issues are ignored or unaddressed.

Martin Sutherland is a Vice-Principal at Laidlaw College in Auckland, New Zealand. He has written extensively on New Zealand Baptist history, Baptist thought in general and theological method. His publications include *Baptists in Colonial New Zealand: documents illustrating Baptist life and development* (2002) and *Peace, Toleration and Decay: the Ecclesiology of Later Stuart Dissent* (2003). He is editor of the *Pacific Journal of Baptist Research*.

ARCHER STUDIES IN PACIFIC CHRISTIANITY

This series explores the experience of Christians in this vibrant region. The best research of new and established scholars will build a more profound understanding of Christian communities, their sense of themselves and their attempts to engage their unique contexts.

CONFLICT & CONNECTION
Baptist Identity in New Zealand

Martin Sutherland

Archer
Press

2011

ISBN 978-0-473-19216-7

Archer Press is an imprint of the New Zealand Baptist Research and Historical Society. PO Box 12149, Auckland, New Zealand

© 2011

For Yvonne,
who first made me a Baptist.

Contents

Preface	xix
Foreword	xxiii
Introduction: situating New Zealand Baptists	1

I. Points of Conflict

Chapter One: Canterbury vs the rest	19
Chapter Two: conflict and connection at Cambridge	33
Chapter Three: the problem of problem pastors	48
Chapter Four: 'downgrade' down under	63
Chapter Five: marking out a space	81
Chapter Six: J.K. Archer and political activism	95

II. Ways of Connection

Chapter Seven: men's ways; women's ways	115
Chapter Eight: *The N.Z. Baptist* as an agent of identity	132
Chapter Nine: from training scheme to college	146

III. Harmony and its Challengers

Chapter Ten: forging unity	167
Chapter Eleven: Machattie and the Baptist Union	180
Chapter Twelve: the roaring 40s	195

IV. Shifting Sands

Chapter Thirteen: hesitating too long - the college 1952-1974	217
Chapter Fourteen: from confidence to confusion	235
Concluding unhistorical postscript	251
Index	255

A Note on Sources and Abbreviations

Despite the progress over recent years the secondary literature on New Zealand Baptists remains thin. No general study has appeared since the centenary volumes in the 1980s. Earlier versions of some of these chapters have appeared in various journals. All have been heavily revised and brought up to date. The principal resources for the historian remain *The N.Z. Baptist* and the New Zealand Baptist Archive, held at Carey Baptist College. The long-running denominational magazine is now available in a digital format, allowing extensive search facilities. Its record of debate and (perhaps more importantly) ordinary Baptist life and witness is remarkable and largely untapped. The archive is similarly rich. Baptists have proved to be good recorders (and, occasionally, obsessive hoarders). Many collections still await detailed analysis. Broader and deeper understanding of the New Zealand Baptist experience will emerge as students and scholars engage this material.

In addition to those signalled in the text, the following abbreviations are used throughout.

NZB	*The New Zealand Baptist*
NZBA	New Zealand Baptist Archive
NZBRHS	New Zealand Baptist Research and Historical Society
NZJBR	*New Zealand Journal of Baptist Research*
PJBR	*Pacific Journal of Baptist Research*

Preface

This is not a history – at least, not in the sense of a chronological account of people and places and organisations. Rather, it is an interpretation of Baptist life in New Zealand, exploring the tension between Baptists' talent for conflict and their desire for connection.

Baptists are never quite sure how to be church. They are the shape-shifters of Christian history. Groups have self-identified as 'Baptist' for at least four centuries, so the name obviously means *something*, but great caution must be exercised in seeking static, essentialist understandings. Whilst emphases and messages echo across the years, there are no simple continuities of style, organisation, moral code or even theological preoccupation. American Tom Nettles has recently argued for an historical Baptist vision which is tightly confessional, most authentic when living within defined doctrinal parameters.[1] But, however useful it might be in his own, North American, polemical context, Nettles' analysis fails to account for the realities of the many Baptist stories worldwide. And that is perhaps the point. Some Baptists do have confessions; some don't. Some are champions for individual liberty; others are not. Some are charismatic, or Arminian, or episcopal - in seeming contradistinction to dispensationalist or Calvinist or radically congregationalist fellow-Baptists. The dynamic of Baptist life is just that: dynamic. Thus, rather than defining Baptist thought by confessions and defended doctrines we may better see it, like the church itself, as *telic*, moving forward, changing and morphing as contexts and demands alter and shift, seeking to reflect a world to come. Rather than *driven* - by logic, institutional form or even text - Baptists may perhaps better be understood to be *drawn* forward, infinitely (if imperfectly) responsive to the rich magnificence of the Kingdom.

The picture on the cover of this book carries some of this sense. The wet sand offers up a striking reflection of the setting sun. The church, imperfectly and with inevitable distortion, is called to mirror a reality beyond itself. It is to show the world to come, in the world that is. The

---

[1] Tom Nettles *The Baptists: Key People in Forming a Baptist Identity* [3 vols] (Fearn, Rossshire: Mentor, 2005-2007).

image is doubly useful for this book. Colonial societies were caught in the tension between reflecting their places or origin and building a life in their new context. They might carry the forms with them, but they could never be the same.

What did it mean to be 'Baptist' in New Zealand? This was the last significant land mass to be settled by human beings and among the last to be substantially shaped by the British Empire. Geographically, environmentally and historically, it is a place apart. Baptists were a small but indicative presence in this intriguing context. Leaving 'Home' in the nineteenth century was no small matter. Only the relatively wealthy might expect ever to return. Leaving, of course, was not the beginning of a story but a moment somewhere in the middle. People left for a reason. Many Baptists were part of an under-recognised English diaspora of those seeking to escape religious constrictions and old arguments. Yet, neither was emigration of itself the end. Baptists, like other colonists, found in the new environment many unanticipated tests. They came with some ideas already formed, but few of these were able to be sustained unchanged in the new setting. There were internal as well as environmental factors. The desire to make connections, to link with other Baptists, meant encountering uncomfortable (sometimes irreconcilable) difference. We can readily see now that this was inevitable. In England, even after three hundred years, the quest to bring together the various elements of Baptist life and thought remained fragile and incomplete. New Zealand Baptists attempted it in one generation. Conflict was inescapable.

The twin themes of conflict and connection weave across and around each other throughout this study. Competing visions of authentic Baptist life are found in the contrasting models of development in Canterbury, Auckland and Dunedin; in the task-oriented Association model and the denominationally aware Union model of connexion; in calls for greater engagement with, or distancing from, politics, the state or other Christian bodies; in disputes over centralised or local identity; in the desire to be seen as a reliable mainstream body and the more freewheeling celebration of life on the edges of Christian witness. The contest was rarely fatal - but neither was it always polite.

The studies in this book seek to explain some of the tensions and to trace the responses of individuals and groups as they struggled to build a religious identity in the new land. Whilst there are lots of people in this story, the selection here is representative rather than exhaustive. There is not much about overseas mission, or social work, or social action, although each enters the narrative at key points. There is not enough in this book about women. The headline conflicts mostly revolved around ministers, and the ministers for most of this period were mostly men. Each of these lenses would grant further insights into New Zealand Baptist life. But you can't do everything. I have chosen to reflect on the values and ideas which have made Baptists disagree and the often closely related forces which hold them together. Quarrels and cohesion, conflict and connection.

Quarrels and disputes can be hurtful things and I realize I touch points which for some may still be sore. As explained below, the major focus is on events from a long time ago. However, as we shall see, the desire to leave past hurts behind can run deep in Baptist life. As one comes close to the present the issues become even more acute. The historian is on risky turf when dealing with events at which he or she was an observer or even a participant. As the final chapter will reveal, I suggest that, in terms of building or maintaining a Baptist identity, the denomination has not done well in recent decades. To analyse is, inevitably, to criticise. I hope those still living who encounter themselves in this narrative do not find the treatment unfair. The last half century has been a difficult time to be a church leader and it needs to be acknowledged that people of good will have consistently sought the best way forward. The interpretations in this book are offered with affection and respect.

Although important sections appear here for the first time, parts of what follows have been seen in other forms over the last decade and a half. This is, nonetheless, a new work and my hope is that the links are clear and the cases are illuminative. The denominational college - a crucial symbol of connection - is the focus of two of the chapters. Whilst this is not intended to cut across another project I am completing, on the history of the college, some of the detail will be common to both. As I reviewed my earlier research I was myself surprised at how consistently the key themes emerged. This book does not tell the whole story. No-one can do that. Rather it brings bits to the surface – some familiar, some never before considered – in an attempt to look at them with fresh eyes. If it succeeds, then I am glad, for it is a story worth telling, and telling again.

Some thanks are needed. I am, first, grateful for the community of Baptists which is the subject of this study. What a diverse, interesting, intriguing, infuriating lot! It has been a privilege to enter their lives, to the degree this is possible for the historian. The research required to bring a project together does not come without cost. Carey Baptist College and

Laidlaw College have assisted with study leave provision. The archive and library at Carey is 'ground zero' for Baptist research in New Zealand. Lesley Utting, Liz Tisdall, Damir Trupinic and Siong Ng, have always been helpful and enabled fruitful delving in this rich and still largely untapped resource. Colleagues have given (mostly) welcome critique and made useful suggestions. Special thanks are due to Laurie Guy for the many discussions on our parallel interests and to Peter Lineham for the inspiration he has been to me as to so many religious historians over the years and for the Foreword he has provided to this volume. Epsom Baptist Church folk have provided encouraging community. They are my spiritual *whanau*, the site of my own covenant and connection. My family has borne the cost of time and distraction which writing entails. Sarah and Andrew have quarried the archives with me at various times; Louisa has attempted to proof-read me into intelligibility. I have dedicated this book to my wife, Yvonne. It is because of her that I first started taking notice of Baptists and she has been an interested ally and help in all my research. Without her this project would not have happened.

Martin Sutherland
June 2011

Foreword

Martin Sutherland's book marks an important step for the understanding of the Baptist community in New Zealand. It is a long overdue work to create the platform for analysis of Baptist history. It is also an engrossing read.

It baffles me that Baptist historical work has been so slow to develop. Like most denominations, there was the usual crop of centenary histories of churches, and then G.T. Beilby's short *Road to Tomorrow* (1957) celebrated 100 years of Baptist work in New Zealand. Finally in 1982 the Baptist Historical Society commissioned four short histories collectively entitled *A Handful of Grain*, by Paul Tonson, Ayson Clifford, Beilby and Stan Edgar.

But in recent years there has been new energy within the Baptist Historical Society, and prominent roles in this have been played by two staff members of Carey Baptist College, Laurie Guy and Martin Sutherland. Between them they have produced two volumes of Baptist historical documents, and a key tool for Baptist analysis has come from the BHS in the form of the production of a searchable database of *The N.Z. Baptist*, the long-lived denominational periodical. Further impetus has been given by the publication over recent years of the *New Zealand Journal of Baptist Research* and then its successor, the *Pacific Journal of Baptist Research*. The opportunity for publication has created a forum for the analysis of Baptist history and has provided opportunity for earlier versions of some of Martin Sutherland's work.

And now this book has lifted the subject still further. It is a marvellous read, as one meets such colourful figures as J.J. North, J.K. Archer and Thomas Spurgeon. The change is not merely one of content. The book represents a depth and a maturity of Baptist scholarship which deserves much praise. Firstly in depth. The skilled use of the minutes of various Baptist Union and College records means that the history is taken under the surface, and controversies are pursued and clarified. The accounts of the structure of the Canterbury rural Baptist community, the development of the Cambridge church, the differences between the southern and northern churches all are significant breakthroughs in understanding their subjects. Secondly in maturity. Small denominations are always at risk of a protective mentality. Too many people in the community are linked to family names, even names in the past. So the result is that the lively dynamism of community formation is softened by concern about the airing of dirty linen. In this book Martin Sutherland challenges the Baptist community to be more mature in exploring its past. As a result he is able to address the key issues that face any developing religious movement; the relationship between its centripetal and centrifugal forces, the organisations (notably the College, the magazine and the annual conference) and the local churches.

This is the real inner 'stuff' of denominational history, and it is critical for an understanding of the church. Martin's knowledge of the wider world of Baptist historiography has given him fine resources to draw on. All religious historians interested in New Zealand will find this study enables them to place the New Zealand Baptist story within the traditions of Baptist history. Hopefully this will also encourage a further development which needs to happen, explaining the contribution of Baptists to the intellectual shape of New Zealand Christianity and the impact of that community on wider society.

Peter Lineham
Associate Professor of History
Massey University, Albany, Auckland.

Introduction: Situating New Zealand Baptists

New Zealand was a very long way from anywhere, for a very long time. Put simply, no-one knew about the place and it was hard to get here. It is probable that there was no Polynesian settlement before the thirteenth century.[1] European attempts at settlement (as opposed to visits to exploit resources such as seals or whales, or missionary ventures to convert) are very recent indeed. Yet the very lateness of the European colonisation of these islands, just gaining momentum at the peak of the Victorian boom, meant comparatively rapid development and a degree of experimentation was possible. This was recognised early by leaders in the colony and articulated most famously by William Pember Reeves, intellectual and politician of the late nineteenth century who celebrated the possibilities for this 'little and latest... nation'.[2] More recently it formed a central theme in the work of James Belich.

> New Zealand is an historian's paradise: a laboratory whose isolation, size, and recency is an advantage, in which grand themes of world history are often played out more rapidly, more separately, and therefore more discernibly, than elsewhere.[3]

In matters of religion the timing and nature of New Zealand colonisation had mixed effects. Institutional ventures were typically the product of broader trends. Early Anglican and Methodist initiatives exhibited all the energies and frailties of the Protestant missionary movement. The Catholic presence too reflected global ecclesio-political issues. Yet for some individuals and groups there was the attractive possibility of fresh air. New Zealand offered new opportunities for religion, just as it did for work, for economic and social advancement, or for political freedom. Emigration had its costs, but it might also have rewards. Many

---

[1] The most recent research, based on radiocarbon dating, suggests 'a recent and rapid human colonization'. See Janet M. Wilmhurst, T.L. Hunt, C.P. Lipo & A.J. Anderson 'High-precision radiocarbon dating shows recent and rapid human colonization of East Polynesia' *Proceedings of the National Academy of Sciences of the United States of America*, December 27, 2010.
[2] See *State Experiments in Australia and New Zealand* (1902).
[3] James Belich, *Making Peoples: A History of the New Zealanders from Polynesian Settlement to the End of the Nineteenth Century* (Auckland: Penguin, 1996), 7.

things were left behind in the old country – some with regret, but others with relief. John Stenhouse has shown that suspicion over the stance of Bishop Selwyn towards Maori land issues had its roots in colonists' memory of the establishment nexus between the landed and the church. In England 'the landed' were the gentry; in New Zealand 'the landed' were the Maori. The suspicion was that the clergy were the pernicious common factor on both settings.[4] Some colonists came to the colony to celebrate their religion; others were keen to shake off oppressive religious structures. Still others – Baptists among them- sought both.

Leaving: an English diaspora?

Much has been made in recent historiography of diaspora studies. Black, Jewish, Italian and, in the New Zealand context, Scottish & Irish population movements have received considerable, often richly productive, attention. However, the possibility and nature of an *English* diaspora has been almost ignored. As Angela McCarthy has recently conceded, 'consideration of the English....is a major lacuna in New Zealand's migration history.'[5] As most Baptist colonists were from England, this suggests some intriguing possibilities. Indeed, the insights of diaspora studies provide a fruitful lens on New Zealand Baptist life. What emerges in turn refines and informs the wider possibility of English diaspora studies.

Most historiographical questions become victims of definition. What makes a movement of people a *diaspora*? The word implies exile, a sense of being not where one began, a confusion over one's true home, one's identity. There are, though, different ways of employing this concept. Narrower definitions of diaspora look primarily to the reasons for leaving and tend to focus on compulsion or distress as motivations for migration. Scottish emigration in the decades following the Highland clearances is a classic example; Irish movement in the wake of the potato famine another. However, the (numerically huge) phenomenon of English emigration seems less easily to fit this restricted approach. A possible reason for the lack of attention to an English diaspora has been the apparent dominance (and therefore assumed cultural power) of English people and structures,

---

[4] J. Stenhouse 'Religion and Society' in G. Byrnes (ed) *The New Oxford History of New Zealand* (Melbourne: Oxford University Press, 2009), 323-356, see esp. 323-327.

[5] A. McCarthy, 'Settlement and Unsettlement' in G. Byrnes (ed) *The New Oxford History of New Zealand* (Melbourne: Oxford University Press, 2009), 173-195, 175.

particularly in the colonisations of North America, Australia and New Zealand. The key elements of compulsion and distress are assumed to be missing. Indeed English hegemony is often cast as the 'other' against which marginalised groups (e.g. the disposed Scots or the starving Irish) must define themselves.

This narrow definition of diaspora has been transcended however. As McCarthy notes, 'other scholars have conceptualised diaspora according to key factors, such as: the dispersal of a population from its homeland and the generation of memories or myths of home; alienation from the host country coupled with a longing and support for home; and the maintenance of a collective identity.'[6] The focus shifts from motivations for leaving and turns instead to the strategies employed for maintaining ethnic identity in the new place.

Opening the arms of diaspora wider in this way allows a more generous embrace. Even the English might be made to fit. The English Diaspora Project at Northumbria University in England focuses on North America and addresses aspects of cultural and ethnic identity.[7] James Belich has written of the 'rise of the Anglo world', consciously emphasising the positive pull of colonisation – the 'boom mentality'.

> The boom mentality...was born in the early nineteenth century, the moment when change seemed to suddenly become commonplace. Previous limitations on the possible were up for renegotiation.[8]

However, these examples continue to reflect the assumption of English self-assurance. Strategies to maintain cultural traditions in America and the drive to extend the Victorian boom are positive factors, signs of strength. Within these broader definitions the English may be granted their own diaspora, but can such a confident, even aggressive movement be truly analogous to the sharper experiences of such as the Scots and the Irish?

More nuanced is Robert Young's call to reappraise the very concept of ethnicity which forms the basis for this broader approach to diaspora studies. Young suggests that, in the Post-Nazi world, 'ethnicity' became a more acceptable category than 'race' (for which it had historically been a

---

[6] McCarthy, 189.
[7] See http://www.northumbria.ac.uk/sd/academic/sass/about/humanities/history/projects/englishdiaspora/ (accessed 25 January 2011) for more information on the project.
[8] James Belich, *Replenishing the Earth: the Settler Revolution and the Rise of the Anglo World, 1783-1939* (Oxford: Oxford University Press, 2009), 203.

virtual synonym). Ethnicity's advantage as the preferred category was that, at least ostensibly, it shifted attention from biology to culture. But for this to be useful it had to imply a unitary, boundaried, definable culture. Does culture anywhere truly fall into such neat packages? Unlikely. Young's view is that, in the case of the English, ethnicity cannot be so constrained without becoming a distortion.

Nineteenth-century England was a place of dynamism and change, 'of perpetual motion', a place where leaving was as important as presence. In Young's analysis, this dialectic of attachment to England, yet distance from it, of continuity and rupture, similarity and difference, became the dominant characteristic of Englishness itself – not Englishness in the sense of the *local* identity of the English, but Englishness as a *diasporic* identity around the world which asserted a grounding in the past and continuity with the centre, and yet at the same time acknowledged the distance of rupture, displacement, migration, colonization.[9] This in turn reflected important features of English life which lie deep in England's history and unique development. Change might have been incremental, but it was constant. Far from a unitary, boundaried culture, 'England and the English have always involved a syncretic community of minorities....There can always be one more.'[10] We might find this dynamism illustrated in such a uniquely English institution as the Common Law. On the face of it a system utterly dependent on precedent and tradition, the Common Law in fact guaranteed that the assumptions and structures of society were never settled. There was always another variation to be made. There can always be one more. By the nineteenth century England's cosmopolitanism - its ability to absorb and to grow with each successive inclusion - was a quality which enabled empire. Yet, it also irrevocably altered the sense of what being English meant. 'Englishness was transformed into an ethnicity unlike any other; because it was no single ethnicity but an amalgamation of many....'[11]

This open, less constrained sense of 'Englishness' raises intriguing possibilities for our understanding of Baptist origins and development. Why was it in England that Baptists emerged at the end of the sixteenth century? If, as I have suggested, Baptist life and thought tends to be

---

[9] Robert J.C. Young, *The Idea of English Ethnicity* (Oxford: Blackwell Publishing, 2008), 7.
[10] Young, 239.
[11] Young, 232.

provisional, incomplete, never resolved, then the extent to which these very qualities were also found in an emerging Early-Modern 'Englishness' makes Baptist groups less anomalous. Anabaptism had broken out when Northern Europe was in flux, only to be neutralised as old structures reasserted themselves. England may well have provided a more naturally fertile soil for the baptistic impulse than had the vestiges of the Holy Roman Empire. Further, though it is beyond the scope of this study, our understanding of the subsequent spread and variation among Baptists may also be informed by these insights. It is tempting, for instance, to speculate that a factor in the unique development of Baptists in the south of the United States (making Southern Baptists unlike any other significant Baptist group) might well have been that the structures and rhythms of the South were shaped more by French than by English influences.

Most importantly, Young redefines any quest for an 'English diaspora'. If there is such a thing it will not be cohesive or unitary. Indeed, if England was a 'syncretic community of minorities' then seeking signs of a broad ethnic identity is misguided. Young's version of 'Englishness' lies in a sense of rupture and displacement – effectively, in diaspora itself. But for the specific experiences of this, for the history, we must turn to the minorities, applying both the broad and the narrow concepts of diaspora to the micro-ethnicities which comprised the kaleidoscope of English culture.

Baptists were one such group.

Once the significance of sub-cultures is accepted, the myth of confident English hegemony dissolves. Indeed, negative drivers for the emigration of specific micro-ethnicities are not hard to identify. Economic disruption, even poverty, was found among many communities. In the England scarred by the effects of the Industrial revolution this should not be a surprise. Rollo Arnold has eloquently described the plight of English villagers who answered the call for rural labourers in New Zealand. 'A combination of social and economic changes had, since the middle of the eighteenth century, turned the majority of village labourers into servile, demoralised men.'[12] Once the tipping point of the 1870s was reached such marginalised individuals and families could readily be wooed by New Zealand immigration agents.

---

[12] Rollo Arnold, *The Farthest Promised Land: English Villagers, New Zealand Immigrants of the 1870s* (Wellington: Victoria University Press with Price Milburn, 1981), 20.

Baptists were certainly not immune from such problems. The English *Baptist Magazine* in 1842 noted the economic factors which appeared to have prompted consideration of New Zealand.

> Letters from various quarters have led us to believe that the thought of emigration has forced itself of late on many reluctant minds, and that solicitude for correct information respecting the state and prospects of other regions is more prevalent among our countrymen now than at any former period. They speak of general and increasing distress, of overwhelming cares and anxieties beneath a constrained placidity of countenance, of unavailing economy and unrequited industry, of diminishing capital, of decreasing trade, and of the startling disclosures of the bankrupt lists. One proposes the formation of a Christian emigration society; another wishes to know whether aid can be obtained to enable him to remove his family to some place where he thinks his difficulties would be fewer than at home; another asks direction to the most eligible of the various lands to which Englishmen may migrate; and minister after minister speaks of the poverty of his friends and the inability of the church of which he is pastor to continue to him a salary, already below his necessities, inquiring for fields of labour open to preachers of the gospel in other regions.[13]

But economic pressures were not the only form of compulsion or trauma which could prompt migration. Religious factors too, though perhaps not quite as obvious as the economic ones, may be identified for specific micro-ethnicities. Here both narrow and broad senses of diaspora apply. Baptists, certainly, were motivated by a desire to escape religious oppression from outside and at the same to leave behind the fruitless internal disputes of their own past. On the other hand they maintained strong connections with Baptists and other Nonconformists in England. The impulse to leave both place and religious context sat in uneasy tension with a vigorous energy to sustain contact with home. Conflict and connection: the New Zealand Baptist experience.

---

[13] This and the following extracts may be found in the *Baptist Magazine* (London, 1842): 353-360 - reprinted in Martin Sutherland (ed) *Baptists in Colonial New Zealand: documents illustrating Baptist life and development* (Auckland: NZBRHS, 2002), 25-28.

Arriving: early Baptist experiences in New Zealand

The first identifiable Baptist in New Zealand was William Wade. Wade's case is indicative of the tensions and restrictions facing English Nonconformists in the early nineteenth century.[14]

From a London Anglican family, Wade became first a Congregationalist and then a Baptist in the 1820s. Attracted to ordained ministry he was thwarted by his mother's opposition, she being 'utterly averse to my entering the Ministry as a Dissenter'. A change of direction to missionary work with the evangelical Anglican Church Missionary Society (C.M.S.) in New Zealand was Wade's attempt to satisfy both his sense of call and his parents' concerns.

> When I made an offer of my services for New Zealand to the church Missionary Society it was with the hope of being employed in a work which seemed to come the nearest of any to that of the sacred Ministry, my non con views hindering me from coming out any other way.[15]

With his wife Sarah, Wade came to New Zealand in 1834. He was intended to be Superintendent of the C.M.S. Press, working with the later more famous printer, William Colenso. The Press, however, was a matter of dispute between the local missionaries and their London authorities and Wade never took up that work. This suited him, as his interest was elsewhere. He wanted to be a missionary, and he wanted to be ordained. This was his opportunity. In August 1835 he was sent to Tauranga to commence mission work. Sometime after, he wrote to Dandeson Coates, Secretary of the CMS in Britain stating his hopes.

> You know, my dear Sir, my early inclination to the work [of] ministry & will not therefore be surprised [were I to] continue as a Missy here at Tauranga rather than [return to] the Press.... Should the Comm^{ee} at Home determine on my return to the Press, I trust I sho^d be found faithful to its duties though unwilling to resume them. But sho^d the Press continue at Paihia & Paihia continue as it was when we were in the Bay I sho^d much doubt whether I could not better serve the cause of Christ by returning to England, if there were any prospect of my entering the ministry there. My desire is to be permitted to end my days

---

[14] On Wade's career in New Zealand see Martin Sutherland, 'A Baptist in the Nest: William Wade and the C.M.S. in New Zealand,' *NZJBR*, 5 (October 2000): 67-83.
[15] Letter, William Wade to Rev. Saunders, Aug. 24/39. Wade's letters are at the Hocken Library, Dunedin. Misc-MS-0323.

here, if the liberty of conscience wh. I have hitherto enjoyed be continued to me.[16]

Wade's determined 'liberty of conscience' would, however, be his undoing. Unsurprisingly, C.M.S. policy could not allow him to move into orders. After five years of frustration and increasingly bitter complaint, Wade left the mission. Conscience, and his right to exercise it as a Dissenter, were prominent in Wade's mind as he wrote a public resignation letter to Dandeson Coates in Jan 1840. His summary is resentful, complaining that his views were known by the C.M.S. at the time of his appointment and seemed then to present no barrier to his service. Yet, when the New Zealand leaders sought to reassign him from the Press, he was caught in a destructive limbo which would prove fatal. On the one side, the local committee would not set up the press adequately - on the other, the parent committee 'will not have a Dissenter engaged in direct missionary work'. Wade found himself to be a Baptist cuckoo in an Anglican nest. Convinced that there was no future for him in the C.M.S., he left New Zealand to commence Baptist ministry in Hobart.[17]

Wade was caught in the peculiarities of pre-colonial missionary New Zealand. Nevertheless, in the 1840s, when more general colonising became possible, religious factors were just as prominent in the discourse of Baptist emigration. The writer in the *Baptist Magazine* may have acknowledged the economic driving factors and potential advantages of leaving for new lands but there was a pointed warning for those considering New Zealand. It is a caution as much indicative of experience in England as it is of concerns for the new environment.

> In this comparatively uninhabited region there is already the germ of a religious establishment. Already there is a bishop! Alas, that church! It haunts us go whither we will. At home it taxes us; it calls us schismatics, points at us with scorn, and frowns on our worship; it proclaims itself our great benefactress, boasts of its unparalleled tolerance, and tramples upon us contemptuously. Abroad it meets us at every turn: in India it circumvents us; in the old colonies it has constructed its fortresses; and if there be a spot of earth in another hemisphere to which an Englishman might repair with hope, it watches his movements, follows him instantaneously, or anticipates his arrival. East or west, north or south, there is no possibility of escaping it; if we sail for the antipodes,

---

[16] Letter, William Wade to Dandeson Coates [1835], 1
[17] See Letter, William Wade to Dandeson Coates, Jan. 13, 1840.

thither it vaults and meets us on our landing.... [A] bishop recognized by the secular governor as his spiritual colleague, cannot fail to be an object of jealousy to all who, being acquainted with the history of episcopalian ecclesiastics and the claims they are now making, are anxious for the religious liberties of the infant colony.

New Zealand never adopted an established church model but this did not mean that the fears of the writer in the *Baptist Magazine* were completely unfounded. Unofficial concessions to the Church of England were (and arguably remain) common. They formed the basis of Baptist concern over religion in schools in the 1890s. Conversely, the very lack of an established church left an identity vacuum for Baptists. In the very different religious context of the colony, whom would they define themselves over and against? If they were any longer Dissenters, what now were they dissenting from? This was a deeper problem and it lies at the roots of the tensions between conflict and connection in New Zealand Baptist life. Could Baptists find a means of self-definition or must they be constantly positioning themselves in relation to others?

In the light of its concerns about incipient Establishment, the *Baptist Magazine* (perhaps imagining there might be strength in numbers) exhorted an organised approach to emigration.

Should any of our friends think of seeking a home in New Zealand, they will do well to act in concert, and in so doing they may probably obtain advantages which otherwise they would lose. In some of our village churches, it may perhaps be worth consideration whether it would not be possible, as a body, to transfer themselves with their pastor to a place where they would be relieved from difficulties under which they are now labouring, and where they might form a truly Christian community with brighter prospects than they have at present in reference to secular affairs.

In the event, only one significant attempt was made at organised settlement. In 1862, a Nonconformist settler group (numbering over a thousand), organised by Baptists but including equal numbers of Methodists and Congregationalists, left England to set up 'Albertland', north of Auckland. The principal religious leader in the group, Samuel Edger, had been trained at the Baptist-aligned Stepney College. Always a radical thinker, Edger's vision was not merely for a settlement free from establishment but from sectarianism itself. Few in the group shared this vision thoroughly. Edger moved to Auckland in 1866 and established himself as leading freethinker. At Albertland there was a good deal of the interdenominational cooperation typical of the colonial environment but confessional loyalties were soon asserted. A Baptist congregation was formed around the influential Brookes family and a chapel erected in 1867. This group was a founding member of the New Zealand Baptist Union in 1882.[18]

Albertland was an exception, which soon complied with the rule. More typically, Baptists would make their way to the new colony as individuals or extended family groups. Often they would settle, comfortably worshipping with other groups - usually Methodist or Congregationalist, sometimes Presbyterian, rarely Anglican – until enough Baptists arrived to set up their own fellowship. There was thus an easy openness to the compromises of colonial life whilst at the same time a deeply retained identification with the religious context they had so recently left. Ken Manley has shown how in Australia 'the earliest colonial churches sought the reassurance that creating replicas of the church life they had known back 'home' provided.'[19] The same is true for New Zealand, although this determination to keep one eye on Baptist heritage could have both positive and negative elements. There was a clear wish to establish familiar structures, but often an equally determined desire to avoid the divisions of the past. These sometimes competing urges may be observed in the formations of churches in Nelson in 1851 (the first to be constituted in the colony) and Christchurch (later Oxford Terrace) in 1863.

Nelson began in classic fashion. Henry Cooper Daniell (1817-1895), a founding member and at some point a local Crown Land Commissioner, recorded that a 'carpenter of the name of Horn ... apparently very seriously impressed' became convicted of Baptist principles, persuading a friend to baptise him, then in turn baptising the other. Horn gathered a group and set up a chapel. This nascent church then wrote to contacts in England, seeking a minister. Decimus Dolamore answered the call and arrived in 1851 to find there had already been a split in the church over Horn's supposed doctrinal errors. There were disputes between the two groups over land grants but the key issues had to do with power and leadership

---

[18] See Peter Lineham's entry on Edger in *The Dictionary of New Zealand Biography* (Vol 2) (Wellington: Bridget Williams Books/Dept of Internal Affairs, 1993), 128. On Albertland and the Minniesdale church see J.L. Borrows *Albertland* (Wellington: Reed, 1969) and P. Tonson, *A Handful of Grain: The Centenary History of the Baptist Union of N.Z.* Vol. 1 – 1851-1882 (Wellington: NZ Baptist Historical Society, 1982), 66-68.

[19] Ken R. Manley, *From Wooloomooloo to 'Eternity': A History of Australian Baptists* (Bletchley, Milton Keynes: Paternoster, 2006),13 and *passim*.

style. Dolamore threw in his lot with Horn's opponents and a new church was constituted with 15 members. Here then was a small group, in the earliest days of the colony, born out of conflict yet determined to find its own way and to connect this with denominational life in England. Daniell was concerned that it be recognised by authorities as 'in the true sense of the word, Baptists.'[20]

Dolamore was also materially involved in the establishment of the Christchurch cause. This church too was the result of Baptists finding one another in the growing settlement and determining to covenant together. Organisers had already been in contact with Dolamore, to determine if he might move to Christchurch to lead a new church. Dolamore indicated willingness, but with important conditions.

> There is another subject on which it is very necessary we should understand each other and if possible fully agree.
>
> The churches in this Province & I heartily concur with them have from the beginning felt it their duty to receive to Baptism & Membership all those they believe to be saved by Divine Grace. Hence they reject the terms *general & particular* Baptist as applying to the churches and regard them simply as Baptist churches or churches of baptized believers. Acting on these principles members of general and particular Baptist churches are alike welcomed by us. So with persons led to Jesus among us and applying for Baptism & Membership. If I believe a person thus applying a Child of God I dare not refuse to baptise him altho. I may think his views on some points not scriptural. Nor can any Christian church refuse to receive him without claiming and exercising an authority not given it by the Lord. That is if they believe him a partaker with them of God's saving grace.

'General' and 'Particular' were of course the distinguishing denominational labels which had for two centuries separated Arminian and Calvinistic Baptists in England. In 1857 a church was formed in Rangiora near Christchurch along Strict and Particular lines but this group was largely based around one extended family and, by the time of the formation of the Union in 1882, had become non-functioning.

The Baptists of Christchurch accepted Dolamore's terms. As had been the case at Nelson, the new Christchurch church was gathered in a traditional manner, thus maintaining continuity with familiar models.

---

[20] Daniell's account is to be found in C. Kershaw and W. Teeboon, *A Short History of the Nelson Baptist church* 1851-1951 (Nelson: 1951), 7-9.

Nonetheless, there was an incipient desire to avoid the doctrinal divisions which had dogged Baptist life in England. Life in the colony meant a chance at a new beginning, as they appeared at least willing to try it.

Conflict and Connection

Such high intentions, however, rarely prevailed. Indeed division and dispute were endemic in the early Baptist causes and never far from the surface across the whole history of these churches in New Zealand. Nelson, as we have seen, was split before it began. The inclusive spirit at Christchurch lasted less than a year. Dolamore resigned in 1864 amid dissension over open or closed communion and approaches to discipline. As we shall see in chapter three, under his successor James Thornton there was to be no calming of the troubled seas.

Conflict, it must be accepted, is a feature of Baptist polity. In 1904. South Australian John Paynter noted that Baptists are distinguished by 'creed and temper, perhaps more temper than creed.'[21] If anything, this feature was going to be magnified in a colonial context. Those who gathered, often via advertisement in local newspapers, may have had little in common except a Baptist background of some stripe. They lacked the shared memory of long-established communities. Before imposing himself on Christchurch, Thornton had previously been minister at Auckland and had had a troubled time there too. By his report, the thirteen members with which he began in Auckland had 'as many different creeds, each contending for the adoption of his own.'[22] Facilities were poor and the transience of the population often dramatically affected church life. We shall see the significance of this at Cambridge. In his survey of 1881 James Upton Davis noted its impact on Hanover St in Dunedin.

> Since its foundation there have been three ministers. Under Mr Parsons 300 joined the church—of whom 40 only remain; under Mr Williams, 180—of whom 80 remain; and under the present ministry, 200—of whom 140 remain. That is to say, in seventeen years 580 members have been received, 420 have been lost, and 250 are still on the books. These

---

[21] Cited in Manley, 226.
[22] J. Thornton, Letter, 1 July 1861 printed in the *Baptist Magazine*, November 1861, 713.

figures are valuable, as showing the great changes to which even a city church is liable in this colony. [23]

Ministry too was a problem. Colonial church life reflected the messiness of the frontier, with mercurial - often brilliant but as frequently deeply flawed - characters coming to the fore early. New Zealand Baptists attracted quite a number of these. James Thornton and William Birch had strangely similar histories. Both caused ructions in Auckland and then subsequently both transferred this tension to Christchurch. If not as aggressively as Thornton and Birch, many of the early ministers floundered in the strange environment.[24] The advent of the Baptist Theological College brought some uniformity to training and the shaping of the pastorate, but the nature of Baptist ecclesiology lends itself to the emergence of charismatic or just plain pushy individuals who find a place, at least for a time, in ministry. A number of these will appear in subsequent chapters. Preachers of more reliable character could still encounter troubles. Charles Crisp Brown was subject to one of the few 'heresy trials' New Zealand Baptists have attempted, doubling his risk by implicating the powerful Spurgeon legacy. Others, more radical, found Baptists in the small Dominion frustratingly conservative. J.K. Archer is an important example, finally opting for party politics as a more effective political arena than what he found to be a disappointingly passive or narrowly preoccupied Nonconformist conscience.

Much of the conflict which can be observed in New Zealand Baptist life may be understood as part of the struggle for identity which was always going to be a challenge in a colony of exiles. Early Canterbury Baptists developed a free-wheeling model which clashed with the more defined denominationalism of the leaders of the Union. The crisis at Napier in the 1930s was not merely the outcome of the earthquake or the fault of the unpredictable Oswald Machattie. It reflected tensions over the centralisation of power which followed the Baptist Union Act of Incorporation in 1923. Personal factors and a wider anxiety to be regarded as reliable and respectable fed the disputes of the 1940s.

The dream that the quarrels of the past might be left behind in the new colony proved elusive. In fact the disputatious history of (mostly English)

---

[23] J.U. Davis, 'The Baptists in New Zealand', *NZB* Feb 1881, 1-4.
[24] The problem was common to new colonies. On the New South Wales experience see Allan M. Grocott, *Convicts, Clergymen and Churches* (Sydney: Sydney University Press, 1980), 218-224.

Baptists merely fed the growing pains of the emerging churches and denomination. The history of New Zealand Baptists is a litany of conflict. Yet this is clearly not the whole picture. Luke Jenkins, as he rued his demise as Principal of the College in 1952, predicted Baptists would disintegrate into a 'sect of Brethrenism'.[25] He was wrong. Churches have faced difficulty and division, sometimes over and over, and yet maintained their life and even flourished. A Union was indeed formed and survived against the odds. Although it came close to schism in the 1890s it has never split. Whilst conflict clearly constantly tested New Zealand Baptists the drive for connection is just as evident, and arguably more powerful.

To focus only on controversy and dispute would be to miss the full story of the development of Baptist life in New Zealand. It is as important to examine the means by which Baptists sought to define themselves more effectively, to forge an identity, even if that identity has never been settled, always contested. In the first formation of the church at Cambridge, forces of both connection and conflict may be observed. Institutions such as *The N.Z. Baptist*, the Missionary Society, the various national organisations and the College became important vehicles for building unity. The concern to downplay or forget past disputes and scandals which is examined in chapter ten reflects an embarrassment about what might be seen as a typical Baptist fractiousness and a desire to present a unified front to other churches and to society at large. In mid-twentieth century a new confidence, led and instilled by J.J. North did emerge, emboldening Baptists to make a claim to be taken seriously. It did not, perhaps could not, last. Indeed its peak in the 1950s marked the commencement of its decline. The quest for a New Zealand Baptist identity would be recast by the charismatic movement and the pressures of the challenging 1990s and 2000s.

Although New Zealand Baptists have never been a large group their story displays the complexities and puzzles of bigger communities of faith. This book does not pretend to resolve or explain all these issues but it does find some shapes in the chaos. It has four broadly chronological sections. In the first part the dominant theme is conflict. Baptists wrestled with each other, wriggled to find space among the denominations and regarded wider colonial society with suspicion. Gradually, however the more profound impulse for connection prevailed. Section Two examines the institutions and strategies employed to forge a credible denomination. James Belich has pointed out that to 'forge' has more than one meaning. The authenticity of

---

[25] Letter, Luke Jenkins to P.F. Lanyon (undated), NZBA, B.1/80.

the Baptist edifice came under severe test. In Section Three it will be seen that whilst the dramatic conflicts of the 'thirties and 'forties could be survived the relative peace and successes of the 'fifties were ultimately the greater threat, leaving Baptists poorly equipped for the upheavals of the 'sixties and beyond. A shorter, concluding section looks across that later period, noting the continuation of some of the themes of the earlier decades but focusing more on broader trends.

Much study of the more recent period remains to be done. The structure and the weight of material in this book clearly give greater attention to the first century of New Zealand Baptist life. Little apology is needed for that emphasis. The early period is not just inadequately understood - among most contemporary Baptists it is largely unknown. For that reason alone it deserves to be highlighted. Moreover, patterns were set in these decades which influence us still.

Baptists are sometimes surprised to learn that they have not discovered every insight - or contrived every problem. There is a legitimate desire in Baptist thought not to be shackled by the weight of tradition. That cannot, should not, must not divorce us from our past. Baptists have a history, and this book attempts to learn from it.

Part I
Points of Conflict

Chapter One: Canterbury *vs* the rest

The immigration of Baptists to New Zealand was a piecemeal affair. Individual cases such as that of William Wade, confirmed by the wider reflections of the *Baptist Magazine* in 1842, suggest a restlessness, a desire to escape religious constriction, but there was no grand plan or design. Unlike the Anglicans, Methodists and Catholics, Baptists did not have a missionary initiative in New Zealand on which to build later structures. The aspirations which drove the Albertland settlement were unfulfilled and, in any case, would hardly have altered this fundamental picture. Being Baptist may have contributed to the motivation to leave England, but it seems to have played little direct role in the way settlement occurred in the new colony. Most came with little more connection than the informal links by which individuals and families called for or followed friends and relations.

It is not surprising, then, that significant regional differences may be observed in patterns of Baptist development in colonial New Zealand. In Wellington, the capital from 1865, progress was very slow. Baptists emerged much more quickly in the Canterbury, Auckland and Otago regions. Of the 25 churches which constituted the Baptist Union of New Zealand at its foundation in 1882, eleven (44%) were in Canterbury, seven in Auckland and two in Otago, with just five from the rest of the colony. Such figures might imply the dominance of Canterbury. Membership statistics, however, suggest a different story. In 1885, when reliable figures first emerge, Canterbury churches had 720 members between them, Auckland was larger at 922 and Otago not far behind at 635.

Canterbury had a higher number of small churches, distributed in a unique pattern. Seven of the eleven were outside the main towns of Christchurch and Timaru. By contrast, in Auckland only two of seven were in such rural settings. Both of the churches in Otago, and all five of those elsewhere in the colony were found in substantial colonial towns. Canterbury thus presents some intriguing points of difference. The pattern of small rural churches is, in fact, exceptional in New Zealand Baptist history. The reasons for this atypical development are worth examining. Canterbury's early Baptist history was influenced by economic and social factors which combined with the particularities of key leaders to encourage the brief flourishing of a unique culture of church settlement. Importantly, it generated a different vision of what Baptist life might be like and set the Canterbury Baptists over and against others in the colony.

An irony of the apparent Baptist success in Canterbury is that this region, of any in the new colony, might have suffered the worst of the disadvantages which we have seen identified by the 1842 writer in the *Baptist Magazine*. Firmly identifying the Church of England as the chief Baptist bogey, the writer was pessimistic about the chances of genuine release from its grip. 'East or West, North or South, there is no possibility of escaping it; if we sail for the antipodes, thither it vaults and meets us on our landing.'[1] Canterbury was indeed planned to be an ideal Church of England settlement. Formed in 1848 to manage the project, the Canterbury Association had the Archbishop of Canterbury as its President. Although the settlement was not a venture of the church itself, Anglicans were to be accorded privileges of land purchase and there were designated funds for Anglican religious and educational purposes. The rhetoric greatly exceeded the eventual reality. No proof of Church of England membership was demanded and a lack of applicants together with a financial crisis led quickly to the relaxation of the original rules. Nevertheless, although 'Anglican Canterbury was never effectively policy', the Church of England had 'vaulted' to Canterbury in a manner more profound and thorough than in any other part of the new colony.[2]

Some Baptists, it is clear, slipped through the net. Nineteen were recorded in a census of 1851.[3] By the mid-1860s four churches had been formed – two in the main town, Christchurch and two in rural villages. Remarkably, in the 1870s no fewer than eight small rural churches were constituted. By 1880 only nine Baptist churches had been formed in the entire rest of the country. By contrast there were twelve in the central part of the Canterbury province alone.

---

[1] *Baptist Magazine* (1842): 353-60, 358.
[2] J. Cookson, 'Pilgrim's Progress – Image, Identity and Myth in Christchurch' in J. Cookson and Graeme Dunstall (eds) *Southern Capital Christchurch: Towards a City Biography 1850-2000* (Christchurch: Canterbury University Press, 2000), 13-40, 18. On the Canterbury Association and Settlement see W.D. McIntyre 'Introduction' to *The Journal of Henry Sewell*, Vol. 1. 1853-7 (Christchurch: Whitcoulls, 1980), 31-67.
[3] J. Hight & C.R. Straubel (eds) *A History of Canterbury*, (Vol. I) (Christchurch: Canterbury Centennial Association, 1957), 248.

Seven of these churches were in what would become, in 1876, the Selwyn County, an extensive local body area which took in the plains and foothills south and east of Christchurch – essentially the land between the major rivers: Waimakariri in the north and Rakaia in the south. That a cluster of Baptist churches should appear together in this area is a remarkable but in many ways explicable development.

Until 1876 local government in New Zealand had consisted of large Provincial Councils. The Canterbury Province had been one of the most extensive and successful of these. However, with the growing strength of central government, the provinces were deemed to be an impediment to progress and were abolished. Canterbury was divided into six counties and three boroughs. Selwyn was without question the most important of the counties. Although it was largely an administrative fiction, lacking integration or cohesion, within the boundaries of Selwyn lay significant resources and profitable industries. At this point in the 1870s it was enjoying a boom. The roots of this prosperity lay in the early years of the Canterbury Settlement. As Christchurch began to grow, its fuel and timber needs quickly exhausted the immediately available native bush. The nearest significant sources lay in the Malvern Hills, fifty miles to the West. From the mid 1850s coal was being mined to supply the town and by 1857 a rudimentary road (a 'coal track') had been cut to Sheffield. By 1875 this had been supplemented by a railway, reaching coal deposits in both the north and south Malvern Hills.[4]

The plains, too, proved bountiful. Farming had been initially an extensive, pastoral activity, with wool the principal product. It was soon discovered that the plains could sustain huge crops of wheat. Canterbury became the grain silo of New Zealand. For two decades from the mid 1870s the 'wheat bonanza' established Canterbury among the wealthiest parts of the country, with Selwyn County a key grain producing area.[5] This combined with a generous plan for the conversion of pastoral leases into freehold tenure to create a land boom and generate a massive increase in the population.[6]

---

[4] G.L. Popple, *Malvern County: A Centennial History* (Darfield: Malvern County Council, 1953), 63-4; 70-71.
[5] G. Cant & R. Kirkpatrick (eds) *Rural Canterbury: Celebrating its History* (Wellington: Daphne Brasell Associates Ltd, 2001), 61-79.
[6] The population of Canterbury more than doubled between 1868 and 1876. See W.J. Gardner, *A History of Canterbury* (Vol. II) (Christchurch: Canterbury Centennial Historical and Literary Committee, 1971), 313.

Baptists in England had not been particularly associated with either farming or mining. The picture does not appear to have been significantly different in New Zealand.[7] The strength of these industries alone does not account for the number of Baptist churches. More important is that Selwyn's general prosperity produced a surge in its population. Indeed, In the 1870s and 80s the Selwyn County had the largest population of any single local body. Even when the borough clusters of the main centres are combined, Selwyn holds its high place, second only to the gold-rush fuelled Dunedin and eventually Auckland.

Populations in Boroughs and Selwyn County

	1878	1881	1886
Auck Brghs	18509	22410	44374
Wellington	18953	20563	25945
Chch Brghs	23411	27800	33651
Dunedin Brghs	35383	43762	47753
Selwyn County	27309	34323	34392

The size of the local general population was clearly a factor in Baptist development. It would be anticipated that as the general population grew, so did the total of Baptists. However, the figures suggest a more subtle pattern than a simple arithmetical progression. There appears to have been a direct relation between the population and the *proportion* of persons identifying themselves as Baptist. This becomes evident when the population statistics are correlated to the percentage of Baptists recorded in each centre. In Selwyn, from 1876-1896, as the population grew towards the mid-30,000s then plateaued, the percentage of Baptists also grew and levelled off in direct relation, peaking at 3.49% in 1886. The relationship was breaking down by 1891 as the population went into decline. Similar patterns are evident for Baptists in Auckland, urban Christchurch and Wellington. The figures for Dunedin, where the proportion of Baptists was higher overall, are less clear. Nevertheless, there seems to be a clear connection between increasing *density* of population and the proportion of that population who will identify themselves as Baptist. Beyond a certain

---

[7] See Brian Smith '"Wherefore then this thusness:" the social composition of Baptist congregations in New Zealand.' *NZJBR* (October, 1998): 71-83.

point the Baptist proportion levels out, even though the population continues to grow.

This phenomenon may be a feature of developing regions everywhere and reflects the nature of gathered church polity. The achievement of a critical mass of population would clearly be conducive to the emergence of Baptist churches. Until these were able to appear, potential Baptists may well have attached to other Christian communities. Something like this appears to have occurred in the farming district of Greendale in Canterbury where from 1865 a combined meeting was held, led by a rotation of Wesleyan, Primitive Methodist, Baptist, Congregational, Brethren and Presbyterian preachers. By 1872, however, the locality was developed enough for the Primitive Methodists, the Presbyterians and the Baptists to found their own separate entities.[8]

There were other local factors at play. The peculiarities of the land sales system, combined with the rapidly increasing population in Canterbury, necessitated 'village settlement' schemes, resulting in a surprising number of small communities dotted around the countryside. One historian has noted that, by the mid-1870s, along with roads and fences, 'other evidences of settled farming existence were most noticeable in [Selwyn and the strip immediately north of the Waimakariri]: the beginnings at road junctions of village clusters of church or chapel, school and library buildings, smithy and hotel'.[9] Economic circumstances and population density combined to generate small towns and a consequent demand for the small traders and artisans among whom Baptists have typically been found.

That the economic and demographic trends were a factor in the history of the small rural churches of Canterbury is certain. However, such material issues alone do not sufficiently explain the atypical development pattern in this region. Auckland and Otago both had growing populations and high proportions of Baptists, but development in those regions took a very different form.

When the Baptist Union was constituted in 1882 there were seven churches in the Auckland region. Of these, only Minniesdale (the Albertland chapel) and Auckland had emerged independently. The other five were in one way or another formed at the initiative of the strong

---

[8] T.W. Adams, undated manuscript reprinted in M. Sutherland *Baptists in Colonial New Zealand: documents illustrating baptist life and development* (Auckland: NZBRHS, 2002), 32-34.
[9] Gardner, 312.

Auckland church. Typical was Cambridge, unusual in being a rural church, some 150 kilometres from Auckland city. In 1881, after a few months of informal Bible study meetings, a group took a step towards church formation, not by independently covenanting together, but by first turning to the Auckland church for assistance. Cambridge is studied in more detail in the next chapter, but this pattern of church planting under the sponsorship of an existing strong fellowship was also followed in Dunedin, where the city church enabled an independent fellowship at Caversham in 1873. Each of these two would subsequently facilitate a number of new causes in Otago.

In Canterbury in the 1870s the picture was very different. In this period there was no single strong church which gradually established others. The development pattern followed in Auckland and Dunedin is not evident. Another strategy was at work which led to the appearance of so many small causes in a short period.

Key personnel were fundamental to the differences between the developments at Auckland and Dunedin and those in Canterbury. From the early 1860s the Auckland church had stable leadership and very effective ministries from experienced Baptist pastors. Phillip Cornford (minister 1862-76) was the son of a Baptist manse and came to New Zealand after missionary service and three English pastorates. He was succeeded by Allan Webb (1877-81) who had been trained in Australia and had already served as President of the Baptist Union of New South Wales. They were followed by Thomas Spurgeon, whose stellar ministry in the 1880s gathered what was for a time the largest Baptist church in Australasia. In Dunedin the key ministries were from two Stepney college graduates: J.L. Parsons (1863-67) and J. Upton Davies (1872-81) and an experienced Scottish minister John Williams (1867-72).[10]

With the influence of such committed Baptist leadership there is little surprise in the pattern of development at Auckland and Dunedin. It was essentially like that in Britain, where a premium on local church based evangelism had gradually supplanted revivalist methods which had enjoyed a vogue earlier in the century.[11] The New Zealand manifestation of this

---

[10] See the biographical entries for these ministers in P. Tonson, *A Handful of Grain: The Centenary History of the Baptist Union of N.Z.* Vol. 1 – 1851-1882 (Wellington: NZ Baptist Historical Society, 1982).

[11] On the evolution of English Baptist methods away from mission societies towards an emphasis on the local church see J.H.Y. Briggs, *The English Baptists of the 19th Century* (Didcot: The Baptist Historical Society, 1994), 297-8.

saw an emphasis on strong fellowships, gradually and cautiously extending the ropes on their tents.

In Canterbury this model was not followed. The reason may well have to do with the individuals who guided Baptist development there in the 1860s and 70s. In contrast to the minister leaders of Auckland and Dunedin these men represented a revivalist line of Nonconformist thought. Indeed, a number of important figures owed their ecclesiology not to traditional Baptist emphases, but to Methodism.

In the first half of the nineteenth century Methodism experienced a series of secessions from the Wesleyan form. At the heart of these splits were issues of polity and practice, rather than credal doctrines. The Methodist New Connexion (1797) sought greater separation from the Church of England and more lay participation. Similar concern for lay participation but also for continued public revivalist preaching spurred the Primitive Methodists (1811) and the Bible Christians (1815). In New Zealand the most important groups were the Wesleyans and the Primitive Methodists.[12]

Key figures in Canterbury Baptist life had backgrounds in Methodist secession. This is not so surprising, when it is recognised that the secessionist groups each moved in one way or another from the hierarchical structures perceived to operate in Wesleyan Methodism towards more 'baptistic' models of church government and participation. For some individuals the transition would continue along these lines until they formally became Baptists. Exactly this religious progression may be identified among Canterbury leaders whose approach consequently mingled both Methodist and Baptist themes.

When the combined meeting at Greendale divided along denominational lines in 1872 the Primitive Methodists appointed Philip Hill as their preacher. The history of that denomination records that 'Mr Hill continued in the work until the end of [1873], when he withdrew

---

[12] New Zealand Methodism lacks a satisfactory modern history. The best recent resource remains E.W. Hames *Out of the Common Way: The European church in the Colonial Era 1840-1913* (Auckland: Wesleyan Historical Society, 1972). The outstanding treatment of the colonial period is W. Morley *The History of Methodism in New Zealand* (Wellington: McKee & Co, 1900) which, though heavily weighted towards the Wesleyan stream, is still the richest repository of detail for any Christian denomination of the period in New Zealand.

from our church.'¹³ Hill then drops from Methodist history, to feature, albeit briefly, as a Baptist. His 'withdrawal' from Primitive Methodism was apparently by Baptist conviction, as he immediately reappears as the founding pastor of a Baptist group at Sheffield. Hill's time was again short, however, as he died in 1876, leaving a congregation numbering seventeen.¹⁴

Hill's short ministry is merely symbolic of the significance of Methodism among colonial Canterbury Baptists. Far more important were the contributions of James Sawle and William Pole.

James Sawle (1835-1920) came to New Zealand from South Australia where he had been involved initially with the New Connexion Methodists but adopted Baptist principles out of an experience in a cooperative fellowship. He settled at West Melton on the Canterbury plains in 1870. There is no record of him receiving training, but he was the first pastor at Greendale and (concurrently from 1873) at West Melton and was a constant on the preaching roster for the region. From 1886 to 1892 he was minister at Ashburton (80 kilometres south of Christchurch). Sawle was a prime mover in the establishment of the Canterbury Association in 1874 and was its second president. As will be seen, the Association was itself a significant factor in the development of Canterbury Baptist life.

Sawle's energy was an effective catalyst for evangelism and church planting but even his contribution stands second to the remarkable ministry of William Pole (1814-79). Pole came to New Zealand in 1867, relatively late in life at 55 years of age, and seems to have been intent on establishing a farm. Instead, he quickly found himself engaged in ministry. He was the first minister at Lincoln Road (1869-76) and was remembered to have been the first minister to preach at Baptist services in South Malvern, Sheffield and Greendale. Like Sawle he was a prime mover in the establishment of the Canterbury Association.

William Pole is particularly interesting, as he had extensive experience as a pastor before coming to New Zealand, initially as a Primitive Methodist. By 1837 he was engaged in a mission in Buckinghamshire, England, where he developed a reputation as a powerful revivalist. From 1844 his work was as an evangelist in Huntingdonshire. Gradually, however, he became convinced of Baptist principles of church government

---

[13] J. Guy & W.S. Potter (eds) *Jubilee Memorial Volume or Fifty Years of Primitive Methodism in New Zealand* (Wellington: Primitive Methodist Book Depot, 1893), 197.

[14] *The Canterbury Evangelist* (August 1876): 16; (November 1876): 40.

and baptism and he was eventually baptised by Philip Cornford (later to be minister at Auckland 1862-76, but then in the town of Ramsey, in Huntingdonshire). Pole began a Baptist church in nearby Buckden which, significantly, quickly set up a number of preaching stations which later became churches. His obituary notes that, 'when he left to come to this colony there were more than twenty local preachers assisting him.'[15]

Pole had clearly not forgotten his Primitive Methodist approaches to evangelism. A similar pattern would be worked out in Canterbury. Indeed the central Canterbury Baptist causes of the 1870s look much like a Methodist circuit. It is a pattern not found among Baptists anywhere else in colonial New Zealand, even where the population was large enough to sustain a Baptist community. Any attempt to explain this anomaly must incorporate the coincidence of pivotal leaders like Sawle and Pole with secessionist Methodist backgrounds.

Baptists made no bones about their differences from Methodists. The issue of believers' baptism was fundamental and left the Methodists lumped with other infant baptisers as lacking the truth. The Canterbury former Methodists were as adamant on this issue as any other more traditional Baptists. Yet it is an undoubted feature of their story that they carried the concerns of the various strands of Methodism into their Baptist life in ways not as evident in other prominent New Zealand Baptists. The revivalism of the Primitives and Bible Christians, the openness to women of the Bible Christians, the lay emphasis of the Methodist New Connexion, the preaching circuit approach of various Methodist groups, these for a time created a fresh expression of Baptist life in the new colony.

Canterbury was the only region to set up an Association prior to the formation of the Baptist Union. In 1874 the Hereford Street church in Christchurch proposed to the Lincoln Road church that they investigate a joint venture in church extension. Lincoln Road, under its pastor William Pole, expressed enthusiasm 'if it were intended to form an association of Baptist churches throughout the Province.'[16] In December 1874 such a body was duly formed with the object 'to advance the cause of Christ'. First and second among the means to achieving this aim were 'promoting the formation of Christian churches' and 'the sustenance of Evangelists'.[17]

---

[15] See Pole's obituary *The Baptist* (April 1880): 46-50.
[16] A.H. Macleod, *The Canterbury-Westland Baptist Association: A Brief History*, (Christchurch: Canterbury-Westland Baptist Asscociation, 1974), 3.
[17] MacLeod, *Canterbury-Westland Baptist Association*, 3.

Associations as vehicles for enhanced evangelism were important in England in the first half of the nineteenth century. In this form they were clearly a legacy of the influence of the evangelical awakening and 'the connexional organisation of the Methodists.'[18] In Canterbury this was reflected in the two major initiatives of the new body. In 1876 an evangelist was appointed. George Johnston would in the next two years itinerate around the province and report regularly on his work. He would be succeeded for a further two years by T.W. Smyth.

A second initiative was to begin a magazine, the *Canterbury Evangelist*. As the discussion in chapter eight will show, the evolving magazine would become a major vehicle for denominational identity. It began, however, as its first name suggests, as a publication aimed at being 'of some utility amongst all evangelical denominations'.[19] This openness reflected the 'loose' Baptist ethos of Canterbury leaders. Key individuals like J.W. Sawle and William Pole may have been convinced Baptists but evangelical fervour was more significant to them than building a denomination.

With the formation of the Union in 1882 the question of the future of the Canterbury Association was raised. The majority voted to continue its existence alongside the wider body but Dallaston voted against continuance and, without the support of his large church, the Association could not be sustained. In 1884 it was dissolved.[20]

The initiative shifted from leaders with Methodist backgrounds and a history of freewheeling evangelism to a more sectarian defence of Baptist principles. To the Canterbury men this also went hand in hand with a loss of interest in evangelism and a failure to promote local initiatives. Concern soon surfaced that the new Union was not facilitating home mission.[21] By the late 1880s the Canterbury Baptists were rebelling. They set up a proto-Association Home Mission Society in 1888. A particularly tense exchange took place in 1891. Rev George Griffiths of Greendale and others took the Union to task for ignoring country churches, reeling back evangelism and relegating the role of laypeople. Griffiths, like the earlier Canterbury leaders, came into Baptist ministry from a Methodist background.[22] His letter was not published but a riposte from Arthur Dewdney, editor of *The N.Z. Baptist*, decried 'the spirit of bitterness and antagonism' it was deemed

---

[18] Briggs, 202-4.
[19] *The Canterbury Evangelist* (August 1876): 1-2.
[20] MacLeod, *Canterbury-Westland Baptist Association*, 5-6.
[21] *NZB* (November 1887): 173-173.
[22] See *NZB* (July 1886): 101.

to display. More specifically Dewdney rejected a number of Griffith's grievances in strong terms.

> [Y]our representation of the West Coast mission grossly misrepresents the Union. The work of Mr. Johnston was an acknowledged failure; there was no 'good footing' to be secured when he left; and even if there were, we had neither the *man*, nor the *means* to do it.
>
> Equally is your reference to the Home Mission committee unjust and ungenerous. It supplied the preaching requirements of the churches, and was prepared to continue to do so at its best, for the only church needing such supply, but you, yourself, and that church - South Malvern - entered into an arrangement and requested the committee to leave it to you. And yet in the face of this you make the assertion you do of it. If you can't be generous, at least be just.[23]

Griffiths did succeed in having a response to Dewdney printed. In terms as forthright as those directed at him he condemned the editor's action, suggesting 'I really think you ought to make an ample apology to your readers for misleading them by printing so scurrilous a letter in the columns of the paper.'[24]

By December 1892 the Wellington layman Thomas Kirk, new President of the Union, was admitting that the cautious mainstream church extension methods had drawbacks. The conservative approach often meant that

> by the time sufficient Baptists have been drawn to the neighbourhood to form the nucleus of a new church the opportunity has passed, the ground has been occupied by other denominations, and our people, being few in number, unite with them in work and worship.....[25]

Kirk also noted the Baptists' failure to utilize local preachers. He cited the example of the Methodists as one worth emulating in this regard.

The areas of weakness Kirk identified in the general approach of the denomination had been the points of strength in the Canterbury model of the 1870s: an early, even if precarious, presence in new towns and the provision of itinerant preachers and evangelists. In the year Kirk gave this address (1892) new regional Associations had appeared, in an acknowledged effort to promote home mission. This time they were to

---

[23] *NZB* (December 1891): 184-185.
[24] *NZB* (January 1892): 5.
[25] *NZB* (December 1892): 178-9.

cover the whole country. Significantly, the Otago and Southland group named itself as an 'Auxiliary' of the Union, as did the Central Districts body when it formed in 1897. Auckland formed an 'Association' the role of which was explained in the pages of *The N.Z. Baptist* by W.R. Woolley, who happened also to be Secretary of the Union. His justification for the Association was a thinly veiled defence of the national body.

> The relation of the Association to the Union may properly be one of simple imitation. The step we have taken is to some extent a tribute to the worth of the Baptist Union; for imitation is the sincerest flattery. We are attempting to do for the District that which the Union has accomplished in the case of the entire Colony...
>
> Then another reason for which the Association has been established is to increase the interest of our members in the Baptist Union, and to make its various and important undertakings more generally known and understood. The Union does not simply furnish a golden opportunity for conference and *talk*, but it is a great *working institution*. ...
>
> Thus the history of the Union, though brief in its record of years, is rich in its record of service. Its grateful testimony may fitly be heard in the words, 'The Lord hath done great things for us, whereof we are glad.'[26]

Canterbury, uniquely among these, reconstituted itself independently of the Union and placed extension and evangelism at its heart. In an assertive summary of Canterbury's concerns, S.R. Ingold demanded that the Canterbury Association be seen as more than a mere clone of the larger organisation.

> The United Baptist churches of Canterbury were prepared to work heartily and loyally with the New Zealand Baptist Union, if the New Zealand Baptist Union were prepared to work with the United Baptist churches of Canterbury.[27]

Ingold listed the relegation of Decimus Dolamore, beloved and respected among Canterbury Baptists and the ongoing isolation of C.C. Brown of Timaru (see chapter four) among complaints against the national body. More general were the concerns over the apparent lack of interest in Home Mission and a perception that the aggregation of power to the Union committees amounted to an abandonment of Baptist principles.

---

[26] *NZB* (July 1892): 97-98.
[27] *NZB* (October 1892): 158-9.

[W]e, in Canterbury, are strictly loyal to our Congregational principles; and, as straws show the current of the stream, so we have thought that in the doings and utterances of the Union and its officials we detected that the flow of the N.Z. Baptist Union was inclined to be swayed from Congregationalism and towards Presbyterianism. This idea first suggested itself to many of us, when the Union passed that resolution, making it incumbent upon any church that had received financial help to consult the Union officials upon the choice of a pastor, should they be called upon to select a new minister. This we take to be a direct blow at our independence, and is placing the churches in a false and humiliating position: false to the Congregationalism we love, and humiliating to themselves before their more (financially) fortunate fellow-churches. The idea was further strengthened when the Union, last year, through its then President, drew attention to the danger menacing our smaller churches of being governed by the most loud-lipped and ignorant of their members. The meaning evidently underlying this statement being, that there is a necessity that the churches should be controlled by some higher power than themselves, to wit - the Committee of the New Zealand Baptist Union. This utterance many of the Baptist churches of Canterbury, being 'smaller churches,' have, rightly or wrongly, taken as an insult to their intelligence.[28]

Unlike those of Otago and Auckland, the Canterbury Association constitution specified that all members of affiliated churches (including, therefore, women) could be delegates to its meetings[29]. At the first opportunity it brought a recommendation to the Union Conference 'that the resolution passed at the first meeting of the Union, interpreting members to mean 'Adult male', be altered to read 'Any adult Baptist'.' The measure was defeated 28-11.[30]

Canterbury had thus placed itself in a very different place from the rest of the Baptist Union. By 1893 a dangerous rift had opened. The national Conference was held in Nelson that year. This was a crucial meeting, debating the touchstone Baptist issue of religious instruction in schools. Yet only two churches from Canterbury were represented, each with only one delegate. What a change from 1882, when Canterbury churches had

---

[28] *NZB* (October 1892): 158-9.
[29] *NZB* (May 1892): 76.
[30] See *NZB* (October 1892): 153; (December 1892): 183.

made up over 40% of those founding the Union. It was a marked decline from the year before when six Canterbury churches were present in Dunedin or from 1891 when five churches sent eight delegates on the longer journey to Wellington. No report of the reborn Canterbury body was tendered at Nelson. However, when the Canterbury Association itself met a month later, in December 1893, it had taken on many of the trappings of an alternative Union. It was employing its own evangelist and publishing a new magazine. In a perhaps unconscious but nonetheless revealing slip, the report for that gathering was published in *The N.Z. Baptist* under the heading 'Baptist Union of Canterbury and Westland.'[31] Schism threatened.

In the event no such formal split took place. As the Union gained momentum and began to implement schemes for training ministers and establishing a stronger financial base, it inevitably exerted more influence. In the first decade of the new century nationally sponsored Home Mission began to bear fruit, particularly in the North Island. Canterbury's momentum dissipated. In the fifteen years prior to 1884, eleven churches had been founded in Canterbury. In the following thirty years only four would be constituted, three of these in the first years of the Association's revival.[32] The generation of Canterbury Baptists which had created the looser, more responsive model of Baptist life in the 1870s was rapidly passing by the 1890s. By 1905 the once pugnacious Canterbury Association was meekly accepting the more passive description of 'Auxiliary'. In 1910 this was formalized, with the union taking over all fundraising.[33] The pioneering phase which had given space to the Canterbury model gave way to concerns for consolidation and sustainable structures. Attention increasingly turned to defining Baptist identity around a narrow band of social issues and in relation to other denominations.

---

[31] *NZB* (January 1894): 6.
[32] Le Bon's Bay and Rangiora in 1895, Kaiapoi in 1897. The fourth was Linwood (1914) which was a plant on the Auckland and Dunedin model, from what had been Dallaston's church, by then at Oxford Terrace.
[33] *NZB* (October 1910): 194. See MacLeod *Canterbury-Westland Baptist Association*, 13.

Chapter Two: conflict and connection in Cambridge

In marked contrast to the almost simultaneous emergence of churches across the Canterbury plains that took place in the 1870s, Baptists elsewhere spread in a more measured fashion. Instead of the optimistic (perhaps naively so) scattering of the Canterbury model, causes elsewhere were generally dependent on the sponsorship of an established city church. The short-lived church at Cambridge in the Waikato is an instructive instance of this more cautious (although, in this case, no more successful) approach. Formed in 1881, it had petered out by the end of the decade. However, we are fortunate that, perhaps because of its close connection to the Auckland church, there are rich sources available which enable us to understand well the fate of this first Cambridge Baptist. Minute books, account ledgers and a surprising number of letters survive, which add nuance and colour to our understanding of both conflict and connection in early Baptist life in New Zealand. Cambridge both illustrates an alternative to the Canterbury model and at the same time directly informs the key themes of this book.

Connectionality

The first Cambridge Baptist church was formed conventionally enough. An historical note in the members' minute book records that

> a few of the Baptist friends consulted together and deeming it desirable that they should occasionally meet to hold fellowship with one another decided to have a monthly Sunday Service and a week-night Bible Reading.[1]

Yet an outstanding feature of the new fellowship was the importance of its connections beyond the local congregation. There appears to have been no attempt to assert the autonomy traditionally associated with Baptist churches. A year after its own foundation Cambridge joined with 21 others to form the Baptist Union of New Zealand but it was with the Auckland Baptist church (first at Wellesley St, then at the Queen St Tabernacle) that the most important links were maintained. There were practical reasons.

---

[1] *Members' Minute Book, Cambridge Baptist church, 1881-1889 (CMM)*, NZBA. file 73/3.

The Auckland church was remarkably proactive in taking up land for future causes. A section had been already secured in the fledgling town of Cambridge and held for a number of years. It was, then, natural (and to its potential advantage) that the new church would consult with Auckland. However, a link was cemented before there was any application to use the property.[2] In July 1881 the group resolved to contact Rev. A.W. Webb of the Auckland church to ascertain 'when he or any of the Wellesley St Deacons should be visiting the Waikato district, so that we might embrace the opportunity of being formed into a Baptist church.' The visit took place on 29 September 1881, when Webb and Thomas Spurgeon arrived 'for the purpose of forming a Baptist church.'

Thus the Cambridge church, though it emerged from a traditional 'gathering' of believers, depended at its formal commencement on senior figures from outside the congregation. This would be a consistent pattern, reinforced in numerous ways. The new body immediately adopted the Auckland church's constitution[3] and at a meeting on 4 May 1882 it was resolved that the church formally affiliate with what was now clearly its parent body.[4] Thomas Spurgeon's presence was thereafter sought at each of the annual anniversary services, with the scheduled dates of these events being changed whenever necessary in order to accommodate his timetable.[5]

By far the most important symbol of this close connection was the senior church's virtual control of the Cambridge pastorate. No choice of pastor was made without the advice, blessing and support of Auckland. The influence began at the foundation meeting. After the formal business Webb proposed that the church consider 'a gentleman who had been labouring as a City Missionary in Perth'. This candidate, later revealed to be David Whytock, had already been approached. If the church were minded to call him for up to three months, Wellesley St would provide financial assistance.[6] Perhaps not surprisingly the new church accepted the offer. In January 1882, at the conclusion of the initial period, Thomas Spurgeon chaired a special meeting at which he 'strongly urged' Whytock's

---

[2] *CMM*, 7 December 1881.
[3] See the compact recorded in the front of the members' minute book.
[4] *CMM*, 4 May 1882. The resolution was carried 'unanimously' although this was possible only because one member, George Smerdon, 'undertook to sacrifice all personal feeling in the matter'. See also the minutes of the previous meeting on March 30 1882.
[5] See for instance *CMM*, 7 September 1882, and 2, 12 & 19 April 1885.
[6] *CMM*, 29 September 1881.

permanent appointment. This duly occurred, again with the promise of assistance.[7]

Exactly a year later a special meeting was receiving Whytock's resignation. His stated reason was that 'his heart was in evangelistic work'. The members appear to have had a different perspective, resolving, 'but not unanimously' that

> as there does not appear to be mutual confidence between the church and Pastor his continuance cannot be for his comfort or the spiritual prosperity of the church and that therefore his resignation be accepted.[8]

The next action of the same meeting was to appoint a deputation 'to confer with Messrs Spurgeon and Knight in reference to the future pastorate of the church.' The Auckland church promised continued support of £50 (one third of the Pastor's salary) for the coming year but urged that Cambridge accept Whytock's offer to supply the pulpit in the mean-time. This advice was followed without dissent.

Thus, at every stage of Whytock's brief term the key decisions were made in deference to the views of the Wellesley St church. The next two attempts to secure a minister were fruitless. In July 1883, in the only instance of an apparently independent decision, the church resolved to call the senior figure Charles Carter.[9] This came to nothing. In November the by now normal pattern was reestablished. A call was issued to Thomas Bray of Greendale on the suggestion of Spurgeon who, it seems, had already discussed the matter in some detail with Bray.[10] Bray's case is interesting as he appears to have written accepting the call only to withdraw by telegram immediately after. Faced with this embarrassment and after 'lengthy correspondence' with Bray, the church was constrained to consult once more with Spurgeon. Another deputation traveled north. This time the outcome was a recommendation that Bray be released from his engagement and a replacement minister be sought from England. Spurgeon was to be the church's agent in this search.[11] The agency gave a virtually free hand. No vetting of candidates by the congregation was expected. On 13 May

---

[7] *CMM*, 15 January 1882.
[8] *CMM*, 15 January 1883.
[9] *CMM*, 29 July 1883.
[10] *CMM*, 29 November and 9 December 1883.
[11] *Deacons' Minute Book, Cambridge Baptist church, 1883-1889 (CDM)*, NZBA file 73/4, 22 January 1884; *CMM*, 31 January 1884 and 3 February 1884; Bray would later be appointed to the pastorate at Mt Eden, another congregation affiliated with the Auckland church.

1884 the Deacons received a photograph of 'the Rev J.G. Wilson our future Pastor who has been selected by Rev. C.H. Spurgeon as pastor of our church at Cambridge.' Wilson arrived from England in mid-June 1884.[12]

Wilson's appointment was for two years, after which he chose not to renew the relationship. This decision was communicated to the Deacons at a meeting on 24 February 1886. Characteristically, the immediate response was to seek the counsel of Auckland.[13] By this point Cambridge's sense of connection appears to have broadened, as advice was also sought from the Baptist Union.[14] Nevertheless the link with Auckland remained decisive. The next incumbent would be G.O. Griffiths, a member of the Auckland church. The invitation to the pastorate was subject to the continuance of support from Auckland.[15] Spurgeon was invited to give the charge to the new pastor at a service of 'induction and recognition', held on 26 September, 1886.

Cambridge's dependence on Auckland continued unbroken through Griffith's ministry. Financial support from the 'mother church' (supplemented from the Baptist Union funds from 1884) was essential throughout its existence. When, in 1887, a new monthly preaching station was planned at Whao/Litchfield, it was undertaken only with the approval of Auckland and the provision from the larger church of pulpit supply to fill the consequent monthly gap at Cambridge.[16] The congregation was in effect a home mission project of its Auckland sponsor. This status would become formalised in the last months of the church's existence.

Covenant and Community

The determination of the Cambridge congregation to maintain its connexional links was matched by an equally determined, though ultimately less successful, effort to build covenantal links within the church community itself. In the founding charter members promised 'to watch, in

---

[12] *CDM*, 13 May 1884. See also the letters of the church Secretary Houghton to Seering Matthews, 9 and 15 August 1882 and to C.H. Spurgeon 13 September 1882. *Cambridge Letter Book* ff 13-17, NZBA , file 074/6.
[13] *CDM*, 24 February 1886.
[14] *CDM*, 21 April 1886.
[15] *CMM*, 29 July 1886. Some consternation was caused to the Deacons when Auckland indicated it would continue support for one year only in the reduced sum of £25 p.a. – *CDM*, 27 August 1886.
[16] *CDM*, 31 January and 21 February 1887.

love, over one another, seeking each other's good, bearing with each other's weaknesses.' This commitment was taken seriously, at least on occasion, though the results were mixed. Applicants for baptism and/or 'fellowship' were visited by Deacons and reports on their faith status brought to subsequent meetings of the church. Of those applying in the first days of the new congregation Eliza Took aged twelve and Louisa Harris aged nine were advised to 'wait a little.'[17] Unusually detailed reports were presented to a meeting in October 1883 when ten candidates were considered. Alice Riley was recommended, as

> she was simply trusting according to the light she has received, but evidently had not studied the Word of God very much. Her parents spoke highly of her and had noticed a marked change in her character for some considerable time.

At the same meeting Manford Scott was particularly endorsed because 'in his daily occupation he was surrounded with more than ordinary temptations and had been enabled by God's help to overcome them.'[18]

Matters were not always so straightforward. On 27 March 1884 a 'Miss Johnson' was nominated for baptism and membership. The necessary reports were favourable but Miss Johnson herself wrote to the church withdrawing her application for membership 'owing to certain remarks having been passed about her conduct in church.' This caused some consternation, with the church resolving that two Deacons visit the aggrieved Miss Johnson to 'explain matters' but that, on the condition that her letter be withdrawn, she might still be admitted as a member. This was apparently what transpired, as Miss Johnson subsequently entered the membership roll.[19]

During this period (mid-1884) the pastorate was vacant pending the arrival of J.G. Wilson. The Deacons attempted themselves to implement the oversight provisions of the founding compact. Visitors were appointed to approach six men who 'were not as regular attendants as formerly'. The visits were not necessarily welcome. Two of the men, John and James Harris, initially declined to receive the deputation at all, though there was one apparent success. Alex. McKinnon, a founding member, had been suspended in 1882 because 'he had fallen away from grace and had several times been guilty of behaviour inconsistent to a member of a Christian

---

[17] *CMM*,13 October 1881.
[18] *CMM*, 25 October 1883.
[19] *CMM*, 27 March and 13 April 1884.

church.' Two years later he resolved to return to active membership.[20] In respect to the others, little was done to follow through on the visits. On 29 October 1884 the Deacons decided that the consideration of these cases 'should stand over until a later date.' The matter was quietly dropped.[21] The new Pastor may have influenced this less aggressive stance as he seems to have preferred a different tactic. Soon after his arrival it was resolved 'that in order to bring the Pastor and church members more intimately together; a tea meeting be held every quarter for members only.'[22] Wilson's successor, G.O. Griffiths, took a sterner approach. In early 1887 he instituted a membership revision which eventually saw 21 names (a third of the total) struck off the roll. In most cases this was for 'absenting themselves from the Lord's table for a period of six months'.[23] In November 1887 a register of attendance at communion was introduced.[24]

In 1888 Mr T. Trewhellan, a member of long standing, filed for bankruptcy. This presented a special case to the church community. The Deacons resolved that Trewhellan be requested to meet with the Secretary, J. Houghton, to 'explain the cause of his failure.'[25] Trewhellan lived in Hamilton and no meeting seems to have taken place. However, he supplied 'a kind and interesting letter'. Trewhellan, the Deacons or both were concerned at the impact the financial failure might have on his future Christian fellowship. The Deacons accordingly resolved 'that a vote of sympathy be tendered to Mr Trewhellan in his present difficulties and a letter commending him to any Christian church that he may meet with.'[26]

Underlying these specific efforts to promote and maintain discipline was the normal run of ordinary services, prayer meetings, Bible studies, business meetings and social gatherings. If greater intimacy was to be built at all, Wilson envisaged it would be achieved in these settings. The record of the members' and Deacons' business meetings from this period provides an important insight into the changing life of the church. The members met approximately monthly during the entire life of the church and in the early years were clearly the main decision making body. Purchases, preaching

---

[20] *CMM*, 27 July 1882 and 28 August 1884.
[21] *CDM*, 16 July, 24 September and 29 October 1884.
[22] *CMM*, 28 August 1884.
[23] *CDM*, 21 February and 23 May 1887. Among those removed was the apparently inconsistent Alex. McKinnon.
[24] *CDM*, 21 November 1887.
[25] *CDM*, 23 April 1888.
[26] *CDM*, 14 May and 18 June 1888.

arrangements, membership questions and the all-too-regular need to fill the pastorate came before these gatherings, which nevertheless rarely attracted more than 10-12 (approx. 25% on average) of the members.

From July 1883 minutes of Deacons' meetings were kept. These recorded details of correspondence received and sent but addressed little in the way of business other than issues to be brought to the members. At least once in this early period the Deacons met merely to confirm the minutes, there being 'no actual business gone into or done'.[27] With the arrival of the more authoritarian Griffiths in 1886, however, the pattern changed. Deacons' minutes become fuller, dealing with questions earlier left to the members. Outstanding in this respect is the handling of the roll revision of 1887. The 21 names were struck off by the Deacons with no reference to the members. Under Griffiths, members' minutes become shorter, with a small agenda largely limited to reports, applications for membership and planning social events. Meetings began to fail to reach a quorum (one because there were not enough males present). [28]

The change in the nature of business meetings reflected the growing tensions and difficulties faced by the Cambridge church under Griffith's ministry. Yet, even in this period, the earlier pattern of soirees, tea meetings, anniversary services and picnics was continued. These were ways the congregation sought to build its covenantal life, evidence of a wish to fulfill the founding promise to 'watch, in love, over one another.'[29] Regular business meetings, social gatherings and twice weekly services, together with specific attempts to provide a framework of discipline were other important means of building community. Cambridge Baptists actively constructed both external and internal forces for cohesiveness. However, neither connectional links nor covenantal commitment would prevent the ultimate failure of the cause.

Collapse

In his short yet pithy analysis of this first Baptist cause in Cambridge, Ayson Clifford identified chronic problems of 'membership, ministry and

---

[27] *CDM*, 18 June 1885.
[28] *CMM*, 1 March and 16 August 1888. There appears to be a confusion of dates around the August meeting. Notes in the minutes suggest the recorded meeting was actually held on 19 July.
[29] This endeavour continued to the end. The last recorded decision of the members was to hold a Sunday School picnic. *CMM*, 2 January 1890.

money'.[30] These three interrelated factors surfaced increasingly in the minutes and correspondence of the church. In the limited space available to him Clifford could not explore far the subtleties of these problems. When these are understood the significance of this combination of constraints emerges.

Finances were a struggle at Cambridge from the outset. At no time in its history was the church able to contemplate continuing without significant aid from Auckland and, eventually, from the Baptist Union. Not surprisingly, the key liabilities were the minister's salary and the building. In November 1882 a tender for the building of the church was accepted and a finance committee set up 'for providing the funds necessary for the erection of the proposed Tabernacle.' The total expected cost was £600. Subscriptions were raised and events planned, but a bank overdraft of just over £200 was nevertheless necessary.[31] By the January 1883 meeting, at which David Whytock tendered his resignation, the treasurer had to report a 'deficit of £14 in the General Fund and wished to know what was to be done in order to provide for it.'[32] There was a temporary improvement but in May the treasurer was reporting that the church was four months in arrears on rent for the Oddfellows Hall 'due to want of funds'. It was agreed to ask the members for a special subscription towards the general funds.[33] An envelope system was introduced, supplemented by the positioning of offering plates at the exits.[34] By March 1885 there was still a 12 pound deficit; in July it had ballooned to £25. Secretary Houghton saw an increase in members as the only solution. It was agreed that the envelope system had failed and that the practice of passing the plate around should be reintroduced. Another special subscription was sought.[35] The shortfalls continued, indeed the situation gradually worsened. On 30 June 1887 the Deacons were forced to respond to a solicitor's letter pointing out that interest payments on the bank loan were two quarters behind.[36] In December the treasurer noted that average Sunday offerings had fallen

---

[30] J. Ayson Clifford, *A Handful of Grain: the Centenary History of the Baptist Union of N.Z.* vol 2. 1882-1914 (Wellington: NZBHS, 1982), 55.
[31] Letter, E.H. Shoard to Messrs Carter & Hogan, 23 November 1882, Cambridge Letter Book f. 2; *CMM*, 30 November 1882, *Cambridge Accounts Book*, NZBA 074/6.
[32] *CMM*, 15 January 1883.
[33] *CMM*, 24 May 1883.
[34] *CMM*, 27 November 1884. By this time a need was felt 'to remind the congregation of the plates standing at the doors'.
[35] *CMM*, 26 March and 30 July 1885.
[36] *CDM*, 30 June 1887.

below two pounds.³⁷ The situation was by now virtually irrecoverable. A year later secretary Houghton applied for an increase of the grant from Auckland, lamenting it was 'almost impossible to pay our way even with the help you have given.'³⁸

The Cambridge church was not alone in feeling the pinch. The Auckland church too was suffering. In reply to Houghton's application for funding, Seering Matthews disclosed that 'we are not meeting our own expenditure...despite the most rigid economy and retrenchment.'³⁹ None of this is too surprising – the whole country was in the grip of a recession, which had been particularly difficult in Northern regions since 1885. This was the context of Trewhellan's bankruptcy. The poor economy also set the scene for the migration of workers in search of employment. The leadership of Cambridge were acutely sensitive to the shedding of members, not only from their congregation (with the Salvation Army apparently being the principal beneficiary) but, more fundamentally, from the locality. Houghton noted 'the exceedingly depressed state of everything in this district'.⁴⁰

In a series of revealing letters Pastor Griffiths reported his view of the situation. In December 1888 he was losing hope.

> The congregations are keeping up as well as can be expected, considering that so many have been compelled to leave the district, and so few coming into the district. I think there is a more united and peaceful spirit reigning in the church than it has ever experienced in the past, but O how ineffectual the preaching is proving for breaking down the strongholds of Satan.⁴¹

Three months later he had accepted the inevitable

> I have come to the conclusion that the best thing that I can do for Cambridge is to retire from the Pastorate of the church. Everything is on the downgrade. The Spiritual life of the church is rapidly deteriorating....Several of the active members are leaving us, - Bro. &

---

³⁷ *CDM*, 28 December 1887.
³⁸ Copy Letter, Houghton to Matthews, 8 September 1888, *Cambridge Letter Book* f.717 (loose).
³⁹ Letter, Matthews to Houghton, 2 October 1888, NZBA 73/2.
⁴⁰ Copy Letter, Houghton to W.R. Woolley, 8 September 1888, NZBA f.719 (loose).
⁴¹ Letter, Griffiths to The Deacons of the Tabernacle Auckland, 26 December 1888, NZBA 73/2.

Sis. Rockliffe have returned to Tasmania, & Deacon Fitzgerald has resigned with the intention of joining the Salvation Army.[42]

Fred Battley from the Auckland church visited Cambridge in May, later reporting 'the church is much weakened by removals and impoverishment of the members and only a mere handful remain. There are only 22 resident members in the church now.'[43]

Cambridge had clearly become trapped in a downward spiral of declining funds and shrinking congregations. It was this that Ayson Clifford had in mind when he identified 'money and membership' as fatal weaknesses. Yet this cycle of causation was not closed. The economic recession was clearly one factor which accelerated the process. Another was Clifford's third element: the ministry. In citing this he had in mind the inability of the church to retain its Pastors. Cambridge had four ministers in its nine years. Yet rapid turnover of Baptist ministers was common in 1880s New Zealand, particularly in small churches. Other rural causes too suffered recession-driven migration and survived into the 1890s. Something more was happening at Cambridge. In Griffiths, it seems, it had a minister with a particular ability to alienate his members.

Griffith's stern approach to discipline has already been noted. He appears to have allowed little room for compromise. Houghton's health collapsed in September 1888 with the unusual result that Griffiths himself delivered the annual report for that year. This report opened in typical form.

> Another year has passed away in the history of our church and has left us with a record in wh[ich] there is much unfaithfulness, the blame of which must rest at our own door.

This hectoring approach produced inevitable tensions. Despite his later report to the Auckland Deacons of a 'peaceful spirit reigning in the church' all was not well between pastor and people. As noted above, Griffiths himself reported the movement of one of his Deacons to the Salvation Army. Battley identified another, T.J. Gerrish, as one 'who has been out of accord with the Pastor'.[44] Gerrish tendered his resignation from all offices in December 1888 but was challenged to provide a satisfactory reason for

---

[42] Letter, Griffiths to T. Spurgeon, 1 March 1889, NZBA 72/2.
[43] F. Battley, 'Report to Pastor and Deacons: Jottings of Interview Friday 3 May 89 with Cambridge church', 1-2. NZBA 72/2.
[44] Battley, 'Report', 1.

doing so.⁴⁵ The resignation was withdrawn in January, only to be renewed in April when it became evident that Griffith was to stay on for a time.⁴⁶

The most startling admission of conflict within the church comes from the engaging successor to Houghton as church secretary, the aged Samuel Crickett. In March 1889, in the wake of Griffith's resignation, he gave his own account of affairs to Seering Matthews in Auckland. At this point he was apparently a supporter of his Pastor.

> I preface my note by saying that I do feel ashamed of my subject, namely: that Mr Griffith should have reason for leaving the Tabernacle in Cambridge....There is a party in the tabernacle who (sic) has of late taken offence at his preaching the gospel in Spirit and in truth. They have felt themselves sadly and badly knocked about with these words of truth spoken on Judas the traitor. The Subject was very well spoken and created great sensation and noise....
>
> Now this party is growing in the Tabernacle and has resolved that Mr Griffiths shall not rule over them and has cried out away with him and I suppose it is as well that he should go, but it is a sad alternative....
>
> And it is vexing to hear members of other churches rejoicing in hope of the Tabernacle being closed and very willing that the Salvation Army should have it as a Barrax (sic). Indeed one of our Bastard Deacons is very willing and indeed anxious that this should be the case. May the Lord help us and keep us from ourselves.⁴⁷

Crickett's unusually informal style is found also in his minutes. On 31 March a meeting fell apart after Griffiths left the room. Cricket described the aftermath.

> There were a number of the members who went outside, to hold a meeting on their own account I suppose, but I do not know what conclusion they came to. But [among] those [who] waited inside, after a conversation in general, it was agreed that a deputation be appointed to wait upon the pastor and request him to wait with them for another Sabbath, when we would by that time know the will and mind of the Auckland church concerning us.⁴⁸

---

⁴⁵ *CDM*, 17 December 1888; *CMM*, 20 December 1888.
⁴⁶ *CMM*, 18 April 1889.
⁴⁷ Letter S. Crickett to Seering Matthews, 26 March 1889. NZBA 73/2. (See also Griffiths' letter to Matthews, 12 March 1889, NZBA 73/2.)
⁴⁸ *CMM*, 31 March 1889.

Cricket's confidence in Griffiths seems to have deserted him by the time Battley arrived for consultation in May. He was not present at Battley's meetings with Deacons and then with the church, although he appears to have written up the minutes. Although Crickett coolly records Battley's impression that Griffith's enjoyed the 'esteem of all'[49] he suggests his own views in the minutes of the next meeting. After noting the view of some that the key cause of 'so many members and adherents being absent from the church' was the attraction of the Salvation Army he confessed 'and your secretary was disposed to blame the pastor, but he would not sustain the charge.'[50]

Whatever Crickett's personal position it is clear that there was real conflict within the church and that much of this tension centred on Griffiths. Battley's solution for the church's future had been to relieve it of the need to support a minister. A 'Home Mission', with a missioner engaged directly by Auckland would be set up for the area. This plan was implemented, with Griffiths appointed to continue in the new role for six months. The experiment was a failure. Griffiths stayed on under the impression that his continued presence was welcomed by the remaining congregation. Battley had badly misread the situation. Griffiths felt betrayed by the lack of support from those who had enthusiastically adopted Battley's proposal.[51] He was succeeded briefly by Rev. E. Barnett whose observation on arrival was that 'between Mr Griffiths and the members that remain things are anything but pleasant, and things have been going from bad to worse for the last six months.'[52] By February 1890 Barnett too was gone. The Baptist cause in Cambridge had finally collapsed.

Cambridge had never escaped the discouraging combination of low membership and inadequate funds matched with significant liabilities. Yet other small Baptist causes had similar problems and managed to limp along. Greendale, in Canterbury, Griffiths' next charge, would survive him more or less intact. The outcome at Cambridge suggests additional, exacerbating factors. The break-down in the relationship between Griffiths and key members was one of these. The abortive attempt by Auckland to set up a Waikato Home Mission revealed the limits of Baptist

---

[49] *CMM*, 3 May 1889.
[50] *CMM*, 30 May 1889. Griffiths later described this meeting as being 'not a very pleasant one' – see Letter, Griffiths to Battley 18 June 1889, NZBHS 73/2.
[51] Griffiths to Battley 18 June 1889.
[52] Letter, Barnett to Woolley, 13 November 1889, NZBA 73/2.

connectionality. Griffiths was left impotent, dependent on a hostile semi-autonomous church, with no ability to direct affairs on the ground. Neither Auckland nor the Baptist Union could dictate terms, even though they sponsored the missioner. Whatever their openness to connectional links, Baptists in colonial Waikato were Baptist enough to guard their independence! The general economic downturn was a second aggravating factor. The recession coincided with a renewal of gold extraction in near-by Thames and the migration of Waikato population there and elsewhere in the search for security. Religious communities were not immune from outside influence. The demise of the first Cambridge Baptist church cannot be understood without a grasp of broader trends.

Insights, however, can flow in more than one direction. Does a detailed study of this Baptist community add to our understanding of wider colonial society?

One of the liveliest debates in New Zealand historiography in recent years has centred on Miles Fairburn's thesis about colonial pakeha society. Fairburn suggests that colonial social organisation was 'gravely deficient' in that

> community structures were few and weak and the forces of social isolation were many and powerful. Bondlessness was central to colonial life. The typical colonist was a socially independent individual.[53]

Fairburn's provocative interpretation has received considerable attention, much of it critical. Most of the contrary views have been based on local or regional studies which have stressed the function of school committees, local boards and councils, women's groups, lodges and churches in establishing and maintaining forces of cohesiveness.[54] Fairburn has responded vigorously, pointing out that, as his proposal eschews universal applicability, hunting for and even finding apparent exceptions proves little.

> Counter examples are entirely inconclusive unless (and this is the vital caveat) they are combined with procedures that assure us that the

---

[53] M. Fairburn, *The Ideal Society and its Enemies: The Foundations of Modern New Zealand Society 1850-1900*, (Auckland: A.U.P., 1989), 11-12.
[54] See for instance the articles in the *New Zealand Journal of History*, Vol. 25, No. 2, (October 1991) and the discussion in J. Belich, *Making Peoples: A History of the New Zealanders from Polynesian Settlement to the End of the Nineteenth Century*, (Auckland: Penguin, 1996), 411-446.

examples represent typicalities or, at least, do not represent aberrations.[55]

This is a trenchant point, the more so as local or regional examples are very difficult to relate to the sort of national statistical information that Fairburn cites. The interface is inherently problematic. The concerns, and therefore the questions, of those holding enough power to gather statistics cannot be assumed to match the day-to-day preoccupations of people living out their lives. Even if some connection could be made, a flood of highly detailed local studies, throwing up examples of strong social fabric, would have only limited value as evidence. Local records by nature will be produced by agents of cohesion, potentially magnifying their importance. Atomisation, by contrast, is likely to generate only silence, leaving few local traces.

The Baptists at Cambridge, then, display very well the countervailing energies at work among New Zealand Baptists. Despite their apparent commitment to connectionality and their attempts to build a strong covenantal community they were overwhelmed by their conflicts and the swirling economic tides. On its own, this case study tends to support Fairburn's analysis. Fairburn does not deny the presence of forces of cohesion; it is just that he concludes they were largely unsuccessful.[56] Sadly, the first Cambridge Baptist church embodied this argument in a near perfect example of failure to achieve 'critical mass'. Despite surprisingly strong centripetal energy from both without and within, the cause failed. Outside support could not nullify economic migration. Internal discipline foundered, relationships broke down, and the membership scattered. Atomisation? Not quite. This local case fits much of Fairburn's pattern but it is as important to note that many of the departing members transferred to other churches or denominations. Moreover the method of church extension found at Cambridge is revealing of attempts to make sense of the colonial environment. While it may have been cautious, and in many ways reflective of English models, it also suggests a willingness to adapt. With the more radical Canterbury model also before us, Cambridge reinforces an emerging picture of colonial Baptists as people who held classical distinctives such as autonomy more lightly than might have been imagined.

---

[55] M. Fairburn, 'A Discourse on Critical Method' *New Zealand Journal of History*, Vol. 25, No. 2 (October 1991), 158-177, 160.
[56] See Fairburn, *Ideal Society*, 158-187.

Cambridge Baptist church was not merely an example of colonial trends or home mission ambitions. It was a site on which a group of believers sought to construct a corporate life and witness. That it failed was for many a tragedy. Among these was Samuel Crickett. It is fitting to close with his lament at the church's imminent collapse as it encapsulates the simplicity of the fellowship's ambitions and the pain felt at its demise.

> Mr Griffith's way-going has deprived me of sleep and of stomach and, while I write, I am weak and stupid for I am now three score and 14 years and the idea of having no place to worship in presses heavy upon me, no place to shew forth the Lord's Death and Love,…without place for communion.[57]

One Baptist, at least, found the prospect of an atomised existence alarming. Cambridge may have foundered amid conflict and recrimination, but the underlying drive for connection, for 'a place for communion', remained strong.

---

[57] Letter, Cricket to Matthews, 26 March 1889.

Chapter Three: the problem of problem pastors

The unique makeup of the Canterbury Association and the history of the short-lived Cambridge church demonstrate the crucial importance of individuals in the sparsely populated colonial period. This was acutely the case with pastors. Two of the most spectacular cases of pastoral conflict were those of James Thornton and William Birch. These mercurial men, two decades apart, caused massive and public disruption in the main churches in Auckland and Christchurch. Yet, examination of their stories provides quite different insights into the shape of New Zealand Baptist life.

James Thornton arrived in Auckland with his family on 14 April 1857. An ordained Baptist Minister from Wales, his avowed intention on emigrating was to commence farming in New Zealand. In the event, he was quickly engaged to preach by the Baptists of Auckland and by August had been called as pastor. On its face, this was a moderately successful ministry. The church grew slowly and soon built its first chapel, in Wellesley St. All was not peaceful however. The church members were divided on the issue of open or closed communion. A number in the closed communion camp withdrew. Thornton himself was also evidently a focus of division. A man of forceful and magnetic personality, coupled with a supreme self-confidence, the mercurial Thornton could sway or bitterly antagonise in turn. On his own admission he resigned 'six or seven times during those five years, perhaps more than that'.[1] He finally left the church in December 1861. The writer of the Jubilee history of the Auckland Tabernacle records that 'his credentials as a minister became disputed, and he was compelled to resign.'[2] After a spell in Sydney, Thornton sought a means to return to New Zealand, this time to Christchurch. It is at this point that the extent of his strange behaviour starts to emerge.

The Christchurch Baptist church had been without a minister since Decimus Dolamore's resignation in June 1864. (Dolamore too had resigned over the church's practice of open communion.) From Sydney, hearing of the vacancy, Thornton offered himself as a replacement. The Deacons were

---

[1] 'The Rev. J. Thornton's Vindication of his Character', *Daily Southern Cross*, 19 February 1867, 6.
[2] *Souvenir of the Auckland Tabernacle Baptist church Jubilee Celebration* (Auckland: 1905), 11.

understandably wary and sought clarification on Thornton's position regarding communion. Impatient with such caution, Thornton simply turned up and challenged the church to appoint him. After a series of fractious meetings the appointment was made in late February 1865

Once again a modicum of success attached to his ministry; but once again questions were raised as to the veracity of his credentials. Members meetings were venues of accusation and dispute, so much so that Thornton's supporters felt the need to give public testimony to their loyalty.[3] Doubts and allegations about Thornton, emanating from Auckland, continued to grow in volume. The charges were certainly remarkable. Word spread that (among other things) Thornton was a bigamist and had falsely claimed missionary experience in China. In characteristically dramatic fashion Thornton returned to Auckland in early February 1867 to publically challenge his detractors.

After he had removed to Auckland, but before his scheduled public meeting, Thornton's situation became (if that was possible) even worse. Disgruntled members of the Christchurch church met in his absence and resolved 'That on account of the peculiar circumstances of Mr Thornton's case as considered by the church that he be not requested to return to the Pastorate of this church.'[4] A more moderate man might have slunk into the night in the midst of this chaos. Thornton, however, was no moderate. Unable for the present to do anything about the Christchurch crisis, he put that to one side. He would deal with the church at Christchurch later.

A series of minor snipes were exchanged in the pages of the *Daily Southern Cross*. On the substantive matters, Thornton certainly had a story. In his public account,[5] the alleged false claim of missionary service was explained as a confusion over the fact that some years earlier he had indeed spent time in China, although this was a business trip. Creating the confusion was the fact that on his return to Wales he worked as a customs official in a suburb of Cardiff in Wales called 'Canton'.[6] The combination of China and Canton had given a false impression of extensive Chinese experience, taken by the confused to mean missionary service. The accusation of bigamy, however, was indeed true. His story was that he had

---

[3] *Christchurch Press* 6 July 1866.
[4] Recorded in A. MacLeod, *Oxford Terrace Baptist church: Centennial History 1863-1963* (nd), 18.
[5] *Daily Southern Cross*, (19 February 1867): 6
[6] There is indeed a suburb of Cardiff called Canton.

married in haste and, as a young, unconverted man had abandoned his first wife and children. It was at this point that he travelled to China and on his return to Great Britain received news (false as it turned out) that his wife had died. Afraid of his brother in law, to whom he owed money, he did not pursue this report in order to verify it. Subsequently, he married again, to a widow he had befriended in Cardiff. By this time he was converted and he later trained and entered Baptist ministry. On his discovery that his first wife was still alive, he felt it his Christian duty to reconcile with her. So, after making financial provision for family number two, he took up with his first wife once more and emigrated to New Zealand to begin a new life as a farmer. By his account against his expectations, on his arrival in Auckland he was approached by the Baptists to help their cause and so his ministry commenced again. Later (as if his life was not complicated enough) his second wife also came to New Zealand with her two children, one of them Thornton's, and lived with Thornton and family number one for a time until they were settled independently in Auckland. Having bared his soul in this fashion, Thornton contended he should be able to continue with his ministry. 'Am I justified in burying my talents because these circumstances transpired in this way?'

The Baptists of both Auckland and Christchurch must have felt that his 'talents' would be safer in the ground. P.H. Cornford, Thornton's successor as Pastor of the Auckland church, was forced into acrimonious public exchanges through the newspapers in the weeks that followed. Delighted critics of religion among the regular writers of letters to the editor seized on Thornton's apparent transparency and directed severe reproof against the Wellesley St church.[7] The controversy was a great embarrassment to the church's leaders. Nevertheless, the storm gradually subsided and Thornton turned his face back towards Christchurch.

With Christchurch having effectively sacked him, Thornton in theory had no standing beyond that of an ordinary member. That constitutional nicety does not seem to have bothered him. As Angus MacLeod in his centenary history describes, Thornton hit back hard.

> At the next meeting, packed with his followers, it was agreed to dissolve the church and reconstitute it on a 'strict' communion basis. Under the new constitution Mr Thornton was still pastor and all the rebels were excluded from membership.[8]

---

[7] See e.g. *Daily Southern Cross* 20, 22, 23, 26, 27 February 1867.
[8] MacLeod, *Oxford Terrace*, 18.

This frontal attack was in turn repulsed at another meeting, on 15 October 1867 at which, it was recorded,

> Mr Thornton and some of his friends behaved in a most disgraceful manner by clapping hands, stamping with their feet, umbrellas, sticks etc, in order to prevent the motions being heard, and it was only by putting a few words at a time that it could be accomplished.[9]

At this meeting Thornton was eventually excluded from the pulpit. Once again, in a pattern typical of his *modus operandi*, claim and counter-claim would appear in the local newspapers. He was not done yet. With his supporters he set up another church and had a spacious building built within a year. This relationship, too, soon collapsed. In February 1869 Thornton was dismissed as pastor. But even this was not the end. The Baptists of Christchurch must have been wondering who could rid them of this troublesome pastor.

Once more Thornton hit the road. He travelled first to Otago and then to Australia on an itinerant mission, ostensibly to raise funds to pay the cost of the breakaway church's new building. He made little contact with Christchurch. In November 1869 he delivered a lecture in Maitland, New South Wales on 'The New Zealand War, its causes and cure'. Reportedly,

> he believed the only way to put an end to the war was to treat the natives as murderers, to seize the ringleaders and make terrible examples of them....Mr Thornton denied that the Maori possessed the intelligence usually attributed, to him, and he believed that he was incapable of a high degree of civilisation; the lowest orders were very low indeed.'[10]

By the middle of 1870 reports were coming in of a suspicious fundraiser touring small towns in Australia, attempting to raise money to rebuild a church which had supposedly been destroyed by the Maori. It was Thornton, and the church was forced to dissociate itself from him. Warning messages were sent to the Baptist churches in Australia.

Here was another point at which most people might have slipped away. Thornton however, seems to have numbered a massive hubris among his personality quirks. Back he came to Christchurch to defend himself against the slanders he alleged had been perpetrated against him. As in Auckland

---

[9] As cited by MacLeod, *Oxford Terrace*, 19.
[10] *Otago Daily Times*, (19 Nov 1869): 2.

three years earlier, he did this through lengthy published statements. As in Auckland the church was forced to defend itself in similar manner.[11]

We are forced to conclude that, whatever his talents, whatever his occasional noble aspirations, Thornton was at base a con man. He finally fades from the New Zealand scene after 1870. These affairs were, of course, excruciating for the churches involved; a desperate embarrassment in a small community. It is hard to imagine a greater pressure being placed on a fellowship. Yet the churches survived. Indeed, they were able in a large degree to carry on business as usual. The original Christchurch group and the breakaway body came back together in 1872. They would next call Robert Morton. Morton's ministry (1871-1876) was highly successful until he too left suddenly under a moral cloud (see chapter ten). Once again the church recovered, entering one of its most fruitful periods.

The power of the drive for covenant, communion and connection needs to be recognised here. Auckland and Christchurch suffered serious wounds under Thornton. They healed remarkably quickly – a testimony perhaps to the deep structures of ordinary church life (tea meetings, Bible studies etc) that we have glimpsed in the Cambridge case. Possibly the healing came too easily, so that lessons were not learned. Maybe the churches of the colony were just particularly vulnerable to the predations of unreliable individuals in these early decades. Maybe it was just bad luck. Whatever the reason, two decades later history seemed to repeat itself almost exactly.

William Birch

The mood of the leadership of the Auckland Baptist Tabernacle in early November 1889 was a mixture of sadness and anticipation. There were certainly grounds for optimism. In the middle years of the decade the church had experienced a period of unprecedented growth under the leadership of Thomas Spurgeon, son of the most famous living Baptist, Charles Haddon Spurgeon of the Metropolitan Tabernacle, London. Thomas had resigned in June 1889 but had continued in the pastorate for five months. On Monday 4 November he was officially farewelled.[12] The regret attending Spurgeon Jnr's departure was tempered by the expectation

---

[11] See the *Christchurch Star* 6 September 1870, 4; 17 September 1870, 2; 20 September 1870, 3. Thornton's hutzpah seems to have known no bounds. His extensive 'Explanations' were published whilst he had been imprisoned at Christchurch for unpaid debts.

[12] See the account of Spurgeon's farewell in *The New Zealand Herald* 5 November 1889.

of the imminent arrival of his hand-picked successor. The Auckland Tabernacle leaders had requested Charles Spurgeon and Dr Alexander McLaren (another outstanding figure in English Baptist life) to select their next Pastor. This they had done. The Rev. William Birch was coming to Auckland from a strong pulpit ministry in Manchester in which he had regularly preached to 5000 and more. The prospects for continued prosperity seemed secure.

Yet William Birch's ministry at Auckland would be brief and disastrous. He would fall out with key leaders, divide the church and bring it into public disrepute. A full eight months short of the expiry of his initial two-year term he would resign. In a tragic echo of the Thornton history, Birch would soon after take up the pastoral charge at Oxford Terrace Baptist church in Christchurch, where a similar debacle would occur.

Little more than these bare facts have been incorporated into the official histories of the church and the denomination.[13] This polite reticence is understandable - few wish to magnify negative episodes. However, rich insight into the Auckland church's view of the experience may be gained through correspondence addressed to Charles Spurgeon and preserved by him in scrapbooks devoted to issues touching the career of his son Thomas.[14] The letters suggest that a combination of factors - theological, political and personal - contributed to Birch's downfall. They also provide significant insight into the evolving relationship between colonial Baptists and their principal 'Home' patron.

On 11 November 1889, Seering Matthews, Secretary of the Tabernacle, wrote to Charles Spurgeon, thanking him for finding the new pastor.[15]

Dear Brother

On behalf of the Tabernacle Baptist Church I have to tender yourself and D^r McLaren its heartfelt, grateful, thanks for your interest in securing as our Pastor so worthy and estimable a man as Mr Wm Birch.

We felt that we were trespassing upon your time and burdening you with yet another care when we asked your help, but the urgency of our

---

[13] See for instance T.F. Hill 'History of the Auckland Baptist Tabernacle' Chap. VII, *The Reaper*, Vol 1 No.10, December 1923, 264-5; A. Clifford, *A Handful of Grain: The Centenary History of the Baptist Union of New Zealand* Vol 2, (Auckland: NZBRHS, 1982), 28-9.

[14] The provenance of the three volumes relating to Thomas Spurgeon (NZBA A/N1577) is unclear. In these notes they will be referred to as SS.

[15] The letter is to be found between SS folios 74 & 5.

case & the loving interest you have always manifested in us during your Son's pastorate over us, was our excuse and plea.

...His first Sunday's services was [sic] the occasion of a blessing to God's own people and the gathering in of not a few from the world. At the after meeting on Sunday evening several young people stood up as a testimony to having that night decided to accept Christ Jesus as their Saviour.

Matthews' sunny optimism rapidly faded. Birch's rambunctious preaching style soon caused disquiet. More important was a discordant theological emphasis which emerged early. By Easter 1890 Birch had sparked controversy - the first of three flare-ups which would eventually cause his downfall. Ironically the focus of the first contention was 'Holiness'. At stake was the degree to which a Christian might expect to attain to holiness in this life. For Birch the righteous life was hugely important; his detractors interpreted him to be preaching 'perfectionism'. A public disagreement with a popular visiting speaker, Henry Varley, culminated on 7 April 1890 in a dramatic meeting at which Birch's provocative manner stunned many of his congregation.[16]

This is the context of Birch's letter of 19 May 1890 to his 'dear friend', Charles Spurgeon.[17] He was critical of the state of his new home town and frankly contemptuous of some of his church officers. Birch denied any improper actions on his own part in the Varley affair. However, by this time reports of his antics were reaching England and part of his intent in writing to Spurgeon was to secure a measure of 'damage control'.

> As a rule, the Auckland City people are crude, low in moral tone, and infected with the spirit of gambling. In this small city I am told that there are about 600 prostitutes, and that most of the traders have failed in business - many two or three times. My teaching therefore that he is only a true Christian who is righteous in all his ways, has cut the Aucklanders 'on the raw.'

> ... Then Mr Varley came saying that 'no Christian can live a day without committing sin'; and when I called a meeting to protest against the inference to be drawn from that idea, a great number of Plymouth Brethren, Conditional Immortality, Seventh Adventists &c. turned up to oppose. I showed Mr Varley's teaching in practical life - 'One cannot help a little sin, you know; so said the sugar, put that lard into the

---

[16] See the newspaper reports SS ff 78-81.
[17] Letter, W. Birch to C.H. Spurgeon, May 19 1890, SS ff 82-3.

butter, water the milk &c., &c., and now come let us go to the Prayer meeting!' This flabbergasted the audience and many of them rose in agitation while four or five of the Tabernacle elders &c rose one after the other, one of them foaming at the mouth, another shaking his hymn book at me, a third running up on the platform. It was a great scene!

...Our Tabernacle church and congregation have stood by me as a whole, and the four of five officials who lost their heads at the beargarden meeting referred to seem sorry for the display they made.

<The people here as a rule are feeble in back-bone. (this sentence is struck out in the original) > Yesterday at the Tabernacle, we had full congregations; and at the evening Lord's Supper, the attendance was larger and the spirit more genuinely loving than any since my arrival. We may not have quite so many women as in January, but we have many more men.

...No doubt, distorted reports will reach England, as one of the Newspapers here has been unfriendly, and you have now the truth of which you can make use if needs be. Yesterday's Tabernacle services especially the Communion, show that the Varley row has welded us together as a church and congregation.

You may depend upon me in keeping to the truth.

A little over a month later Birch wrote again.[18] By now he was overtly antagonistic towards a group of his officers. At this point the crucial issues remained theological but Birch's descriptions reveal the 'racy' language for which he was becoming notorious among the staid Baptists of Auckland. Once again there was an element of self-justification in this communication with Spurgeon. Birch, already contemplating a return to England, was anxious lest his reputation be besmirched and his prospects jeopardised.

I have been ill two Sundays from blood poisoning caught while visiting a woman on her death bed where the dreadful smell was enough to knock a cow down, but I am rapidly recovering and hope to be at work next Sunday. As I have preached seven or eight times each week since my arrival, the quiet and rest even tho' from fever is enjoyable.

The work at the Tabernacle goes on as well as can be expected. The last Sunday I was there, an ordinary service, every seat was occupied, and, a

---

[18] Letter, W. Birch to C.H. Spurgeon, June 23 1890, SS ff 86-7.

novel feature for Auckland, more men than women. The collection average is better than for several years past.

I do not wonder that your son resigned. One or two of the officers are cantankerous, as men are whose bowels move only once a week.

...I have some enemies, who hate me as if I were a second 'Old Nick' - they are Plymouth Brethren of the rank sect and various Antinomians in several churches, several Tabernacleites, to whom Mr Varley was like a God-send. Their idea of religion is as Chalmers said, 'that selfishness which under the guise of sacredness sits down in placid contentment with the single privilege of justification.' They have a theological or imaginary faith, and with much apparent delight embrace the idea that 'the sin we cannot help' (or as I say, the sin we like) is excusable - that the robe of righteousness blinds God to the wilful sin of the justified!! No wonder that Auckland is chiefly ruled by mammon, music, races and self-indulgence.

My impression is that some of the Antinomian Calvinists or Plymouth Brethren may send home garbled accounts to the Home religious press and you are at liberty to publish this letter in reply.

Birch was becoming increasingly alienated from his officers. The relationship would never recover. Two further crises would follow the 'Holiness' row. To concern over Birch's theology would be added anger at his politics and indignation at personal affronts. The colour of the reaction is eloquently represented in the two letters of R.B. Shalders which follow. It is useful at this point, however, to set out the chronology of the breakdown of Birch's Tabernacle ministry.

In August and September 1890 Birch, the Trades Hall preacher from Manchester, gave active support to striking miners. On Saturday the 6th of September he addressed a large gathering of unionists at a meeting held in the natural amphitheatre of Mt Eden's crater. The following morning he preached on 'The Land Question' and in the evening sparked a walk-out of his congregation by inviting a miners' leader, John Abbot, to share the podium at the Tabernacle.[19]

The officers of the Tabernacle found all this intolerable. A flurry of activity quickly followed. At an emergency joint meeting of Elders and Deacons on Tuesday 9 September they concluded that Birch's part in the 'strike question' deserved the 'highest censure'. In addition they listed the

---

[19] See the reports in *The New Zealand Herald* Sept. 9 1890.

following grievances: the lack of 'spiritual food' in his sermons, his disregard for the constitution and his unpleasant handling of the officers. They summoned Birch to a meeting with them on Thursday 11 September 're his relationship with the church.' It is unclear what understandings were reached at the Thursday meeting, or even if Birch appeared. What is known is that the officers drew up resolutions calling for his resignation, planning for pulpit supply and even drafting his resignation letter![20]

Birch was not yet ready to go. At a special meeting of the church on Monday 15 September he apologised for his actions over the strike. The resolution from the officers that he resign was defeated by 97 votes to 77. Two weeks later, at an ordinary members' meeting on 29 September a similar resolution was moved but ruled out of order by Birch, who insisted on retaining the chair throughout.[21]

A stand-off had now been reached. No reconciliation would occur. The church limped through the summer. The end came rapidly when, on 23 February, Birch was held to have personally insulted two of the leading women in the church, Mrs Gaze and Mrs Batts, both wives of officers. To a members' meeting held that same evening Birch refused to apologise and by a letter dated 24 February 1891 he resigned on certain financial conditions.

R.B. 'Bishop' Shalders recounts these events and the whole sorry affair in two letters to Charles Spurgeon.[22] The first (14 April 1891) covers a number of specific incidents. It also makes telling comment on Birch's preaching.

> ... I had hoped that he would at least command our sympathies, if not our intelligent appreciation. For more barren sermons I have seldom heard. I have read 5 vols of his sermons and, beyond anecdotes, there is little in them save two themes (and glorious themes they are: salvation thro faith in the precious blood and a holy walk as an evidence of the faith). As a teacher he is inferior to a well taught Sabbath School teacher and had I not had your printed sermons, which I have revelled in for 15 or 20 years, and my own studies and reading for my local efforts, I should have been a starveling indeed. As to doctrines of

---

[20] Loose-leaf notes and minutes taken at these meetings are to be found in NZBA A5/25 013/3.
[21] See reports SS ff 94-8.
[22] Letters, R.B. Shalders to C.H. Spurgeon, April 14 1891 and May 22 1891, SS ff110-111 & 112-113.

Sovereign grace, he is totally ignorant of them and some of the doctrines he has are sadly astray.

The second letter on 22 May, 1891 was if anything more desperate. Shalders' earlier confidence that the Tabernacle congregation would not suffer unduly seems to have been misplaced. There is more comment on the preaching but by now he was openly questioning Birch's sanity and a note of complaint entered as he questioned how Spurgeon and McLaren came to endorse one so theologically unsound in the first place.

> I wrote to you last month enclosing [manuscript illegible] slips from the daily papers re Mr. Birch and, thinking you might like to know the present position of matters relating to our Tabernacle, I report Mr. Birch is gone to Sydney, he said for three months. I hope he will not return here to further damage the interests of true religion in our city. Only about sixty members have left the Tabernacle but the congregation is largely affected - only about half filled. Those who have left have opened the old Baptist Chapel five minutes walk from the Tabernacle and have styled themselves the *Free Union church* or Union Free Church. Baptist principles seem to be a discount with them as it is a conglomeration of views held by various individuals, without any common bond of union. They seem rather to have gathered around the standard of a man (Mr. Birch) rather than on central truths. I scarcely think they will continue long, unless Mr. Birch returns, which I hope you will use your influence to prevent. So many elements can scarcely keep long united.[23]
>
> As for Mr. Birch, I am puzzled to know what his principles are. I enclose some extracts from his sermons, which are so far from the teaching of the scriptures that I cannot account for your sending us such a man, except you were entirely ignorant of his views, which you should not have been, and the greater wonder is that Dr. McLaren, who lives in Manchester, should have allowed you to send him. There's not a minister in Auckland would let Mr. Birch into the pulpit. I believe two or three of the ablest think he has been a curse to Auckland. It would take too long to recite their expressions to you which they have made to me but the complete testimony of all is his [manuscript illegible] have

---

[23] The Union Free Church eventually became the Baptist City Mission and joined the N.Z. Baptist Union in 1898. Through this group was founded the work which grew into the Manurewa Children's Home. The church disbanded in 1906. See Clifford p 62 and Hill 264-5.

swallowed up his intellect and principles. So we charitably conclude, as numbers say, he is off his head.

... I feel deep interest in the cause here. I am not a novice (66 years of age) I am one of the first of the members and aided or rather compiled the constitution form so well it is my command. I am not circulating these extracts (not wishing to be drawn into controversy), merely printing them to show the wanderers the truth and to prevent them asking Mr. Birch to return. He is certainly <u>*down-grade with a vengeance.*</u> I trust the Lord will give him his Spirit and lead him back to the truth of Christ and him crucified.

Mr. Birch is awfully sweet on you, he calls you his 'dearest and most intimate friend.' He says he has ate with you, slept with you, washed your feet and all and sundry things beside. I always take a discount off his statements. The secretary of our YMCA has just returned from Sydney and stayed in the same hotel and he informs me Mr. Birch told them he had 100 conversions in his meeting at our Choral Hall where he preached before leaving Auckland, and before he left he told us at a Ministers' meeting they were all in tears, when there was not one, nor have I heard of one conversion at the Choral Hall.

I am sure his head is gone wrong, but he is a man of great power, especially over the girls. At one meeting of girls he had, he flattered them by 'How very fair and pretty you all look' and 'How neatly you all are dressed and so beautiful' and 'Would you not like to be a missionary wife?' So he bears captive the fair sex. Sometimes in his sermons the ladies have had to cover their faces and one left and could not come again and has not yet.

The deference of the Auckland church to the counsel and prestige of Charles Spurgeon is notable. This respect was no doubt boosted by the high regard in which Thomas continued to be held at the Auckland Tabernacle, even after his departure. Nevertheless, as the tone of Shalders' second letter indicates, a realisation was growing that Spurgeon senior's advice was not infallible. On this issue a further letter gives an intriguing slant. Although not from Auckland it is preserved, like the letters already examined, in Spurgeon's scrapbook. It is addressed to one of Spurgeon's assistants at the time when news of Birch's affairs was filtering through to England. The signature is unclear but, whoever penned it, its frank contents indicate that Birch's behaviour was no sudden aberration, and that Spurgeon had been warned.

34 Devonshire Road

Liverpool   2 May 1890

Dear Mr Brown

You thought me wrong in my judgment about Spurgeon's sending Mr Birch - eh? Well what do you think now? Pity you hadn't taken my advice my Brother & got C.H.S. to telegraph & stop him.

Next time you are in Manchester walk into the Exchange & ask the first man you meet if he knows W. Birch *Jnr* (who W.B. *Snr* is nobody knows) & *why he left Manchester*. The answer will be a revelation. I say no more. Except that I do heartily wish CHS could be brought to wash his hands of this business. Possibly his letters from Auckland may have let him see by this time that I was not to (sic) far wrong when I warned him through you of the worse than folly that be …(illegible) perfectibility. Now don't my dear Brother let him get further into the net. He had better say 'Peccator' ['I have sinned'] in the Sword and Trowel & have done with it *before any more comes out*.

believe me

always yours

(signature unclear)

As with Thornton, New Zealand Baptists were not yet done with William Birch. Birch did return to Auckland, as Shalders feared he might, to lead the breakaway Union Free Church. He did not stay long. In April 1892 he was called to Christchurch to replace the impressive Charles Dallaston, who had succeeded Morton and set the now Oxford Terrace church on a good footing. Just why the choice would be made for Birch is a mystery. On 1 March 1892 the *Star* carried a Press Association note summarising his history.

Pastor Birch, who had trouble with the Tabernacle congregation, causing numbers to secede and form a Union church, of which he has since been the Minister, has accepted a call to the Oxford Terrace church, Christchurch.[24]

It is inconceivable that the Oxford Terrace church was not aware of this background. Is it just possible that a Canterbury-Auckland rivalry, already manifesting itself in Canterbury's complaints about the Baptist Union, was a factor? ('If he fell out with Auckland he might well suit us!')

---

[24] *Star* 1 March 1892, 3.

Whatever the reasoning, come he did, and the outcome was disastrous. The church name was soon changed to Christchurch Baptist Tabernacle and Birch introduced the raw mission style of preaching which had rankled in Auckland. As he had in Auckland, Birch took an interest in the Trades Union movement.[25] The church began to divide over his ministry. As MacLeod describes events: 'realising this, a deputation from the Deacons waited upon him to discuss the matter, but Mr Birch was the kind of man who felt that anyone who disagreed with him was lacking in spiritual zeal.'[26] Birch nonetheless offered his resignation, which was ultimately accepted by only a small majority of members in August 1893, less than 18 months after his arrival.

Birch immediately moved to found a Central Mission. At the inaugural meeting he stated 'that a large number, perhaps the majority of the people did not seem to be in sympathy with the churches, and the Central Mission was an attempt to bridge the gulf.'[27] This is a clue to understanding Birch. Although clearly a difficult personality and quite unsuited to pastoral ministry, he was not James Thornton. He was, rather, a radical proponent of what would later be the social gospel, willing to overturn traditional church practice to build his bridges. At the Central Mission, for instance, 'the Sunday morning service was to be a free and open meeting to all the workers and friends, the usual pulpit-preaching being dispensed with.'[28] In March 1893 he addressed the Wesleyan Conference. 'He thought religion was not losing ground, though the churches might be. They should confine themselves to the socialism of the Sermon on the Mount.'[29] Through 1894 he was agitating for better care of the unemployed and destitute, eventually succeeding in setting up a Christchurch Benevolent Society.[30] He left New Zealand in 1896 to pursue interests in an International Peace Federation.[31]

Thornton and Birch, though with uncannily similar patterns to their ministries in New Zealand, reveal quite different aspects of colonial Baptist life. Both were difficult individuals to work with but there perhaps the similarities end. Thornton was a crook, a man with a history of deception

---

[25] He was elected an Honorary member of the Tailoresses' Union in June 1892 – see *Star* (9 June 1892): 4.
[26] MacLeod, Oxford terrace, 42.
[27] *Star* (31 August 1893): 2.
[28] *Star* (31 August 1893): 2.
[29] *Star* (8 March 1894): 1.
[30] See e.g. *Star*, (5 Dec 1894): 4.
[31] *Star*, (9 April 1896): 2; (2 May 1896): 7.

and half-truth who was inevitably found wanting despite his over-confident bluster. He is an extreme example of the ministry problem. In the earliest decades few top quality pastors would willingly expose themselves to the challenging conditions of the new colony. Slow communications made the checking of credentials difficult and the desperation of churches looking for teaching made smooth talkers appealing, at least for a while.

Birch represents something else altogether. Shalders complained of the thinness of Birch's preaching. This may be accepted as true, and just one among many signs that his calling lay elsewhere than the teaching pulpit. His disastrous stints at the Auckland and Christchurch churches suggest the ministry supply problem lasted well into 1890s. We shall see that by 1900 a new generation would be agitating to cut through this chronic problem, with better local training initiatives. But there was more to Birch, a committed depth shows him to be a different person altogether from Thornton. His Central Mission era in Christchurch deserves recognition and further study. In some senses he too was a victim of colonial circumstances, where the niches possible in larger, established populations were often denied. Beyond that, Birch's unacceptability also demonstrates the essential conservatism of New Zealand Baptists. Other radical pastors such as J.J. Doke, A.H. Collins and J.K. Archer, though much more successful as ministers, would come against the same diffidence on social action. Doke[32] and Collins would leave the country for other settings. Archer would direct his energies to the party political sphere.

The churches, meanwhile, managed to survive. The conflicts surrounding Thornton and Birch were painful and embarrassing. The public nature of the spats did little to build a sense of respectability for the Baptist cause. It was probably inevitable that these types of conflict would be found in the colonial context. Baptists were finding their way, but without a reliable map. We have seen them struggling to find authentic structures at regional, national and local levels. As the next chapter will show, theological dispute would also be part of the shaping of Baptist identity in New Zealand.

---

[32] On Doke see Laurie Guy, *Shaping Godzone: Public Issues and Church Voices in New Zealand 1840-2000* (Wellington: VUP, 2011), 99-101, 242.

Chapter Four: 'downgrade' down under

A telling measure of the strength of any organisation is its ability to cope with dissension. One might imagine that Baptists would have some skills in this area, as we assume they have had plenty of practice. As we have seen, different visions of how to be Baptists on a colonial frontier caused tension among New Zealand Baptists. Conflict within churches has been so endemic as to threaten some sort of sorry normality. Serious doctrinal disputes across wider Baptist connections have been rarer, but often profound and always indicative of other stresses within the community. Baptist organisations have shown a remarkable resilience despite these battles. The Charles Spurgeon initiated 'Downgrade' controversy of 1887/8 is a famous case. Although, as E.A. Payne lamented, the controversy 'cast a shadow over the Baptist denomination for more than a generation,' the Union was able to survive the defection of its most prominent individual - a signal of the diversity and depth of its membership as well as a pragmatic concern to preserve unity.[1] Not so familiar is a parallel controversy played out in New Zealand over the same period. Parallel, but not the same. As in Britain, the New Zealand crisis ostensibly turned on theological purity but, due to the distinctive character of the colonial context, its course and immediate outcome were quite different. Nevertheless, an examination of the controversy reveals the remarkable degree to which the concerns of the denominational leadership mirrored those of their counterparts at 'Home' even as they sought to shape themselves to a new environment.

When the Baptist Union of New Zealand was formed in 1882, the colony was enjoying the final glow of a period of optimism and expansion.

---

[1] Payne's treatment is found in *The Baptist Union - A Short History* (London, Carey Kingsgate Press, 1959), 127-143 and 'The Down Grade Controversy: A Postscript' *BQ*, Vol. XXVII, No. 4 (October 1979): 146-158. More recently M.T.E. Hopkins has rounded out the picture considerably in 'Spurgeon's Opponents in the Downgrade Controversy' *BQ* Vol. XXXII, No. 6 (April 1988): 274-294 and 'The Down Grade Controversy: New Evidence', *BQ* Vol XXXV, No. 6 (April 1994): 262-278. See also M. Nicholls, The Downgrade Controversy: A Neglected Protagonist', *BQ* Vol. XXXII, No.6 (April 1988): 260-274.

This prosperity was not just economic. Church attendances climbed during the 1880s, Baptists benefiting with the emergence of a few large churches. Yet there was little progress in the forging of a uniquely New Zealand version of Baptist life. Denominationalism had been somewhat self-consciously transplanted and was yet to face the tests of the 1890s.[2] Britain continued to provide all the models, the most conspicuous individual example being Charles Spurgeon. Through the 1880s no human figure was more revered among New Zealand Baptists. Spurgeon's publications were widely available and eagerly read; his pronouncements respectfully reported in the denominational magazine. Most importantly, his emissaries were everywhere. Lacking a training scheme of their own, New Zealand Baptists of necessity sourced most of their Pastors from English Colleges. For those few men who left the colony to train, Spurgeon's Pastor's College was a natural choice. To that small group was added those induced to emigrate from Britain to assist struggling causes in the new land. In the decade and a half from 1877 more than half of the ministerial arrivals in the 1880s were Spurgeon's graduates. Standing out among these was Charles's own son and eventual successor at the Metropolitan Tabernacle. From 1882 Thomas Spurgeon was the hugely popular and successful pastor of the Auckland Tabernacle. It became the largest church in Australasia during his time. Although many of the Pastors' College graduates served only briefly in New Zealand, in a Baptist community which could boast only one recognised minister for every 1025 adherents their collective impact was considerable.[3]

In a context so open to Spurgeonic style and concerns a student of the master could expect to be well received. Thus, when Rev. Charles Crisp Brown arrived in the colony in 1884, armed with a letter of recommendation from Charles Spurgeon, he was welcomed. Yet, before long, Brown would find himself at the centre of a colonial 'downgrade'. The controversy would provide a focus for underlying tensions within the fledgling Union. Personal, pragmatic and theological issues would be at stake, all magnified by reports of the unfolding English crisis. The Brown affair highlights both the degree to which the Baptists of New Zealand perpetuated the assumptions and forms of their British counterparts and the inadequacy of those structures for the colonial context. Moreover it

---

[2] See the editorial on 'Undenominationalism' in *NZB* (August 1881): 104.
[3] Figure from an analysis in *NZB* (March 1887): 40-41. Baptists had the lowest ministerial ratio. Comparisons include: Church of England 1 in 901; Presbyterians 1 in 816; Congregationalists 1 in 458; Wesleyans 1 in 430.

represents a third arena in which the themes of conflict and connection which this book explores were played out. Canterbury Baptists contested for a looser brand of church extension and branding than eventually prevailed. Cambridge was an example of the 'tighter' approach and also an exemplar of the interplay between local conflict and the underlying desire Baptists had for connection. The Thornton and Birch cases demonstrate the fortitude of local churches in the face of bad (at moments egregiously bad) leadership. In Brown's case the conflict was not local but colony wide. It was not about practice (such as open or closed communion) but about more esoteric points of doctrine. Personal factors were certainly important, but these were about more than character, as with Thornton and Birch. They were as much to do with loyalty and the still strong threads linking the colony to church life in England. Crucially it was the first test of whether the new Union could or should govern its corporate life. It fell into two phases.

Phase One: 1885-1888 conflict and expulsion

In 1885 C.C. Brown became minister of an almost defunct cause in Timaru in South Island. The church was in recess - divided, with the status of its property in some confusion. Although it had been a founding member of the Union, it was suspended for a year between the 1883 and 1884 Conferences, whilst enquiry into its affairs was made.[4] Brown thus took on a church which already had a history of tensions with Union leaders. Nevertheless, under his energetic ministry, baptisms, members and optimism returned. A series of ebullient reports from the Timaru cause appeared in *The N.Z. Baptist* late in 1885.

Yet, in the wider Baptist community, there was growing doubt about Brown himself. In particular, disquiet was felt at his theological views. By his own account, Brown, whilst still a student in the early 1870s, had 'abandoned the belief that the wicked would suffer eternal punishment.' He became convinced of the 'Life in Christ only' position of the Congregationalist Edward White.[5] Brown apparently made no effort to hide his views from his New Zealand colleagues but it was not until 1886

---

[4] See the several entries regarding Timaru in the Minutes of the Union Committee, October 1883 - October 1884. NZBA B1/119.
[5] *NZB* (April 1888): 57-8. On White see R.T. Jones, *Congregationalism in England 1662-1962* (London: Independent Press, 1962), 248-50, 264-5.

that discomfort at his doctrinal position was transformed into action. It was the beginning of an increasingly bitter process of censure and alienation.

The founding constitution of the Baptist Union of New Zealand was almost silent on doctrinal matters. The sole clause with any theological edge merely affirmed that 'the Union fully recognises that every separate church has liberty to interpret and administer the laws of Christ, and that the immersion of believers is the only Christian Baptism.' There was, accordingly, no constitutional ground for censuring Brown on the basis of doctrine alone. Nevertheless coercion was attempted.

Encouraged by early signs of renewal under Brown's ministry, the Timaru church applied to the Union Committee (the executive body of the New Zealand Union) for a grant to assist in supporting its new minister. This was granted, in the sum of £20, but on the condition that Brown was not to promulgate his conditional immortality views.[6] Bridling at this interference in what they regarded as local matters, Brown and his church appealed to the Conference in November 1886. They were unsuccessful. After a long debate the gathered delegates endorsed the actions of the Committee. A stand-off ensued and the grant remained unpaid. More importantly, hints of further trouble surfaced. During the Conference debate, Thomas Spurgeon cited a letter from his father in which Spurgeon senior distanced himself from Brown's views and effectively repudiated his letter of endorsement.[7] This sounded a personal note which would echo through the affair. The Spurgeon factor would increase in importance as the controversy developed.

---

[6] One of the first decisions of the Union Committee (approved at the 1883 Conference) had been to reserve to itself the right to insist that churches receiving grants confer with it over matters of Pastorate and Constitution - see the Minutes of the Union Committee 11 October, 1882 (f. 2). The claiming of this right would later be cited by groups concerned at the increasing power of the Union executive body.
The Union Committee minutes of 16 October, 1885 (f. 27) record a decision to make a grant to Timaru and two other churches, payable 'as soon as the Union exchequer will permit'. By the publication of the Official Report in February 1886, unspecified 'conditions' were signalled. See *NZB* (February 1886): 3. At the Conference in 1886 the restriction on promulgating Brown's views was acknowledged and endorsed by the delegates. Disquiet at this action prompted H. Olney of Christchurch, a trustee of the Union, to fire the first shot in a campaign to rein in the Union executive - *NZB* (December 1886): 186-7.
[7] The reading of the letter is not recorded in the minutes of the Conference but Thomas Spurgeon spoke in the debate and later referred to his use of his father's note at that gathering. See *NZB* (May 1888): 74.

The matter was now public. Through 1887 a series of articles by senior figures were published in *The N.Z.Baptist*, attacking Brown's position. Brown replied in the pages of *The Bible Standard*, a publication promoting the conditional immortality view.[8] So prominent was the debate that the matter could not be kept from the agenda of the 1887 Assembly. Again, the Union Committee took the initiative. On its behalf President Philip Cornford moved for the expulsion of this troublesome minister.

That, in the judgement of this assembly, the Rev. C.C. Brown, of Timaru, has identified himself with the distinctive views of another body, and is hereby requested to withdraw.

This meat was too strong for the delegates. An amendment was accepted, subsequently became the motion and was passed, 'without a dissentient', to the effect:

That this Union regrets to know that Mr Brown holds and gives prominence to the distinctive views of the body represented by Mr Aldridge[9], and considers it right to declare that such views are not in accordance with the views of the Union.[10]

The matter might have stopped with this censorious inaction were it not for Brown's provocative conduct in reading aloud the testimonial from Charles Spurgeon which he had brought to New Zealand. As has been noted, his right to claim this influential endorsement had been challenged a year before by none other than Thomas Spurgeon. Brown's timing was not good. On the same day on which it expressed its strong disapprobation of Brown's activities, the Union elected the junior Spurgeon as its new President.

That Brown's persistence in using the great man's name would rankle is of little surprise, particularly as the affairs of Charles Spurgeon were at that

---

[8] There were cross-currents in this debate. P.H. Cornford published a series of articles on 'Immortality' in *NZB*, June-September 1887. Cornford, a respected senior minister was President of the Union in 1887. George Aldridge, the editor of *The Bible Standard*, responded in a parallel series - *The Bible Standard*, July-October 1887. Rev. Charles Carter, a noted Baptist scholar and linguist, defended Cornford - *NZB* (August 1887): 113-5. Brown responded to Carter in *The Bible Standard* (September 1887): 129-131. Carter replied to Brown in *NZB* (October 1887): 146-149 to which Brown in turn responded in *The Bible Standard* (November 1887): 161-164.
[9] George Aldridge was a leader of the Conditional Immortality Association in New Zealand and editor of *The Bible Standard*.
[10] Minutes of the Conference of the Baptist Union of New Zealand, 17 November 1887 (ff. 65-66), NZBA B1/172.

time on everyone's mind. Spurgeon had resigned from the British Baptist Union in October 1887. In the same issue of *The N.Z. Baptist* which reported the 1887 Conference it was noted that 'misapprehensions and misrepresentations are rife concerning the import of the action of the Rev. C.H. Spurgeon in relation to the Baptist Union in the Mother Country.'[11] News of the developing crisis at 'Home' would run parallel with exchanges over the Brown affair through the next crucial year.

Brown himself immediately invited further criticism. He wrote a pugnacious account of the Conference for *The Bible Standard*[12] and, travelling north, spoke in similar vein to public meetings sponsored by Conditional Immortality groups in Auckland and the then still prosperous mining town of Thames. In these addresses he explained his views, celebrating what he regarded as his justified escape from expulsion and the 'very harmless resolution' which was eventually passed. To this - effectively a claim to victory - Brown's Baptist critics took umbrage. There was more. Brown provocatively linked his cause to the simmering English 'Downgrade'. The report of the Thames address records that Brown made reference 'to Pastor Spurgeon and his secession from the Baptist Union because it would not preach the doctrine of eternal torment, which in [Brown's] opinion, was an awful blasphemous doctrine, while it was not supported by the Bible.' This daring criticism of his former mentor was spur enough to Brown's Baptist detractors, but even this was eclipsed by his concluding reference to 'the tendency of many orthodox ministers to preach anything for money, and also to the fact that few cared to debate or search the scriptures.'[13]

Brown's personal propensity for controversy found a ready match in the new editor of *The N.Z. Baptist*. Rev. Lewis Shackleford had arrived in New Zealand in 1884, the same year as Brown. After a brief, unsuccessful pastorate at Wanganui[14] he took up the cause at Greendale in Canterbury. Shackleford was appointed editor at the 1887 Conference and was

---

[11] *NZB* (December 1887): 184.
[12] *The Bible Standard* (December 1887): 185-6.
[13] See the report in and subsequent letters to the Thames *Evening Star*, reprinted in *NZB* (January 1888): 5-6. The meetings were also reported in *The Bible Standard* (December 1887): 191. Brown denied making the statement about money but the *Evening Star* stood by and indeed reinforced its report - See *NZB* (February 1888): 27-8 and (March 1888): 43.
[14] On Shackleford's brief tenure at Wanganui see A.K. Smith Manuscript 'History of the Wanganui Baptist church' held in the Carey Baptist College Library, 9-12.

intimately involved in the handling of Brown's case at that gathering. With one other, he had been commissioned to confer with Brown 're his status in connection with this Union' before the resolutions on the question were brought to the floor.[15] Through 1888, in the pages of *The N.Z. Baptist*, he would pursue the controversy with vigour and some venom.

In January and February 1888 Shackleford allocated extensive space to Brown's Thames address and the angry correspondence which attended it. In the March issue he and Brown clashed head on. Responding to his critics Brown laid down the gauntlet to the Union.

> At the next Conference, let a resolution be carried to the effect that all members of the Union must subscribe to the doctrine of eternal torments for every soul outside the number of the elect. This will change the basis of the Union. As I could not subscribe, I should immediately tender my resignation.[16]

Shackleford responded to this challenge by linking the controversy theologically and personally to Charles Spurgeon and the English 'Downgrade'. The article in *The N.Z. Baptist* which immediately preceded Brown's provocative dare was a long report, taken from *The British Weekly*, on attempts to reverse Spurgeon's withdrawal from the English Union. This juxtaposition can hardly have been coincidental. A paragraph complimentary to Spurgeon as a 'common-sense Englishman' is printed side-by-side with a response to Brown by Shackleford which appropriates the revered name whilst casting grave aspersions on the integrity of his opponent. It is important enough to be quoted at length.

> It will be sufficient to allude to one point only in Mr Brown's letter. He says: 'When I joined the Union it was known I held 'Life in Christ Only' views.' He came, we believe, furnished with a letter from the Rev. C.H. Spurgeon, which was deemed sufficient guarantee that Mr Brown was not the kind of man he has since shown himself to be. How came he by that letter? The question opens a chapter of history which we are afraid is not altogether to Mr Brown's credit. It is convenient for Mr Brown to make the issue between the Union and himself one of doctrine; but we hold…that the question at issue is primarily not so much a doctrinal one as a moral. Is it likely, in the light of recent controversies at Home, that the Rev. C.H. Spurgeon recommended Mr Brown to the Baptist Union of New Zealand, knowing that he held and

---

[15] *NZB* (December 1887): 183.
[16] *NZB* (March 1888): 42.

intended to teach what he holds and teaches? We put the question to the common-sense of our readers.'[17]

Despite Shackleford's claim to have shifted the controversy from 'doctrinal' to 'moral' grounds it is clear that the real issues were personal. Spurgeon senior, so esteemed in the Colonies, was under intense pressure at 'Home'. For Brown to continue to claim his endorsement at this time, whilst holding the very views Spurgeon rejected was beyond toleration. Shackleford's appeal to the 'common sense' of his readers - a quality already attributed to the great man - subtly marked Brown as the outsider.[18]

Stung by this new tone, Brown appealed directly to Spurgeon for confirmation of the authenticity of the testimonial. In a letter dated 6 June 1888 he outlined the dispute, explained his own views and proceeded 'simply to beg from you the favour of half a dozen lines to the effect that *you* do not charge me with double dealing, dishonesty or want of morality in connection with your letter of recommendation.'[19] Brown's hope was to be able to publish these 'lines' in *The N.Z. Baptist*. Spurgeon, it seems, did not accede to his request, as no such statement appeared. Indeed the controversy disappeared from the pages of the denominational paper for a time after the June issue. It was clear, however, that the Brown matter was not yet settled.

In the September issue of *The N.Z. Baptist* notice was given of a motion to add to the Union's constitution the following clause: 'That the Constituencies and List of Members may be revised by the *Committee*, and their decision shall be duly notified to the persons concerned, who shall have the right of appeal to the Assembly.'(original emphasis).[20] The mover was Rev. Alfred North.[21] North had been a member of the Union Committee since its inception and was the key individual in the Union leadership. In his motion, North was proposing a considerable appropriation of power by the executive body of the Union. No overt link

---

[17] *NZB* (March 1888): 42.
[18] This isolation was reinforced through 1888, as relevant columns were headed 'Mr C.C. Brown and the Union'. Here too was a double implication, as reports of the English Down-grade fallout were generally headed similarly 'Rev. C. H. Spurgeon and the Baptist Union'.
[19] Letter, C.C. Brown to C. H. Spurgeon, 6 June, 1888, NZBA Spurgeon Scrapbooks Vol. 1, f 69.
[20] *NZB* (September 1888): 136.
[21] On North see S.L. Edgar, *Alfred North*, N.Z Baptist Historical Society Monograph, 1955.

was made to the Brown case (North was preparing another motion, of which no public notice was given, dealing directly with that matter) but the effect of the constitutional change would be to allow a speedy means of expulsion.

At least one body of Baptist leaders made the connection between North's motion and Brown.

> 'Oct. 26/88 A meeting of Pastors and Deacons of the Tabernacle and Mt Eden churches was held at [the] Tabernacle to consider matters as far as possible that will come up at the conference in [Christchurch]. The matter of the Rev. C.C. Brown was especially referred to. A motion will be submitted to Conference requesting him to withdraw from the Union. It was moved by Rev. Bray, 2nd Mr Stone that the delegates agree to support this motion, also the motion of which Rev Mr North has given notice in [The] Baptist.'[22]

Further significant resolutions of this crucial meeting will be referred to below. It is clear, however, from this first motion that the expulsion of Brown and North's proposed constitutional change were held to be in tandem.

The Seventh Annual Conference of the Union was held in Christchurch in November 1888. Thomas Spurgeon was in the Chair. In the first session, North's constitutional amendment was passed 'with one dissentient.' (It would be intriguing to know who, but the record is silent as to the name.) Almost immediately after, North moved 'That in the judgement of this Assembly, the Rev. C.C. Brown has so far identified himself with another denomination that he ought no longer to continue a member of the Union, and that therefore he be, and is hereby requested to withdraw.' After a lengthy debate, during which Brown vigorously defended himself, the motion was carried by a total of 31 votes to 5. Brown 'bowed to the decision of the Assembly and accordingly withdrew.'[23]

On the face of it, in expelling Brown the New Zealand Baptists had responded to doctrinal controversy in a way markedly different from their fellows in Britain. The British Baptist Union, at its Conference in April that same year, had reached a compromise solution, driven by the desire to prevent a damaging split. Charles Spurgeon, unhappy that the compromise formula had failed to achieve a purified Baptist Union, declined to retract

---

[22] Minutes of the Mt Eden Baptist Church, 5 November 1888. NZBA M13/a.
[23] Minutes of the Conference of the Baptist Union of New Zealand, Tuesday 13 November 13, 1888, 72-4.

his resignation. The New Zealand outcome appears almost the polar opposite. The result was not the withdrawal of the concerned conservative, but the exclusion of the heterodox *provocateur*. Unlike its British counterpart, the New Zealand Union had apparently exorcised the Downgrade demon.

But had it? A careful consideration of the underlying causes of Brown's demise suggests a challenge to that sharp contrast. The concerns of the New Zealand Baptists were in fact very similar to those in Britain. Only the context in which those concerns manifested themselves was different. Individual factors and the unique challenges of a colonial situation played key roles in the outcome.

The importance of Brown's polemical approach must not be discounted. The Baptist Union of New Zealand was very small, its ministerial cohort even smaller. Brown marked himself as an outsider early in the controversy and had little hesitation in criticising leading ministers. His aggression was matched by that of Shackleford, whose brief tenure as editor of *The N.Z. Baptist* included the period in which the dispute reached its public height. With cooler heads controlling it than these two, the course of the controversy may have been very different.

There were broader forces at work. In an illuminating article on the British controversy, Mark Hopkins has identified the role of denominational rivalry in provoking public response to Spurgeon's allegations.[24] The cloud cast over Nonconformity in general gave opportunity for criticism, even gloating, from sectors of the Church of England. In New Zealand the situation was quite different - there was no established church - but this tended to intensify, rather than calm sectarian sensitivities. With no obvious ecclesiastical adversary in the colony those with Dissenting origins lacked both a clear sense of their own identity and the negative incentive to unity which goes with having a common enemy.

Of particular concern to Baptists in the 1880s was the presence of activist churches in the Life and Advent movement. Occupying a similar place on the ecclesiological spectrum, these churches were distinguished from the Baptists largely by their views on conditional immortality and the end times. Although Brown maintained throughout that his denominational loyalties were not divided, he found a naturally sympathetic audience among these groups. He spoke to their meetings and contributed to their magazine *The Bible Standard*, in whose pages he was

---

[24] Hopkins, 'Spurgeon's Opponents', 277-280.

lauded in the hope that his influence be felt within the Baptist denomination in the direction of leading many to a knowledge of 'sound doctrine'.[25]

That denominational rivalry played a large role in the reaction to Brown is manifest from the wording of the resolutions concerning him. As has been noted, in 1887 both the original resolution calling for his withdrawal and the weaker censure eventually passed lamented that Brown had 'identified himself with the distinctive views of another body.' A year later the wording was more direct. Brown's withdrawal was not sought for heresy, but because he 'has so far identified himself with another denomination.'

As in Britain, denominational standing was a factor in the outcome of the controversy but it was not the whole picture. There were other parallels between the British and colonial crises. Most importantly, an overriding concern for unity was common to both. The evidence shows that Brown's exclusion was engineered to avoid a crippling split.

Throughout the 1887/88 row, the colonial protagonists kept an eye on the unfolding events in London. If there were fears in Britain that the downgrade might lead to a damaging split in a Union which had lasted more than half a century, these were magnified exponentially among the leaders of a fragile body of a mere twenty-six churches, which had been in existence only half a decade. Moreover, the risk of division implicit in the British controversy became explicit in New Zealand at the Conference in November 1888.

Though principled, Charles Spurgeon's action in resigning from the British Union in October 1887, soon after the start of the controversy, was a tactical blunder. He had fired all his guns and had thereby excluded himself from direct intervention in the ensuing debate. His 'son Tom' did not make the same mistake. At the 1888 Conference, after the motion demanding Brown's withdrawal was moved but before it was debated, a letter was read from Thomas Spurgeon's Auckland Tabernacle and the associated Mt Eden church recording 'an emphatic protest against Mr Brown's proceedings in Auckland and elsewhere after the Union meetings of last year.'[26] The juxtaposition of the motion and the written protest made the clear inference that the defeat of the motion and the consequent

---

[25] *The Bible Standard* (December 1887): 191.
[26] Minutes of the Conference of the Baptist Union of New Zealand, Tuesday 13 November, 1888, 72.

continued presence of Brown would be unacceptable to the Auckland group. Whilst neither the minutes of the 1888 Conference nor subsequent reports of proceedings in *The N.Z. Baptist* record an explicit threat as to the consequences of a failure to expel Brown, *The Bible Standard* declared that 'it was generally known that if by any mischance [Brown's] name remained on the Union's rolls...a serious disruption would at once take place.' The report goes on to quote Alfred North as declaring 'the laws of self-preservation demand the withdrawal of Mr Brown from our ranks.' [27]

The Bible Standard was hardly a sympathetic witness to the actions of the Baptist Conference. There is available, however, clear substantiation of its claim that disruption was threatened. It is found in the record of the meeting of Auckland church leaders on 26 October to which I have already referred. The first resolution of this meeting has been cited. There were three more. The second reads as follows:

> 'That a presentment from the Tabernacle and Mt Eden churches be made to the Conference expressing disapproval of the Rev. C.C. Brown's actions subsequent to the Conference of 1887.'

A third resolution appointed three of their number to draw up the 'presentment'; the fourth makes the seriousness of the move clear.

> 'That in case the motion of Rev. North's be not carried, the delegates be requested to notify the intention of the Tabernacle and Mt Eden churches to withdraw from the Union at the end of the session.'[28]

A clear risk of disruption thus hung over the Conference of 1888. By retaining the threat of possible resignation, withdrawal or division, Thomas Spurgeon's party was able to influence events more powerfully than had his father in Britain. Nevertheless, it was Charles Spurgeon's downgrade crusade which had raised the spectre of disunity over the very doctrinal questions with which Brown was identified. Indeed, it is arguable that the key personality in the New Zealand controversy, in its first phase at least, was not Brown, Shackleford or North, but Charles Spurgeon.

Spurgeon's personal prestige among N.Z. Baptists in the late 1880s was incalculable. Brown himself had recognised the value of an endorsement from the great preacher. Conversely, he miscalculated in citing that blessing again in the midst of the controversy. To associate Spurgeon's name with the very doctrines he was at that time heroically fighting was

---

[27] *The Bible Standard* (December 1888): 178.
[28] The Mt Eden church members were invited to approve the resolutions, which they duly did - Minutes of the Mt Eden Baptist church, 5th November 1888.

highly offensive. When to that impertinent blunder was added the presence and enormous influence of Spurgeon senior's favoured son - Pastor of the largest church in the country, about to enter his Presidential year - it is clear that Brown faced impossible odds. The charge of denominational disloyalty, important as it was, paled next to the coincident threat of secession if he was not firmly dealt with. The power of that threat depended on the Spurgeon prestige.

It should not be missed that in New Zealand the Union model was new and still the not-yet-secure alternative to the Canterbury approach. Its backers needed it to succeed. Brown was from a Canterbury church. The key engineers of the expulsion in 1888 were from Dunedin (North) and Auckland (Spurgeon). Faced with the defection of an influential Union group, the New Zealand Conference opted to sacrifice the individual. In this, far from taking the opposite tack to its British counterpart over the downgrade question, the New Zealand Union mirrored the fears and anxieties of the 'Home' body. The immediate outcome may have been different but the pragmatic concerns which prompted it were the same. As the affair entered a second phase it would become evident that the 1888 'resolution', wrought under those assumptions, was inadequate.

Phase Two: disquiet and reinstatement 1889-1892.

The history of Charles Crisp Brown and the N.Z. Baptist Union did not end with his expulsion in 1888. He was welcomed home enthusiastically by his Timaru church.[29] Although Timaru did not formally withdraw from the Union, the church was not represented at the 1889, 1890 or 1891 Conferences and it failed to pay the annual subscription required under the Constitution and Rules of the Union.

The Union Committee was not inclined to tolerate Timaru's non-participation. North's constitutional amendment of 1888 was soon brought into play. On 15 November 1890 it was resolved 'that the church at Timaru be struck off the list according to Rule 22 of the Constitution, no subscription from the church having been received.' This was a severe reaction, considering Timaru had been seeking financial support only a few years before. It was particularly unfortunate given the fact that the decision

---

[29] See the report in the *Timaru Herald* (21st November 1888).

was made five days after Timaru's chapel had burned down.[30] Perhaps because of this unfortunate turn of events, the resolution was not actioned.[31]

However, there was a rapid twist in affairs which would have long-term consequences. After steeling themselves to build anew, the Baptists in Timaru were presented with the 'providential' opportunity to purchase a better building at a bargain price from the local Congregationalists. The net result of these dealings was that within two months of the fire they were able to report that 'happily the Timaru church is perfectly sound financially.'[32] This 'providence' would come to haunt Brown and his church.

The Committee reapplied the pressure. In November 1891 an expanded resolution was made in the following terms:

> That in view of the evident lack of sympathy on the part of the Timaru church with the Union, as evidenced by their abstaining from contributing to its funds, and their refusal to send delegates to Conference, it be removed from the list of churches comprising the Union.[33]

Other developments were catching up with the Committee. As outlined in chapter one, significant cracks were beginning to widen in the Union structure. Among the complaints was that the concerns of smaller, regional churches (and most of them were in Canterbury) were discounted. The increasing tendency of the Committee to exercise centralised power was also resented. In his strongly worded letter, printed in *The N.Z. Baptist* in October 1892, Cantabrian S. R. Ingold decried the continued isolation of Timaru and its minister and protested a gradual arrogation of power to the Union Committee.[34] The problem lay with the very idea of a Union. A single body was inappropriate for a scattered Baptist community in a colony in which communications were rudimentary. Further, centralised authority could only be acceptable if even representation was guaranteed. This was theoretically possible in Britain, as the much larger number of

---

[30] The destruction of the chapel on 10 November was notified in *NZB* (December 1890): 184-5. In a letter to the editor Brown and his officers notified a £200 loss and seek financial assistance.
[31] Minutes of the Union Committee, 15 November 1890 (f. 71).
[32] *NZB* (January 1891): 3-4.
[33] Minutes of the Union Committee, 21 November 1891 (f. 77).
[34] *NZB* (October 1892): 158-9.

churches militated against the domination of a few. In New Zealand, distortion was inevitable, and ultimately resented.

In this atmosphere, the Timaru church exercised its right to appeal to the 1892 Conference against the Committee's decision to remove it from the list. With the appeal was lodged the provocative demand that Brown be reinstated as a ministerial member. The fate of these two petitions is revealing.

The case of the church was relatively straightforward. In the first session of the 1892 Assembly, Tuesday afternoon 15 November, it was unanimously resolved 'that the Conference having heard the appeal of the Timaru church is of opinion that the action of the Committee though perfectly justifiable at the time should not be insisted upon now that assurances have been given of the loyalty and sympathy of the church towards the Union in the future.'[35] By this wording the Conference managed simultaneously to indicate complete support for the Committee and satisfy Canterbury's delegates.

The case of C.C. Brown was much more difficult, as to re-admit him would mean overturning a decision of the Conference itself. The Committee considered the matter on Tuesday morning 15 November and met with Brown that night, a meeting at which Brown is recorded as making 'a full expression of regret for the course he had taken.' He was asked to give a written assurance that 'he would refrain from any similar action in the future.'[36] This he duly did, and the Committee agreed to recommend his reinstatement. At no time did Brown indicate that he resiled from his doctrinal views. The presenting issue remained his provocative behaviour in parading his difficulties with the Baptists among the other churches during 1887/88, which had provided the formal grounds for his expulsion in 1888. Importantly, the Committee's recommendation to the Conference preserved the earlier disquiet over Brown's views in stressing 'that the resolution passed at Wellington at the session of 1887 remains in force' (see above).[37]

This recommendation was brought to the floor of the Conference on Thursday 17 November. A long and inconclusive debate ensued, in which 32 of the 41 delegates present spoke. No vote was taken and the

---

[35] Minutes of the Conference of the Baptist Union of N.Z., Tuesday 15 November 1892, (f. 120). (The entry is mistakenly headed 'Tuesday Nov. 16th.')
[36] Minutes of the Union Committee, 15 November 1892 (f. 81).
[37] Minutes of the Union Committee, 16 November 1882 (f. 82).

Committee was asked to consider the matter further. This it did, only to adhere to its original recommendation. On Friday 18 November, after a further twenty speeches, the motion was put to the Conference and passed by 26 delegates' votes to 15. Brown was thereby received back into full standing.

The Committee had been wary about readmitting Brown. It had demanded written assurances and had had these read over again when asked to reconsider the question. Nevertheless it maintained support for his reinstatement in the face of an obviously uncomfortable Conference. This was a remarkable turn-around, given the history of the affair. Yet this decision too, just like the one it reversed, was largely pragmatic. A number of factors, similar in type to those which bore on the decision to expel Brown in 1888, were present again in 1892. This time they pointed to a very different result.

Personality factors had changed. In 1892, Brown displayed a contrite and conciliatory attitude. His principal protagonist during 1888, Lewis Shackleford, was no longer in the country. More significant was the waning of the Spurgeon factor. Things had altered in this area in several ways. By November 1892 the British Downgrade was but a memory in New Zealand. Charles Spurgeon himself had died early in the year; Thomas Spurgeon had returned temporarily to Britain. Spurgeon junior's former church base in Auckland, which had played such an important role in 1888 was struggling to recover from a disastrous pastorate under his successor, William Birch. There was, accordingly, little momentum from this quarter to maintain Brown's exclusion.

In 1888 Brown's contacts with an unfavoured rival group contributed to his exclusion. In 1892 the concerns of a more acceptable denomination militated towards his reinstatement. Once more Brown was the central figure. At issue was that 'providential' purchase of the Congregationalists' building in 1890. At the same time as it was considering its position on Brown's case, the Committee was receiving representations from Congregational leaders who were unhappy with what they saw as the Timaru Baptists' opportunistic appropriation of the building for no more than the cost of the outstanding mortgage. The Congregationalists asked the Committee to 'use its influence with the pastor and officers of the Timaru church to restore the property on equitable terms.'[38]

---

[38] Minutes of the Union Committee, 17 November 1892 (f. 83)

This development was not communicated to the Conference itself. The Committee was thus placed in an invidious position. Baptists had historically close links with Congregationalists. It was noted in *The N.Z. Baptist* that, in England, talk of union between the groups was as common as 'roast mutton in the bill of fare of a colonial restaurant.'[39] In New Zealand an 'intimate relation' had developed between the two bodies, symbolised by a combined Baptist/Congregational cause in Thames.[40] The Committee were thus anxious to maintain good relations. Yet how could the Committee claim sway over a minister and church it had excluded? 'Influence' with Timaru would obviously require concession to the demands for reinstatement.

In the end the price was felt worth paying. The more so, as once again the threat of disunity hung around the question of Brown's status. The open dissatisfaction with the Union in Canterbury now provided further drive for a reversal of the 1888 expulsion. Although a significant number of delegates maintained their opposition to Brown, all the Canterbury delegates voted for reinstatement as, to a man (and they were all men), did the Committee.[41]

Between 1888 and 1892 everything and nothing had changed. Changes of personnel, the decline of the Spurgeon influence and the concerns of a favoured denomination set up a situation very different from that which had pertained in phase one of the Brown affair. Unchanged, however, was the pragmatic concern to preserve the Union in some semblance of cohesion. The inclusive outcomes of 1892 were much more in line with the result of the British Downgrade in 1888 than was the decision to expel Brown in 1888. Nevertheless, the fundamental interests of the leadership of the New Zealand Union had always been similar to those of their 'Home' counterparts. Doctrine was important, but unity was essential. Conflict was not to trump connection.

Brown would remain minister at Timaru until 1895, when a further financial squeeze forced the sale of the church back to the Congregationalists. He resigned in October that year. The loss of both their building and their pastor was too much for the church, which soon

---

[39] *NZB* (January 1892): 9.
[40] See *NZB* (December 1890): 185 and (July 1892): 102-3.
[41] A full list of those voting for and against Brown's reinstatement is given in the Conference Minutes, 18 November 1892, (ff 125-6).

after went into recess. Denied the support of the Union Committee, Brown did not serve in another Baptist church.[42]

The conclusion of the affair was hardly more satisfactory for the wider Baptist community. The Union had survived its first major test but underlying tensions between local churches and the national body remained unresolved. The search for a viable identity, with structures and forms appropriate to a new country, had barely begun. Moreover it was now clearer than ever that Baptists could not consider their own affairs in isolation. All the denominations were finding their way in the new colony. Baptists needed to recast their net of allegiances. Government policy, in the form of the Education Acts, was now forcing Baptists into a wider sphere of conflict and connection.

---

[42] See the Minutes of the Union Committee, 15 November 1895 (f. 117) and the brief obituary for Brown in *NZB* (February 1926): 31.

Chapter Five: marking out a space

The twenty-three Baptist delegates meeting in Nelson, New Zealand, in December 1893 concluded their conference divided. They had failed to agree on the place of religion in state schools. The division revealed a gap between radical Baptist views and the emerging ecclesiology of the colonial churches. This chapter explores the parameters and consequences of this divergence of view. The need for colonial Baptists to adapt ideas to an environment which was short on resources and infrastructure will be noted, as will the implications of Baptist approaches for our understanding of the nature of wider evangelicalism in such societies.

Timothy Larson has argued that the political positions taken by the Free Churches in Britain in the nineteenth century have not been properly understood. He traces this to a failure by historians to appreciate the significance of the ecclesiologies of these denominations, suggesting that this is especially true for the gathered churches of 'old Dissent' (notably Congregationalists and Baptists). Unlike other 'evangelical' groups, such as the Wesleyan Methodists, these argued consistently for the removal of state influence from religious matters. This was not merely a call for the disestablishment of the Church of England (although it included that) but extended to divorce laws, Jewish emancipation, education, even liquor laws. What Larsen's analysis suggests is that, especially with regard to public policy issues, 'evangelicals' should not simply be lumped together with the aim of identifying *the* evangelical attitude or response.[1]

The term 'evangelical' is of course slippery to begin with. As an interdenominational designation it has been notoriously imprecisely classified. David Bebbington's inclusive definition includes no ecclesiological element. In New Zealand the popular (as against the historian's) use of the word has taken a number of trajectories. From the 1920s, with the influence of Rev. Joseph Kemp and the founding of the Bible Training Institute in Auckland, the term took on for some a sharper doctrinal content, increasingly defined over and against 'modernism'. In the

---

[1] Timothy Larsen, 'Free Church Politics and the Gathered Church: The Evangelical Case for Religious Pluralism', *Fides et Historia* XXXIII, 1 (Winter/Spring 2001): 109-19, reprinted in *Contested Christianity: The Political and Social Contexts of Victorian Theology* (Waco: Baylor University Press, 2004), 145-156.

colonial period its meaning appears to have been looser. In 1902 Presbyterians approached other 'evangelical' groups for discussion over the possibility of church Union. Those deemed 'evangelical' were the Presbyterians, Methodists and Congregationalists, along with some Anglicans. Baptists were not approached on this occasion and, in any case, made it clear they did not see any chance of Union. The meaning of the term at this time seems to have orbited around two suns. The first, evangelistic fervour, was common to all parties. Preaching to wins souls for Christ was crucial. The second centre of gravity varied. For Presbyterians the word carried the memory of the magisterial reformation, a heritage within which, in different ways, each of its preferred conversation partners could be held to fit but in which Baptists, with their roots in the radical reformation, looked uncomfortable. They might be included as evangelicals, but not for the purposes of union. There was little argument from Baptists themselves. Happy to count themselves as evangelicals, Baptists too knew evangelism alone was not the total picture. For Baptists the necessary extras were adult conversionism and voluntarism. By these lights all paedobaptists inevitably had ground to make up but, on the evangelism measure, Congregationalists and Methodists (especially Primitive Methodists) ranked well. Presbyterians were a bit suspect but, given the strong voluntarism of the colonial church, they could be accorded the benefit of the doubt. Anglicans on the other hand, with what Baptists rated as merely a territorial approach to salvation, failed to make the cut. Divergences within evangelicalism thus turned on convictions about the church.

This was fundamental to Baptists. Themes of conflict and connection lie at the heart of the quest to find a Baptist identity in a strange land. Already we have seen them manifest in competing visions of denominational organization, in local church life and in disputes between Baptists over doctrine. There were, however, two further spheres in which identity was uncertain and contested: ecumenical connection and the public square. The next chapter will concentrate on the second of these, through the case of J.K. Archer. In this chapter both are in view, as Baptists located themselves in the debate over a public issue which all the churches of the time agreed was of huge significance.

The 1893 Baptist Conference was held when the dissatisfaction of Canterbury was at its height. Only two Canterbury delegates were present. It was one of the smallest since the formation of the New Zealand Baptist Union a decade earlier yet it generated one of the liveliest debates. The question was the place of religion in state education. Larsen has identified this as a key point of difference between evangelical Free Churches and other evangelicals in Victorian Britain, citing those who 'became convinced that no religious instruction should be offered at all in state schools.'[2] The question provides a useful test case in New Zealand, as the importance of ecclesiology in the debates has already been established. As is often the case with New Zealand religious history, we are indebted to Ian Breward, whose 1967 study *Godless Schools?* set a benchmark for insightful analysis of an important and long-running controversy.[3] In this chapter I will revisit those issues, exploring further than Breward was able to the nuances and variations of Free Church, especially Baptist, positions.

The 1877 Education Act excluded religious instruction from state primary schools. Various moves had been made to soften or confuse the purity of this principle. In 1890 a Private Schools Bill had been submitted. Regarded as a screen for state funding of Catholic and Anglican schools, this was opposed by other protestant groups. Nevertheless, some Protestants sought the inclusion of Bible teaching in the state curriculum. In order to track these debates it is helpful to note the models of religious instruction in schools which developed over the period. Five models, ranging from least to greatest religious input, may be identified.

1. No religious element at all in state schools – (the *status quo* under the 1877 Education Act).

2. The 'Nelson System' whereby schools could elect to open late or close early on one day a week to allow for religious instruction outside the state curriculum. (This exploited a loophole, identified by the Nelson Presbyterian Minister James McKenzie, and gradually gained official acceptance from 1897).

3. The use of the Lord's Prayer and scripture readings to begin the day.

4. Bible knowledge as part of the curriculum but with no instruction or explanation of the religious meaning of the text.

5. Full religious instruction as part of the curriculum (possibly following the system implemented in New South Wales, whereby clergy might supplement general lessons from teachers).

---

[2] Larsen, 153.
[3] I. Breward, *Godless Schools?: A Study in Protestant Reactions to the Education Act of 1877* (Christchurch: Presbyterian Bookroom, 1967). The description here of the general course of the controversy is drawn from Breward.

The Presbyterians petitioned Parliament for religious instruction in 1892, with an extra specificity being added from 1893 with the advocacy of an 'Irish Text Book' (of scripture portions) which would supply the necessary teaching and learning resource. This was model four. Anglicans and Methodists took a similar line. Catholics, stung by the repeated denial of state funds, vigorously opposed these moves, suspecting a protestant plot (a view only strengthened by the reference to the Irish text). The move failed but agitation on the issue continued. In 1903 a 'Bible in Schools League' was formed to promote religious instruction and to seek a referendum on the question. Lacking success, the movement faded. It was revived from 1912, only to again fall short of its target with the outbreak of War in 1914.

Catholics, with their developing parallel system, maintained strong opposition to these campaigns. The Presbyterians and Wesleyan Methodists consistently backed them, as did the Anglicans (although with some equivocation as to whether proposals went far enough). Notably, each of these protestant groups operated out of an ecclesiology which assumed a role for the state in the preservation of true religion. Anglicans and Presbyterians had a history of establishment; Wesleyans, of the Methodist groups, had maintained the strongest attachment to the state. (Wesleyan Missionaries were, for instance, on the whole more fervent advocates for the Crown during the New Zealand Wars than many from the Church of England.)[4]

If there were passionate advocates, there were also opponents of the Bible in Schools movement within New Zealand Protestantism. There is a correlation between these and those who gravitated towards a Free Church ecclesiology. James McKenzie, instigator of the Nelson system, had roots in the voluntarist United Presbyterian Church, which combined groups which had seceded from the Church of Scotland in the eighteenth century over the issue of establishment. McKenzie saw no gain in churches seeking state backing. 'Let the church turn from the door of Caesar, with its broken wire bell, and attend to what is her happiest and most imperative duty' (the nurture of children).[5] The Primitive Methodists were another case in point. The 'Prims' had separated from the British Methodist Connexion in 1811 over concerns that the Connexion was too willing to follow the state's

---

[4] See Y. L. Sutherland 'Te Reo O Te Perehi: Messages to Maori in the Wesleyan Newspaper Te Haeata 1859-62' (unpublished M.A. thesis, University of Auckland, 1999), 132-168.
[5] *Christian Outlook* (28 April 1894), cited Breward, 38.

direction. New Zealand Primitive Methodists James Guy and E. Drake made submissions against the Bible in Schools movement in 1895.[6]

Congregationalists and Baptists had a more obvious heritage of dissent from state interference in religion. On the Bible in Schools issue, the positions of each evolved between 1893 and 1913.

Congregationalists began the period adamantly opposed to any religious instruction in schools in the conviction that 'it is not the duty nor the right of the state to teach or control religion.'[7] By 1903, however, a change was evident. The Congregational Union joined the Bible in Schools League and indicated an openness to model four. A decade later, having in the meantime seriously considered union with the Presbyterians and Methodists, the Congregational Assembly expressed 'cordial approval' of the revived league. Whilst remaining committed to model four and rejecting model five the Assembly now favoured a referendum to determine the question. In both 1903 and 1913 there was significant opposition within the denomination to these concessions to State religious instruction, but this was a clear minority.[8]

From the start, the Baptists were divided on the questions. This is evident in the debate at the 1893 Conference. Rev A. H. Collins of the Ponsonby Baptist church put forward the motion

> That this Assembly, being convinced of the urgent importance of the adequate religious instruction of the young, we unanimously affirm: (1) That it is not the function of the State to teach religion and that it has neither the right to control nor enforce it; (2) That in view of both open attempts and covert desires to obtain State aid on behalf of denominational teaching, it is a public duty to resist every effort to alter the present Education System of the Colony; (3) That, while recognising the supreme value of home training, it is the duty and within the power of the churches to provide religious teaching for the young.[9]

---

[6] Breward, 33-34. The Primitive Methodists merged with the Wesleyans in 1913 and their individual voice on the issues disappeared.
[7] Resolution of the 1895 Congregational Assembly, cited J.B. Chalmers *'A Peculiar People': Congregationalism in New Zealand* (n.p.: Congregational Union of New Zealand, n.d.), 171.
[8] See Chalmers, 171-3.
[9] See the account in *NZB* (December 1893): 185, 188.

Collins' motion contains a number of crucial elements to which I will return. It was not accepted by the Conference. An 'amendment' (so called, although it effectively negated the motion), promoting the use of the Irish Text of Bible selections, was put but it gained only the vote of its mover, Rev James Blaikie. Next, Rev. Alfred North moved that schools be allowed to open with Scripture and the Lord's Prayer (model three). This too was lost, though narrowly. In the end the Conference, again by a small margin, made a very Baptist decision not to decide.

> This Assembly declines to commit itself, or the Union it represents, to any action in regard to the Bible-reading-in-Schools movements, and leaves each individual member at liberty to act as his (*sic*) judgement and conscience dictate.

In terms of the models identified above, the Baptist Conference was in 1893 divided between models one and three. Model four was clearly rejected; models two and five were not considered.[10]

As was the case with the Congregationalists, by 1903 the situation had changed considerably. R.S. Gray, formerly minister at Nelson and now at Christchurch, had secured support for religious instruction in schools at the 1902 Conference.[11] He and other Baptists attended the Bible in Schools League conference in 1903 and, at the Baptist Conference in November that year, Gray and H.H. Driver of Dunedin, presented a report endorsing the work of the League and favouring model four, the model least approved a decade earlier. After 'a long, but able, debate' the report was adopted. Nevertheless, the opposition led by Rev. T.A. Williams of Thames was significant and controversy carried on in the pages of *The N.Z. Baptist* for several months thereafter.[12]

The matter resurfaced with the revival of the League in 1912. H.H. Driver moved 'That we give general approval to the platform of the league.' An amendment offered by R.S. Gray to exclude the 'right of entry' provision in model five was passed but the Conference was once again so divided over the substantive issue that, as in 1893, it was decided that 'no official pronouncement be made.'[13] A year later the same level of

---

[10] Versions of the 'Nelson System' were emerging as a pragmatic solution in some places but it had not been formally defined and proposed in 1893.

[11] *NZB* Supplement (January 1903): 9.

[12] *NZB* (December 1903): 188-189. See also *NZB* (February 1904): 219; (March 1904): 236; (April 1904): 252-253; (May 1904): 267; (June 1904): 284 for a vigorous exchange between T. A. Williams and H.H. Driver.

[13] *NZB* (November 1912): 214. See also *NZB* (December 1912): 224.

disagreement emerged. No policy on the Bible in Schools League could be adopted. However, a motion seeking positive official provision for the Nelson System (model two, the least intrusive change) was adopted with only one dissenting vote.[14]

The Baptists had in many ways followed a path similar to the Congregationalists, only with greater internal division. From effective opposition to any but the most minimal religious element in 1893, to a majority for model four in 1903; too divided to endorse the League in 1912 but virtually unanimous over the Nelson System in 1913. The vacillation and indecision should not be allowed to mask the issues. It is clear that the views of Baptist advocates for the League like Gray and Driver matched almost exactly those of the Congregational majority. On the other hand the opponents in each denomination were very strongly opposed indeed. Some (e.g. the Baptist T.A. Williams and the Congregationalist W. Saunders) became active in the National Schools Defence League, a body in direct opposition to the Bible in Schools League.[15]

How are we to interpret these events? In particular, what do they say of the usefulness of Larsen's thesis for understanding Baptists in colonial New Zealand? Presbyterians and Wesleyan Methodists generally favoured religious instruction in state schools. Congregationalists and Baptists initially opposed the notion and at best were cautiously supportive. This appears to fit Larsen's pattern reasonably neatly, with 'gathered' churches preferring greater distance from the state. Yet the reality is more complex than that simple reading allows. By the early years of the twentieth century the Free Church tradition in New Zealand had evolved in ways which made it quite different from its antecedents in mid-Victorian Britain. A closer examination of the debates reveals the extent and significance of this transformation.

We must first note the precise nature of the caution expressed by Congregational and Baptist supporters of the Bible in Schools League in 1912-13. Those advocating endorsement of the League's platform in both cases added the rider that they rejected the New South Wales provision of 'right of entry' for clergy. Their objection, then, was not to religious instruction by the state as such, but instruction by other *denominations*. The issue was more sectarian than a mere matter of separation of church and state. These advocates (a majority among Congregationalists and probably

---

[14] *NZB* (November 1913): 210.
[15] Breward, 60.

the stronger group among the Baptists) seem not to not fit Larsen's pattern at all. They were as disturbed as any Methodist or Presbyterian at the absence of religion from the public square in New Zealand. They were more concerned, however, that Anglicans or Catholics might proselytise their children. As the observer of the 1912 Baptist Assembly assessed the situation,

> the dread of the priest lies heavily on these people, and though they dearly love the Bible and long that all children should read and obey it, they fear lest the priest should gain undue influence over the pupils of the Primary Schools.[16]

A glance beyond the issue of religious instruction, to other public questions of interest to Baptists, confirms the suspicion that Larsen's thesis does not sit tidily with the New Zealand experience. On the one hand Baptists were certainly opposed to any state subsidy of churches but, unlike Larsen's mid-Victorian Free Churchers, both Baptists and Congregationalists in New Zealand vigorously opposed liquor licensing and gambling from the outset. There was little reluctance to legislate for morality in 'Greater Britain'.[17]

Yet it is just as clear that a more purist Free Church ecclesiology of the type Larsen identifies did exist among those opposed to the Bible in Schools League. Here we return to the 1893 motion from A.H. Collins. It begins with obvious Free Church positions. The state has 'neither the right to control nor enforce' religion and there should be no 'state Aid on behalf of denominational teaching'. This much is familiar, but there are twists.

Firstly, it is a 'public duty' to oppose moves to compromise the existing secular system. There is no hint in Collins' motion of a withdrawal from society. Indeed, far from it. Collins himself was an activist who took a leading part in labour questions of the day. There was no shrinking pietism in this approach. Larsen identifies a 'fresh sense of self-confidence' among British Baptists and Congregationalists in the nineteenth century. The new assurance came from the embracing of evangelicalism and the rise in numbers this generated. 'They now saw themselves as a force in the land

---

[16] *NZB* (November 1912): 214.
[17] New Zealand Colonists often used such phrases as 'Greater Britain', 'Brighter Britain', 'Better Britain' to communicate their sense that they could create a parallel but improved society in their new setting. On the significance of this concept for colonial New Zealand history see J. Belich, *Paradise Reforged: A History of the New Zealanders from the 1880s to the Year 2000* (Auckland: Penguin, 2001).

that had the potential to provoke change.'[18] This reforming activism need not be seen as an abandonment of Free Church principles. Indeed it could be a fulfilment. Taking up Troeltsch's analysis of 'church-type' and 'sect-type' groups, Larsen pinpoints a largely unexplored possibility.

> Much has been written about the process whereby a sect evolves over time into a church. Those who narrate this trajectory often take great delight in chronicling the increasing worldliness and respectability of such groups. There is a much more complicated and interesting process than this one, however, in which a sect, finding it has become considerably larger and more influential, then seeks to use its new position to apply sect-type values and insights to the structures of society.[19]

Baptists, at 2.3% of the population in 1896, were not a large group in New Zealand, but they were present in greater proportion than in England. Moreover, they had an added factor which could generate the sort of self-confidence that evangelical revival had done for an earlier generation: they had come to a country with no established church. This they took to be an epochal endorsement of their position. They began to wonder if the whole world might not become Baptist and they began to shed the negative trappings of their past.[20] In response to the Bible in Schools debate at the Baptist Conference of 1903, for instance, Rev. John Muirhead saw no need to be defined by anyone else, pointing out that 'in England Non-Episcopalians are Free Churchmen and Nonconformists; in New Zealand they are Free Churchmen but not Nonconformists....The fact is there are no Nonconformists in New Zealand.'[21]

With such a sense of new possibilities Collins regarded it as a 'public duty' to resist the erosion of secular state education. Williams, too, openly opposed the Bible in Schools League, aligning himself with rationalists and atheists if necessary. J.K. Archer arrived from England in 1908 to be minister of the Napier Baptist church. A disciple of the radical Baptist John Clifford, Archer became a leading labour activist, eventually being appointed to the Legislative Council (see next chapter). The nature of this

---

[18] Larsen, 146.
[19] Larsen, 151
[20] See for instance the claims made in the letter from J.N. Prestridge reprinted in *NZB* (November 1908): 208.
[21] J. Muirhead, 'Nonconformist or Free Churchman', Letter to the Editor, *NZB* (December 1903): 181. See similar arguments raised earlier by Bible in Schools advocate J.G. Fraser *NZB* (September 1896): 129.

activism needs to be understood. It was not of the type Breward identifies in Rutherford Waddell who declared 'we refuse absolutely to regard the state as a secular institution.'[22] The state was not regarded as a key partner. Rather, this assertive ecclesiology placed the state perpetually under the judgment of Christ, exercised through his church. Williams, writing in 1896, allowed no concession to an ungodly magistrate.

> The state is Christian only so far as it submits to the will of Christ in its legislation and policy....The state is divine only so far as it is imbued with Christian principles. If the state refuses this submission, and violates any of these principles it becomes in that measure unchristian and undivine.[23]

In 1910 J.K. Archer put it this way.

> Moses appeared to Christ [in the transfiguration] because all law worth calling law came from Christ. Moses disappeared from Christ because all legislative functions are now merged in Christ. No law can have the consent of Christians unless it has the assent of Christ. Antiquity, ubiquity, utility do not count.[24]

This approach deeply qualified the standard protestant political ecclesiology which accorded the state a providential role of its own. In the radical Free Church model the state was not a main act. The real action was in the new society, coming to be in the gathered church. The state was always on probation. It had, in the interim, a separate set of responsibilities, but the church was charged to call it to account at all moments, and to resist it when it failed to measure up.

This radical commitment to the gathered church is a characteristic of Free Church ecclesiology which is not always fully appreciated. It is emphasised in the second twist in Collins' motion. The final clause reads 'that, while recognising the supreme value of home training, it is the duty and within the power of the churches to provide religious teaching for the young.' This reservation of a role for the church in religious education beyond the family – an opportunity denied to the state – is another connection with Larsen's analysis. As he points out 'Dissenters believed

---

[22] *Outlook* (13 August 1912). See Breward, 41.
[23] T.A. Williams, 'Religious Instruction in State Schools' *NZB* (November 1896): 165-167, 166.
[24] J.K. Archer, 'Jesus Only' (Union Sermon to the 1910 Baptist Assembly), *NZB* (January 1911): 11-13, 11.

firmly that they knew what the church was'.[25] The church was thus the 'starting point' for theology and practice. The gathered, covenanted community was a new society, which would flourish if freed from the pernicious effects of state interference. Collins had contended that religion 'can only be learned when the fire leaps from heart to heart, and the emotions of the scholar are touched by the emotions of the teacher.'[26] Williams similarly declared 'I regard religion as too sacred and too exalted to be entrusted to the keeping of state-paid agents, that I demand that none but the religious shall teach it.'[27] An 1898 Leader in *The N.Z. Baptist* declared that only by the removal of religion from the state 'shall we be able to boast that we have shut out the secular intruder from God's holy temple.'[28] This is counter to what has been taken to be a process of secularisation to which the Free Churches unwittingly contributed. Larsen contests this view.

> They saw the separation of church and state, not as the creating of a godless government, but rather as the creating of a purified church....What some might see as the church's retreating from its strongholds in society, evangelical Dissenters viewed as the state's being forced to retreat from its squatter holdings in the land of Zion.[29]

This strand of Free Church thinking might have led to a radical form of church, prepared to stand over and against both the state and prevailing structures of society. Collins for instance looked for a time 'when the capitalist will cease out of the land.'[30] Williams called for a brave rethink on the plight of New Zealand Maori.[31] But these were minority voices. What actually developed was more like militant sectarianism than insurgent Christianity - identifying its enemies more in other faith communities than in the systemic evils of society. That Gray and Driver were more concerned about blocking denominational interference in religious education than in seizing the initiative from the state was a symptom of this drift. Even such apparent radicals as the temperance leader A.S. Adams were deflected into single issue activism.

---

[25] Larsen, 150.
[26] A.H. Collins, 'Our Secular Education – A Reply to 'Holdfast', Letter to the Editor, *NZB* (May 1894): 78-9.
[27] T.A. Williams, 'Religious Instruction in State Schools' *NZB* (August 1896): 113.
[28] J. Thomas, 'Our Message for the Times' *NZB* (January 1898): 1.
[29] Larsen, 155-6.
[30] Cited M. Davidson, *A History of the Ponsonby Baptist Church*, 6.
[31] T.A. Williams *NZB* (May 1900): 66-67. See Driver's reply *NZB* (June 1900): 82-83.

Why did the Free Church social radicalism described by Larsen fail to flower in New Zealand? Among the Baptists at least the gradual change from an imported to an indigenous leadership was a crucial factor. In 1893 Collins had just arrived from Britain, as had his key supporter at the Conference that year, Rev. W. Drew. Both spoke out of their English experience. Williams too had been formed for the ministry in England. He arrived in 1895. Archer, similarly, was radicalized in Britain and came to New Zealand in mid-career. These men may be seen to have represented the after-guard of the radicalism Larsen finds. They found surprisingly little fertile ground for their radical visions and lost heart in their chances of propagating them among New Zealand Baptists. Collins left the country in 1902; Williams in 1919. J.K. Archer came to see little hope for progress through the churches and invested his energies into secular politics.

In contrast to these imported ministers. Gray and Driver were colonials, home grown. These men were comfortable seeking legislative change on the very questions (religious education, prohibition, gambling) which Larsen's free radicals wanted removed from state interference. The difference of context is profound. The New Zealanders did not have the automatic bogey of an established church against which to define their approach. On the other hand, by the mid-1890s, they did have before them the record of an interventionist Liberal government. Far more than in Britain, the resources of colonial society were concentrated in central government. In the debate over religion in schools, Dunedin layman J.G. Fraser made these differences specific. In the colony, he pointed out, the state was different, more democratic and inclusive, than that in Britain. Moreover, only the state had shown itself capable of providing free, 'commodious and well-equipped' schools.[32]

Few Baptist leaders were willing to retreat to a pietistic separatism by which 'the church can sustain no relation to social problems.'[33] Yet engagement in the New Zealand context would inevitably entail interference by the state. A half-way house, with only some elements of the stance that Larsen identifies, developed. The generation of Gray, Driver, J.J. North and A.S. Adams did, in a real sense, set out to 'apply sect-type values and insights to the structures of society'. However, Free Church values in the New Zealand of 1900 had developed a different set of

---

[32] *NZB* (September 1896): 129.
[33] A.S. Adams 'The Relation of the church to the Social Problems of the Age' (Presidential Address, 1906) *Baptist Handbook* (Wellington: N.Z. Baptist Union, 1907) 9-23.

priorities from those in Britain in 1850. In the absence of an established church, pure separation of religion and state was less critical. The opportunity was taken to attempt to impose other 'sect-type values' such as positions on drink and gambling. These became the focus of the social conscience of New Zealand Baptists.

But this was a half-way house. Calls for state-led solutions tended to halt at these points. On other matters, notably those relating to labour, Baptists held back. Adams called for the relief of oppressive conditions but specifically eschewed any entry 'into the strife of class with class'.[34] There was plenty of interest in the issue. A public 'mass meeting' on the relation of church to Labour was held during the 1907 Assembly. A panel of ministers 'displayed...a sympathy with the aspirations of Labour, and a hostility towards the iniquities which selfish capitalism inflicts on the toiler.' Nevertheless the way forward was not connected to legislation. The panel operated 'with a belief that the solution of all economic difficulties must be a moral and religious one.'[35] Disruption of public life and militant unionism drew little support. H.H. Driver for instance, at the time editor of *The N.Z. Baptist*, had no sympathy with the Unions during the maritime strike in 1913.[36]

Ambivalence over labour issues was common to all the churches before World War One. Gradually, however, a point of contrast emerged. Baptists did not adopt social gospel approaches in the way that other 'evangelical' bodies such as the Methodists and Presbyterians did from the 1920s. In 1922, as the Methodists at their Conference were adopting a new Social Creed, the Baptists, at theirs, were being reminded of 'the pre-eminence of the spiritual.'[37] In his Presidential address of 1932, J.J. North called for a renewed church, centered on Christ, and was lukewarm on social radicalism.

> We shall utterly fail if we merely preach a social gospel. That would be an attempt to bribe the democracy. Others will outbid us there....The social results that are visualized by our religion, and they are very precious results, are fruits from deep roots.[38]

---

[34] Adams 22-3.
[35] *NZB* (November 1907): 262, 274.
[36] *NZB* (December 1913) 225-6.
[37] See A. Davidson, *Christianity in Aotearoa: A History of church and Society in New Zealand* (Wellington: Education for Ministry, 1991), 107; *NZB* (November 1922): 297.
[38] *NZB* (November 1932): 352.

The importance of ecclesiology in this divergence of approaches between 'evangelical' groups must be recognised. Evangelicals may have been united on matters relating to conversion, even personal morality, but there were clearly *evangelicalisms* with regard to public policy. Baptists in New Zealand failed to develop an approach to public issues which radically reflected their particular view of the church. What emerged instead was a colonial compromise, a willingness to seek political backing on a few things, whilst withdrawing from meaningful engagement on others. This essentially defensive strategy represents a developing if desiccated sense of identity. It had its own coherence but it did little to transform the social order. As we shall see in the next chapter, there were a few individuals who sought direct involvement in politics in the first decades of the new century, but in general Baptists sought solutions in different places. For such as J.K. Archer, radicalised in a more clearly delineated environment, it was a frustrating abandonment of the Free Church vision and calling. Only with the arrival of an ecumenically-minded leadership in the 1940s did Baptists again engage directly with government, but then less as radicals than as bulwarks of respectability.

Chapter Six: J.K. Archer and political activism

New Zealand Baptists like to regard themselves as activists. The energy created and released by the Baptist way of being church has been channeled into evangelism, social service and protest. Political activism, by contrast, has been less common, its appearance patchy and little understood. Thomas Dick (1823-1900) of Dunedin was an outstanding nineteenth century individual, prominent for thirty years in province and parliament. J.W. Sawle, one of the principal figures in the flourishing of the Canterbury Baptist Association in the 1870s, attempted a political career in the 1890s. He stood unsuccessfully for the Ashburton seat in 1890 (as a Liberal) and 1896 (for Isit's Prohibitionists). The campaigns were bruising - opponents characterising him as 'weak' or of the 'extreme radical left' because of his Land Tax views. Sawle later moved to Taranaki, where in 1902 he became a Liberal candidate for Egmont, only to withdraw for health reasons. These, though, were unusual. More typical of the first five decades of Baptist life in New Zealand was a suspicion of the political process. Editor of *The N.Z. Baptist* in 1887, Alfred North, felt constrained to make a case for voting on the 1887 General Election.

> If it be true that we are responsible for the use we make of the power we have, it must be true that the power we possess as citizens should be used by us, and not wrapt in the napkin. The assumption that politics are too worldly for the Christian man to deal with is to the last degree absurd.[1]

North had identified a colonial quietism on political matters which would become characteristic of many Baptists. The picture appears different for the first few decades of the twentieth century. Howard Elliot of Mt Eden, for instance, caused a sensation with his Protestant Political Association in the years around World War One. Indeed a spike in activity in this period has been suggested by Barry Gustafson.[2] Yet the apparent flowering of direct political activism among Baptists was illusory and the individual cases were exceptions to the rule. The reasons for this are

---

[1] *NZB* Editorial (July 1887): 104.
[2] See B. Gustafson, 'Intervention in the Public Square', *Bulletin of the New Zealand Baptist Historical Society*, No. 8, July 1980, 2-7.

complex but they may be glimpsed through a study of the most prominent Baptist political protagonist of the time.

Faith and Politics

Rev. John Kendrick Archer (1865-1949) features prominently in Gustafson's analysis of 'intervention in the public square'. He seems to have personified the denomination's consciousness 'of its social and political responsibilities as well as its task of evangelism.'[3] A formidable figure, Archer served his denomination variously as President, as minister in several churches and on numerous committees and boards. At the same time he was as active in politics: President and Vice-president of the New Zealand Labour Party, Parliamentary candidate, three-term Mayor of Christchurch, member of the Legislative Council. No other figure in New Zealand history has combined political and clerical roles to such a degree.

Gustafson was not the first to note Archer's importance. N.R. Wood contributed a long biographical essay some years earlier.[4] Yet, neither Wood's nor Gustafson's interpretation of Archer is satisfactory. A more rounded picture is possible - one which has implications for our understanding of Baptist life and N.Z. society. Much of the basis for this reinterpretation comes from an examination of material not previously studied. In a major antiquarian exercise E. Harrison, of Grimsby in England, transcribed local records of Archer's pastorate there between 1903 and 1908.[5] From the other end of his career, Archer's speeches to the Legislative Council provide numerous insights into his view of himself. Neither of these sources was employed by Wood or Gustafson.

In his history of the formation of the New Zealand Labour party, Gustafson includes Christian principles among 'sentimental' motivations for involvement in the labour cause. Archer, he suggests, fits this category.[6]

---

[3] Gustafson, 'Intervention', p 3.
[4] N.R. Wood, 'John Kendrick Archer: Baptist Minister - Christian Socialist 1865-1949', *Bulletin of the New Zealand Baptist Historical Society*, No. 7, October 1970. See also the undergraduate research essay of M. Frost, 'J.K. Archer', University of Canterbury, 1989.
[5] In 1977 the N.Z. Baptist Historical Society received a 102 page manuscript from Mr E. Harrison, J.P. of Wolsham, England. The product of Harrison's antiquarian efforts relating to Archer's pastorate in Grimsby (1903-1908), it consists of transcripts of newspaper accounts of Archer's activities, including several important letters.
[6] B. Gustafson, *Labour's Path to Political Independence: The Origins and Establishment of the New Zealand Labour Party 1900-19*, (Auckland:AUP, 1980, 158 (in the biographical

There is, admittedly, some evidence for this view. Archer's early encounters with deprivation had a deep emotional impact. Late in life, he spoke movingly to the Legislative Council of miners he saw in his youth.

> There was not a man of forty years of age among them who was not warped and twisted in his body by the conditions under which he worked. Many of those men living round about my home were living in hovels that I have never heard of, except among the Negroes engaged in the cotton industry in the Southern States of America.[7]

Gustafson's taxonomy, however, is misleadingly simplistic. It does little justice to the intellectual core of Archer's Christian commitment. To the Legislative Council in 1941 Archer declared

> As I see it, the Labour movement - and this is why I am in it; if I did not believe this I would not be in it - is an attempt, a very imperfect and incomplete attempt, but a real attempt, to put into practice the teachings and the spirit of Christ.[8]

Later he affirmed that 'the teaching of the Bible, rightly understood, is the most radical teaching in the world.' The phrase 'rightly understood' is important. Just what sort of Christianity drove Archer? The answer provides an important element in a reinterpretation of his life.

In 1906 the popular preacher, Rev. R.J. Campbell of the City Temple, London, caused a storm with his adoption of the findings of 'higher criticism'. In his 'New Theology' he repudiated the Fall and appeared to question the Trinity, the Incarnation and the Atonement. Archer's mentor John Clifford (1836-1923), although differing on some details, was one of the most prominent churchmen to come to Campbell's defence. On 27 January 1907 Archer himself responded to the controversy, preaching to his Grimsby congregation on the 'New Theology'. A report of the sermon reveals an approach far from the fundamentalism assumed by Gustafson.

> What was theology? Simply a statement of man's religious beliefs. God had no theology. All the theology in the world was man's making....There were some things their forefathers believed in, that never could be believed in again by intelligent man. For instance the

---

note on H.E. Holland). See also Chapter 11 'Wowsers and papists: religion and the rise of Labour', 120-131.
[7] New Zealand Parliamentary Debates (N.Z.P.D.), Vol. 260, p 1086, 9/10/41. See also Vol. 250, p 146, 8/3/38 and Vol. 263, p 178, 2/7/43.
[8] N.Z.P.D., Vol. 260, p 641, 12/9/41.

belief that God made this wonderful world in six days of twenty four hours each, the belief in a hell of literal burning, the belief in verbal inspiration of the scriptures...were beliefs of the past. He did not believe in the Bible because it was called the Bible but... because he believed it to be true and if modern scholarship could show him it was not true,... he would give it up and go into the world and work for his living.[9]

Archer maintained a lively appreciation for theological development. In a debate on the question of capital punishment he censured another member of the Legislative Council who suggested a dualistic explanation for 'the murder-complex'.

It is not... a sort of conflict between God and the Devil. That is a very obsolete way of stating the position. No up-to-date theologian would state it that way and I would suggest to the honourable gentleman that he should brush up his theology and read a few up-to-date books.[10]

In the same debate he set the question in the context, not of divine judgment or retribution but of theistic evolution.

The unfolding of God's great plan for the creation of the world...was not finished in six or seven days, but is still going on. In that light we see that this bill is a step along the evolutionary path.[11]

Archer's faith was intimately linked with his political views, but his was no conservative reaction. Gustafson was wrong to place him among those with 'impeccably fundamentalist and evangelical credentials'. Although he was a committed, warmly evangelistic theist, Archer is better associated with more liberal theology.

There were, of course, many Christians - even 'modernists' - who took little part in political affairs. Archer's militancy drew on more than Christianity - whether 'sentimental', 'fundamentalist' or 'up-to-date'. Other influences shaped and directed him.

---

[9] Harrison 72-3. Clifford had a very open attitude to doctrine. 'My attitude towards Creeds...is of persistent investigation with a high resolve not to be misled by terms or confused by the clouds that emerge from the hoary past....The "doxies", "ortho" and "hetero", have interested me and do still, but the main purpose of my spirit...is to live at the vital centre and work from it.' See S.J. Marchant, *Dr. John Clifford, C.H.: Life, Letters and Reminiscences* (London: 1924), xiv-xv.
[10] N.Z.P.D., Vol. 260, 639, 12/9/41.
[11] N.Z.P.D., Vol. 260, 640, 12/9/41.

Heroes and Mentors

John Clifford was undoubtedly a significant figure in Archer's life. Also one who combined Baptist ministry and political activism, Clifford briefly taught Archer and gave a testimonial as to his qualities when Archer was called to Napier from England in 1908. From this patron Archer drew inspiration and encouragement. Clifford also imparted economic and political views. Nevertheless Clifford's role was primarily that of a mediator, exposing Archer to a wide range of radical thought.

Chief among these was one of Clifford's philosophical guides, John Ruskin (1819-1900). Archer acknowledged his debt to Ruskin in one of his first speeches to the Legislative Council. Another member, Waite, had quoted from Ruskin's *Unto This Last*. Archer regarded his use of the text as invalid.

> I imagine the Hon. Mr Waite has never read it, or, if he has read it, has never understood it in its completeness....I have the book here, one of the greatest books in the world next to the Bible. I have carried this book with me for thousands of miles during the last thirty or forty years. I have read it wholly or in part hundreds of times...If Ruskin's teaching as an whole were accepted, we shall very soon get to an ideal state....[12]

Archer's claim to have 'carried this book...during the past thirty years' seems to have some foundation. Certainly Ruskin features in his speeches from early on. At Grimsby on 13 April 1905 Archer based a speech to a local literary society on *Unto This Last*. He outlined Ruskin's thoughts on education, welfare, wealth and labour. Ruskin, he admitted, 'was not a socialist but he pioneered social reform and paved the way for socialism.'[13] Wood records that, in New Zealand in 1912, Archer included Ruskin in a series on 'Big Brothers of Humanity'.[14]

In part a reaction against industrialization, Ruskin's political economy gave much attention to education and advocated a planned economy and full employment. Many of these themes came out in Archer's own thought and life. He too was convinced of the value of schooling. He was a local School Board member at Hepstonhall Slack and education was one of the main themes in his 1919 campaign for the Invercargill seat.[15]

---

[12] N.Z.P.D., Vol. 249, 123-4, 4/11/37.
[13] Harrison, 43-4.
[14] Wood, 8.
[15] Wood, 4. *Southland Times* 11 October 1919: 6; 12 December 1919: 10.

In the Legislative Council Archer displayed an almost utopian faith in learning. Taking China as an example he said it 'could not be a cultured nation when...90% of the people [are] illiterate. When we have cultured nations, there will be no war.'[16]

Ruskin developed a novel theory of work and labour. Work should be treated as a 'luxury'. One could have either too much or too little.[17] Thus it should be policy to evenly distribute the amount of work. Archer's views on working hours were similar.

> Looking at it from the point of view of the benefit to the people themselves, it is desirable that everyone should be at work, and it is quite obvious that if everybody is to be at work all of us must only work a few hours a day...we have to set our minds to the problem of what is the smallest number of hours that all people must work in order that they all may be at work and in order that all may have a sufficiency of the necessaries of life.[18]

As will be seen, in 1918 Archer identified 'covetousness' as the root of society's ills. In the Legislative Council this became 'selfishness' but the message was the same. Private enterprise benefits 'the worshippers of mammon' and 'the private enterpriser who wins great success is a public plunderer.'[19] Here too are echoes of Ruskin, who insisted that the reason merchants are held in poor regard lies 'in the fact that the merchant is presumed to act selfishly... [The public] must not cease to condemn selfishness; but they will have to discover a kind of commerce which is not exclusively selfish.'[20]

Ruskin was not Archer's only favourite. The Italian patriot Giuseppe Mazzini (1805-1872) appealed even more as a man who added militant action to his theories. Archer admired him as

> a preeminently religious man who was three times sentenced to death by his own Government. He lived for years as an exile in England....But his memory today is reverenced and almost worshipped from one end of Italy to the other.[21]

---

[16] N.Z.P.D., Vol. 249, 75, 3/11/37.
[17] J. Ruskin, *Unto This Last* (London: 1860), 100-1 note *.
[18] N.Z.P.D., Vol., 250, 145, 8/3/38. See also Vol. 249, 852, 1/12/37; Vol., 264, 833, 31/3/44.
[19] N.Z.P.D., Vol. 264, 416, 11/3/44.
[20] Ruskin, 28-29.
[21] N.Z.P.D., Vol. 251, 223, 6/7/38.

In Mazzini's political economy, the will of the people was guaranteed, their need to organise recognised, the evils of property rights deplored, and an internationalist conception of humanity advanced.[22] Each of these themes finds an echo in Archer's speeches. He too professed a confidence in the people: 'I am sufficiently democratic to believe that the mistakes of democracy are preferable to the sins of autocracy[23] and strongly supported organisation of labour:

> the right to combination is one of the fundamental rights to life..So far as the workers are concerned, my view is that wherever they do not combine and are therefore unprotected they are maltreated.[24]

He was clear on the relative importance of property: 'when the rights of property and the rights of the people clash, the rights of property must be subordinated to the rights and needs of the people'[25] and was inspired by an internationalist vision - 'the great idea of the brotherhood of nations...to which we hope all nations of the earth will ultimately belong.'[26]

Two other themes, elemental in Archer's political philosophy, were shared with Mazzini. Among the latter's 'foundations of belief' were 'the unity of the human race' and 'the constant, unlimited progress of mankind'.[27] These very themes were espoused by Archer in 1938. 'There is no such thing as an individualist life, and the more civilisation progresses the more interdependent we become.'[28] In the closing words of his last major speech in the Legislative Council his optimism again shines through.

> I believe that the poet Browning was right when he said, "the best is yet to be".... In spite of all the things we are in the midst of, a great evolutionary process is going on which will have good results for the good of man and the glory of God.[29]

In his speech in the Address in Reply debate of 1944, unity and progress again feature. If the root problem of society was 'covetousness/selfishness', then 'Unification' was his solution.

---

[22] On Mazzini see G. Salvemini, *Mazzini* (London: ET 1956).
[23] N.Z.P.D., Vol. 256, 853, 7/10/39. See also Vol 261, 81, 19/3/42. cf. Salvemini, 61.
[24] N.Z.P.D., Vol. 250, 147, 8/3/38; cf Salvemini. 162-3.
[25] N.Z.P.D., Vol. 249, 850, 1/12/37 cf. Salvemini, 165.
[26] N.Z.P.D., Vol. 249, 75, 3/11/37. See also Vol. 260, 306, 27/8/41.
[27] Salvemini, 18-19. These themes are also found in Clifford (cf his description of the preacher's task in Marchant, 97).
[28] N.Z.P.D., Vol. 251, 223, 6/7/38.
[29] N.Z.P.D.,Vol. 273, 441, 18/7/46.

I submit that the real alternative to what is called private enterprise...can be summed up in one word - 'unification.'

I mean unification of possessions, interests and activities. That is the great family idea, the fatherhood of God and the brotherhood of man...The Bible stands for unification of individuals, unification of groups and unification of races...'That they may all be one'...that is the Lord's prayer...It means Unification.[30]

'Unification', although articulated in this form only in the final years of his life, was the sum of Archer's ideology. An amalgam of the teachings of Christ, the Bible, Ruskin, Mazzini, and Clifford, its final form was the creation and property of Archer himself. This unique and sophisticated view of life and society provided the intellectual underpinnings for his career.

A Fighting Man

Not all who held radical views become activists. Ruskin generally stayed above the fray; Clifford vigorously pursued political causes but declined a political career. Archer, by contrast, actively sought office. This drive involved factors beyond mere ideology. Two are crucial: Archer's idiosyncratic personality and the New Zealand religious and social context he encountered. Of these, the first has been courteously skirted in earlier studies; the second hardly recognised at all.

The course of Archer's life might suggest that he was driven by simple ambition. He stood unsuccessfully for Parliament no fewer than four times and sought nomination for a safe seat (Lyttelton) at least once. He sought and gained high positions in the New Zealand Labour Party. He gained numerous Local Body posts, standing three times successfully and once unsuccessfully for the Mayoralty of Christchurch.[31] At the age of 72 he accepted appointment and subsequent reappointment to the Legislative Council. The scale of the public offices he sought gradually expanded: from school board to Poor Law Guardian whilst still in England; to local bodies, Mayoralty and Parliament in New Zealand. Archer's career seems to have

---

[30] N.Z.P.D., Vol. 264, 416-8, 11/3/44.
[31] In addition to the mayoralty he held posts as vice-President of the Labour Party 1922-25, 1927-28, 1929-31; President 1928-29; Invercargill Borough Councilor 1915-16 and Christchurch City Councilor 1921-25, 1931-35. He was a member at various times of the Canterbury Hospital Board and the Christchurch Tramway and Fire Boards - See Gustafson, *Labour's Path*, 153; Wood, 18-20.

followed the pattern typical of any ambitious politician. However, it is clear that Archer's motivation transcended crude power seeking. His ideology was genuine and clearly played a major part in his choices. Nevertheless, certain personality traits helped set the pattern of his life.

When Archer died in 1949 a series of memorial speeches were delivered in both houses of Parliament. Each testifies to his pugnacity. Archer was a natural controversialist. As his own speeches reveal and as his colleagues readily avowed, he did not avoid conflict. Indeed, he appears to have relished it. Walter Nash, speaking on behalf of the Government, noted that 'he was as fearless as any man I ever contacted'. Nearly twenty years later, less than a year before his own death, Nash wrote of Archer that

> he spoke with a directness that far exceeded the normal, caring not so much it seemed to me for what the rate payers he represented, or the people on the City Council said or thought.[32]

Sydney Holland (no ally, although from a prominent Canterbury Baptist family) noted much the same in his memorial tribute in 1949.

> Mr Archer was...not very careful whose toes he trod on. If he felt a thing ought to be said, nothing on earth would stop him from saying it...he would sooner lose an election when there was a fight than win one without a fight.[33]

In the post-war, overwhelmingly male world of the New Zealand Parliament these assessments of Archer may have been the mere stuff of eulogy. In Archer's case, however, the descriptions carried more than an element of truth. He spoke in similar terms of himself.

> So far as I am concerned the most miserable moments I have had in my public career have not been when I was criticized but when I have been complimented.[34]

Later he makes the point more directly.

> I love a fight and a fighting man, and, if ever we reach a state when there is nothing to fight about, the best thing will be to go home and do some useful work elsewhere. It is in the clash of ideals that we get progress.[35]

---

[32] N.Z.P.D., Vol. 286, 983, 3/8/49; letter Nash to N.R. Wood 7 September 1967.
[33] N.Z.P.D., Vol. 286, 985, 3/8/49. Rev. Carr, in his tribute said of Archer 'He liked a fight, but he liked a fair fight and a clean fight.' - N.Z.P.D., Vol. 286, 987, 3/8/49.
[34] N.Z.P.D., Vol. 260, 480, 4/9/41.
[35] N.Z.P.D., Vol. 263, 1144, 26/8/43.

He admired the same quality in others. In a tribute to H.T. Armstrong he declared

> I have never had sympathy with men who are what Tennyson calls. 'faultily faultless, icily regular, splendidly null, dead perfection, no more.' I used to like my friend...when he got warmed up and when others were warmed up too. I have a lot of faith in men who, with their eloquence, get warmed up and warm other people up when they deserve it.[36]

Passion, the cut and thrust of argument, these were of the utmost importance in Archer's approach to public life. As a result he was a vigorous debater. He could be sarcastic, acerbic and humorous.[37] He clearly enjoyed the fray. There were drawbacks. Archer was sometimes guilty of placing polemic before accuracy. On occasion he had to withdraw statements about preceding speeches, seemingly because he gave more energy to reacting emotionally than to listening analytically. Speaking to the Customs Act Amendment Bill in 1942 he delivered a scathing condemnation (based on doubtful evidence) of the Liquor Trade. Despite the strength of his rhetoric (or perhaps because of it!) Archer's speeches were often ignored by others in the Council. On this occasion, however, his errors were so egregious as to provoke a series of responses.[38]

If the 'fighting spirit' attributed to Archer was not imagined, neither was it a feature only of his Legislative Council years. An examination of his career both in England and New Zealand reveals numerous incidents which suggest he was most at home when embroiled in battle.

Almost immediately after his arrival in Grimsby Archer became involved in local affairs. In March 1903, responding to criticism of a temperance mission, he wrote to the local paper questioning the motives of the critic. This man, one H.J.F. Crosby, claimed to have been, initially, a supporter of the mission. However, on some point he felt he had been deceived by the mission organisers. Archer, in a reply replete with strong phrases, alleged a hidden agenda behind Crosby's strictures. 'Surely we need no brewer's lackey to speak for us.' Crosby was 'working out his pigmy

---

[36] N.Z.P.D., Vol. 261, 901, 2/12/42. The quotation from Tennyson (which Archer repeats in 1943 - Vol. 263, 1144, 26/9/43) appears also to have been a favourite of his mentor Clifford - see Marchant, 56.
[37] See e.g. N.Z.P.D..Vol. 256, 721, 6/10/39; Vol. 260, 305-6, 27/8/41.; Vol. 263, 178, 2/7/43; Vol. 271, 294-295, 8/11/45.
[38] N.Z.P.D., Vol. 261, 345-350, 9/5/42. See also Vol., 249, 154, 4/11/37; Vol., 249, 851, 1/12/37; Vol., 256, 316, 26/9/39.

vengeance'. If any had been deceived it was 'the drink buyers...who impoverish themselves for the enrichment of the brewery shareholders...and allow themselves to be hoodwinked by the newspaper claptrap of brewers' paid agents.'[39]

Archer's five years at Grimsby witnessed a series of battles over the drink question. The most dramatic began in October 1903, after another letter from Archer to the paper. The leading candidate for the local mayoralty was a respected councillor by the name of Evison. Evison, however, was 'of the trade'. In October 1903 Archer wrote to the editor, protesting at Evison's candidature. He had been requested to do so by the Temperance Union but, he later acknowledged, 'the terms of the letter are mine'. The 'terms' were strong. Despite disclaiming any personal attack, Archer declared that 'a publican as a mayor is a discredit, a disgrace and a scandal to the town'.[40]

The letter caused a local storm. Although his own church affirmed their confidence in him, at least one other temperance leader dissociated himself from the letter. Crosby, the target of Archer's letter in March, suggested a 'good ducking in the horse pond' for Archer. Evison was duly elected but, refusing to let the matter drop, sued for libel. Archer refused to apologise. The case was heard in February 1905, the jury finding against Archer and awarding £25 damages. In addition Archer was left with a legal bill of some £250 (his annual stipend at this time was £160).[41]

The libel writ does not appear to have slowed Archer down. In the interval before the case was heard he conducted a campaign against gambling and was fully active in the local activities of the 'Crusade against the Education Act' of 1902.

Education had been a bone of contention for Nonconformists for many years. After the 1902 Act the issue hinged on the payment of rates. The Act allowed local authorities to levy a general rate which included a sum to subsidise Church of England schools. Many Nonconformists refused to pay that portion. The national figure leading the opposition to the Act was Archer's mentor Dr. John Clifford. It is therefore not surprising to find Archer himself heavily involved at the local level.

---

[39] Harrison, 4-5.
[40] Harrison, 13-15.
[41] Harrison, 17-28.

At Grimsby Archer and many others refused to pay the disputed part of the rate. Several times during his five years at Grimsby Archer had a distress warrant issued against his property to recover the unpaid amount.[42] At a hearing on 21 March 1906 Archer was appointed spokesman for the resisters. By this time it appears he had gained a reputation. The Stipendiary Magistrate allowed him to speak on the condition he was 'not going to hear a long political speech'. Archer's address barely complied with this ruling but was, in any case, of no avail. He later wrote yet another letter to the paper, protesting at the Magistrate's remarks about the resistance.[43]

In 1907 Archer was elected (as a Labour Party candidate) to the Grimsby Board of Poor Law Guardians. Here too he was soon the centre of conflict. At one of his first meetings he challenged the Finance Committee on a decision over tendering. Harrison records that 'personalities were brought into the discussion and the Chairman had to call order'. A year later on 2 March 1908 Archer was calling into question the distribution of work to tradesmen, alleging favouritism. None was established.[44]

The picture we have of Archer at Grimsby is of an activist pursuing several causes at any one time in addition to his pastoral duties. In the Evison case he was not merely active but provocative. Not just causes but controversy itself seemed to attract him. In 1908, bidding farewell after accepting a call to Napier, New Zealand, he was explicit in his relish for battle. A report of his address includes a revealing statement, which would later be echoed in the New Zealand Legislative Council.

> One of his greatest delights was the thought that he had made a few enemies at Grimsby. He should be sorry to go away feeling he had the good word of everybody.[45]

Archer quickly became part of the Labour movement in his new home. He also stamped his character on the Napier church. Early in 1909 he preached against Britain's increased Naval expenditure, inviting comment from his congregation. Two of his Deacons contested his view. This 'breeze at Napier' reached the pages of *The N.Z. Baptist*. He later

---

[42] See Harrison, 6, 12, 29, 36, 40, 48, 55, 64, 75.
[43] Harrison, 55-58.
[44] Harrison, 75, 82, 93-96.
[45] Harrison,101. cf N.Z.P.D., Vol. 260, 480, 4/9/41.

acknowledged to the church that 'he had always been a fighter.'[46]

The 'fight' could come from anywhere. In 1917 Archer was appointed Chaplain to the Army camp at Featherston. Immediately he volunteered for front line duty. His application was declined on the grounds of age but the incident is indicative of his attraction to action.[47] In other settings he would deliberately incite a reaction. During one of his Christchurch mayoralty campaigns he was reputed to have responded to a question about ratepayers concerns at proposed expenditure with a direct 'Damn the Ratepayers!'. His opponents made much of this strong statement by an ordained Minister. In his tribute on Archer's death, Holland suggested, probably correctly, that this was a provocative ploy to put some life into the campaign and get some free publicity.[48] Wood suggests that Archer's predilection for the provocative statement cost him valuable votes in his attempts to get into Parliament. To the Baptist Assembly held in Christchurch during his mayoralty Archer confessed that 'the town clerk who accompanied him on most occasions spent his time whispering, "Don't do anything rash".'[49]

As this track record might suggest, Archer was in his element during his years in the Legislative Council. Wood records that 'he said it was the best job and the best paid job he had ever had'. In her memorial speech, Mrs Dreaver (another member of the Council) recalled a visit to Archer during his final illness. Archer was anxious for news of the Council. 'He never tired of hearing what was happening in Wellington. He still lived in the Council, as it were, although he could not leave his home.'[50]

Without question Archer enjoyed the political hurly burly for its own sake. His activist and irascible personality played a large part in shaping his career. Throughout his life he pursued the greatest action, constantly seeking the eye of the storm. 'I want to be in a place where there is something to be done - where we are expected to do it, and to attempt to

---

[46] Wood, 7-8; *NZB* (May 1909): 323.
[47] Precisely in what capacity Archer sought to serve is unclear. Wood (12) implies he wished to go as a Chaplain. Wilson, Leader of the Legislative Council suggests that 'Mr Archer volunteered on three occasions for active service.' - N.Z.P.D., Vol. 286, 977, 2/8/49. Holland also talks of Archer's desire for a 'combatant' role - N.Z.P.D., Vol 286, 986, 3/8/49.
[48] N.Z.P.D., Vol. 286, 985, 3/8/49.
[49] Wood, 19-20.
[50] Wood, 21. N.Z.P.D., Vol. 286, 980, 3/8/49.

achieve some results.'⁵¹ Beilby notes that 'the dust of battle was never far from J.K. Archer.'⁵² This was no accident. He liked it that way.

A Decision for Party Politics

To the emerging image of a modern, informed Christian socialist, naturally drawn to political controversy, must be added the peculiarities of the New Zealand context in which he spent the second half of his life. New Zealand had appealed to Archer for its radical reputation. What he found disappointed him. He was particularly frustrated at the indolence of the churches. In 1941 he would declare

> I have been a churchman all my life, and for the last fifty years I have been waiting and watching and hungering for the church to take its proper place alongside the forces of progress in the interests of social reform. I want that a thousand times more than I want anything for myself.⁵³

In New Zealand, the Christian activism for which Archer yearned was missing. When he set out for his new home he had not fully grasped how different the context was from that pertaining in England. There, under such leaders as his friend Clifford, Nonconformists were a powerful force in political life. Indeed, in the first decade of the twentieth century, Nonconformist influence was at its peak. In New Zealand, although occasional individuals were active, 'Nonconformists' as a group had little political profile.

Reasons for this are not hard to identify. One was a function of size. There were less than 5000 Baptists in New Zealand in 1910. Other 'Nonconformist' groups were bigger, but the wide spread of the population meant there were few centres of activity and intellectual development.

'Nonconformist' has been deliberately placed in quotation marks. As I have already suggested, the term is anachronistic, barely applicable to the colonial situation. In New Zealand there was no legally privileged, established church as in England. 'Conformity' and its opposite were thus stripped of their sense. For Archer this would have far-reaching

---

⁵¹ N.Z.P.D., Vol. 263, 1144, 26/8/43.
⁵² G.T. Beilby, *A Handful of Grain: The Centenary History of the Baptist Union of N.Z.*, Vol. 3 - 1914-1945, (Auckland: NZBHS, 1984), 98.
⁵³ N.Z.P.D., Vol. 259, 221, 26/3/41. He did not regard the whole of church history as a write-off. He acknowledged failures but proudly pointed to such achievements as the abolition of slavery - see N.Z.P.D., Vol. 260, 1048-9, 8/10/41.

consequences. He had come from an environment where historically-defined Nonconformists had obvious political grievances. The Education Act which he had opposed in Grimsby was just one rallying point.[54] In New Zealand the 'Free Churches were much less conscious of disputes with the Church of England. They were more inclined to define themselves in opposition to the Roman Catholics than to the Anglicans. Political issues where they emerged were often barely disguised 'anti-popery'. As will be seen, both J.J. North and Howard Elliot represent a sectarian framework quite different from that of Archer. This is no coincidence. Both were among the first generation of Baptist ministers who grew up and were trained in the colonies (North in New Zealand, Elliot in Australia) where the weight of Anglican establishment did not apply but where strong Catholic working class communities were present. In Elliott's case, anti-Catholicism came to merge with opposition to socialism.

When he came to New Zealand in 1908, Archer thus entered a context quite different from that he had shared with Clifford. 'Nonconformist' churches displayed little interest in political campaigns beyond issues such as temperance and gambling. As a body they certainly did not identify with the emerging Labour party with which Archer was naturally aligned. This unanticipated feature of church life contributed to both his disillusionment with merely religious activism and his increasing attraction to party politics.

Despite the fact that he spent a working life as a minister Archer appears to have found the pastoral role increasingly restrictive. Indeed, between 1914 and 1918 he appears to have gone through a personal crisis. This is the period Wood calls 'the broken years'. Archer was successively minister at Invercargill for two years, minister at Vivian Street in Wellington for sixteen months and then Army Chaplain for eighteen months. Wood puts this transient interlude down to Archer's willingness to serve wherever called. This is too simple an analysis. These years were more like a 'mid-life crisis', during which Archer, unsettled and dissatisfied, was forced to reconsider his call. Throughout this period, his involvement with party politics gradually increased. He made contact with the New Zealand Labour movement soon after his arrival in Napier, serving as editor of the

---

[54] Baptist political activism peaked in England in the last third of the nineteenth century. On reasons for this and its subsequent decline see D.W. Bebbington, 'The Baptist Conscience in the Nineteenth Century', *Baptist Quarterly*, Vol XXXIV, (January 1991): 13-24 and 'Baptists and Politics Since 1914' in K.W. Clements (ed), *Baptists in the Twentieth Century* (London: 1983), 76-95. See also Bebbington, *The Nonconformist Conscience: chapel and politics, 1870-1914* (London: 1982).

United Labour Leader in 1913.⁵⁵ This continued the association he had begun in Britain. From 1914 onwards he would be increasingly involved in the political side of the movement. By 1918, secular politics had become the preferred channel for his socialist Gospel.

Some hint of this process can be traced in the two major statements he made as Union President. The first (a new-year message published at the start of 1918, when he was still a Chaplain) reflects both his own struggle and his criticism of the churches.

> Life in Camp demonstrates beyond all dispute, that our manhood, in overwhelming proportions, is not merely out of touch with the churches, but is positively full of wrath and resentment at the churches...
>
> [The churches] are splitting theological hairs, emphasising ecclesiastical differences, winking at and even indulging in economic sins, instead of setting up the Kingdom of God.
>
> We need to dream Spirit-filled apocalypses of our own and then strive to get them actualised.⁵⁶

By the October 1918 Assembly Archer had 'dreamed his own apocalypse'. His Presidential address, entitled 'Covetousness', was a sweeping critique of society and a call to radical discipleship.

> We must take the machinery of government out of the hands of the robbers...We must transfer from private to public hands the business of producing and distributing the necessities of life...Politicians laugh at prayers; but they tremble at votes...It is up to Christians in general and Baptists in particular to lead a movement for the consecration of the ballot box to Christ and humanity.⁵⁷

'Covetousness' marks the maturing of Archer's creed and the end of his crisis. By the date of its delivery his candidacy for the parliamentary seat of Invercargill seat had been announced. Before the end of the year he accepted a call to his final and most lengthy pastorate, Sydenham, in Christchurch.

Archer was serious about his Invercargill candidacy. It is clear that he was ready to give up his pastoral responsibilities if elected to Parliament. After initially declining the call to Sydenham, he eventually accepted only

---

⁵⁵ Gustafson, *Labour's Path*, 153; Wood, 9.
⁵⁶ *NZB* (January 1918): 4.
⁵⁷ *NZB* (December 1918): 184-9, p 189.

on the condition that he be able to continue his political activities.[58] From this time forward he was constantly running for, or holding, some political office. The Sydenham charge was not neglected but Wood's assertion that the church took priority is hard to sustain. The six years of his Mayoralty of Christchurch took up much of Archer's time, particularly during the early years of the Depression.

From 1919, though he was faithful, even enthusiastic, in the discharge of his pastoral duties, J.K. Archer's focus was primarily on public life. This was not a repudiation of his calling. On the contrary it was its full flowering in a new environment. His speeches in the Legislative Council were replete with biblical imagery and quotation. As Archer put it

> I am in a very peculiar position. When I speak here my friends tell me I am preaching sermons. When I preach in the pulpit, they tell me I am talking politics. I really do not know which is right.[59]

Both were right. The imperatives of the Gospel, shaped by experience and frustration, married to his predilection for action and conflict, made Archer's religion and political stance indivisible.

Had he stayed in Britain - where the Nonconformists provided a larger, more politically organized platform - it is possible Archer would have continued to direct his energies to the church's radical activities. He may never have had to grapple with the crisis he faced in New Zealand between 1914 and 1918. This was a turning point. In it he displayed a willingness to honestly appraise his commitments and an ability to redirect his considerable energy. Perhaps more importantly, in this crisis Archer's career merged with a now familiar story.

In New Zealand, the churches struggled to adapt largely British forms to a new environment. The corporate identity of English Nonconformity evolved in the face of centuries of legal and structural constraint. In the new country, few such limitations survived. Categories such as 'establishment', 'Nonconformity', 'Dissent' and 'Free' are thus of only limited use in New Zealand. Protestant denominations, removed from the framework in which they arose, have struggled to establish a new sense of identity. Imported forms and structures have proved to be provisional only.

---

[58] In his speech at the Sydenham Jubilee celebrations 'he turned to traverse briefly his difficulty, on leaving his military chaplaincy to determine whether any church would leave him free to make his contribution to public life and social service. Finally he accepted Sydenham.' - *NZB* (November 1930): 360.

[59] N.Z.P.D., Vol. 264, 415-6, 11/3/44.

For Baptists, with roots deep in 'Old Dissent', the fresh air of the new territory presented remarkable opportunities. Some achieved rapid prominence in fields only barely opening up to them in Britain.[60] There were problems too. One was the blurring of accepted links between religion and politics. By 1918, J.K. Archer had adapted, resolving his personal struggle by choosing the podium above the pulpit. Few followed his lead. Indeed, on Archer's election to the Christchurch mayoralty in 1925, J.J. North counselled other ministers not to follow his example.

No political service that a man can render can compare in real and abiding value with what he can accomplish as a whole-time minister of the Gospel of Christ. We bid our ministers remember that.[61]

Though Baptists have sounded their trumpets on a narrow range of moral issues, less obviously religious causes have created more confusion than action. In any case, they might make Baptists appear extreme or fragmented – not a good look when you are endeavouring to establish your credibility in the mainstream. 'Spirit-filled apocalypses' are messy and might be better kept as unactualised dreams.

---

[60] Examples are Thomas Dick in politics, Thomas Kirk in botany and education and T.W. Adams in silviculture and education.
[61] *NZB* (June 1925): 142.

Part II
Ways of Connection

Chapter Seven: men's ways; women's ways

As the men and women of Archer's disillusioned and alienated generation made their way back to New Zealand at the close of World War One it was clear that a new type of society would have to emerge. This would take time. War-time Prime Minister William Massey, utterly committed to keeping New Zealand part of the British Empire, would lead the country until the mid-1920s. Depression would intervene. Not until the election of the First Labour Government in 1935 would the parameters of a new social contract become clear. Massey recognised the fragility of New Zealand's economic base. To him the best response was to cling to the economic power of Britain. Labour would emphasise a different aspect of the same reality - just as stark, but with a more local solution. In a former colony with a shallow pool of wealth no private body was stable enough or big enough to provide secure philanthropic support. In Britain this might once have been imagined to be the church's role. In post-Depression New Zealand it would be the Welfare State.

For Baptists too, a significant transition would take place. The assumed links with English Baptist life remained strong, but they could no longer dominate. The wild colonial energies, already dissipating, were brought under some sort of order. Conflicts would continue and rogue ministers would still appear, but the centre was strengthening. A New Zealand way of being Baptist would begin to emerge.

The shape of the transition may be glimpsed in the careers and contributions of two individuals from the most influential family in the first century of New Zealand Baptist life: Alfred North and his son J.J. North. Alfred North was a graduate of Rawdon College and a key advocate for the denominational, rather than the association model. He was editor of *The N.Z. Baptist* in the 1880s and through 1885 conducted a determined campaign to ensure a missionary society would emerge. It was clear that such a move would be a huge undertaking for the fledgling denomination. North, however, overrode any objections on the grounds of lack of resources or administrative capacity. He resisted, for instance, the proposal that New Zealand join a combined Australasian organisation. New Zealand should stand confidently alone. After all, as he stressed, 'the commencement of the English Baptist Missionary Society was by a few men....At this conference we are more in number.'[1] The church was called to engage in the grand task of mission. There was nothing New Zealand Baptists could not do. If they were but faithful to that calling, all else would fall into place.

Yet dreams were not to be so simply fulfilled. Alfred North's optimism notwithstanding, neither the Union nor the Missionary Society worked well in their first years. The Union was threatened by potential splits (over C.C. Brown and Canterbury) within its first decade and the Missionary society, though able to send out a succession of committed young women to Bengal, faced scandal and near collapse on the field by 1899 (see chapter ten). Both had been formed prematurely; both were barely sustainable in the colony. New Zealand was not Britain. In the new environment few of the old rules applied. In this skinny, mountainous country where communication was difficult and people were few the focus of Baptist life was initially centrifugal, local. The needs of the two central organisations drew increasing energy and some resentment from the churches. Baptists' sense of themselves and their relationships with others would have to adapt. Mere replication of denominational forms was not going to be enough.

The nature of Baptist identity would need to be recast. Nonconformity was no longer viable. As Archer found, the options for political activism were also different. The notion of being a community of contrast would not disappear, but it had to change its target. The second generation of Baptist ministers, especially those who were shaped and trained in the colonies, marked themselves out as different, not so much from Anglicans or Presbyterians but from Catholics. Indeed anti-Catholicism for a time threatened to consume them.

The Rev. Howard Elliott, some time minister at Mt Eden in Auckland, was the notorious leader of the Protestant Political Association (P.P.A). By 1918 this organisation boasted four times as many members as the Baptist Union. Most were drawn from amongst Presbyterians and Methodists but there was ample support from Baptists. Indeed, it is a measure of the sectarianism of New Zealand Baptists at the time that, in 1916, Elliot was a close contender with J.K. Archer for the Presidency of the Union. Archer was ultimately successful but not before two rounds of voting were required. Elliot eventually went beyond 'acceptable' sectarianism, planting sensational false allegations against Catholics to test whether the P.P.A.'s

---

[1] *NZB* (November 1885): 166.

mail was being intercepted. The Baptist Union officially dissociated itself from his extreme actions but, significantly, questioned why there should be censorship of the P.P.A. when none was applied to the Catholic Tablet.[2] In 1920 the Conference expressed thanks to Elliot for his work against the recognition of the Catholic *Ne Temere* ruling over mixed (i.e. Catholic-Protestant) marriages.[3]

Elliott's case had been referred to the Union executive by the church pastored by Alfred North's oldest son. John James (J.J.) North, was an outstanding figure in New Zealand Baptist history. A hugely popular minister, he was the key intellectual figure in Baptist life in the first half of the twentieth century. In 1924 he would be appointed first Principal of the new denominational theological college, combining wide learning with charismatic personality to shape a generation of ministers. Erudite, open to critical scholarship, appalled by Elliott's excesses he might have been but J.J. North was nonetheless himself relentlessly anti-Catholic. Through the pages of *The N.Z. Baptist* and in other publications he maintained a steadfast opposition to 'Romanism'. In 1919 he preached a twelve-week series on its evils. In one of his most popular publications, a short book entitled *Protestant and Why* he concluded that 'Rome is at variance with the Gospel and history refuses to countersign her claims.'[4]

The apparent contradictions between this sectarian stance and North's otherwise moderate views are lessened when it is recognised that North's fundamental objection to Catholicism was what he saw as its authoritarian control of its adherents' beliefs. 'We are a free people and the perpetual menace to freedom is the church which claims lordship over thoughts and research and politics and life.'[5] (In private conversation he would be just as scathing of what he saw as the repressive structures of Plymouth Brethren.)[6] To be Baptist, in North's eyes, was to stand firmly against any

---

[2] *NZB* (November 1917): 169. See Gustafson, 'Intervention', 5-6 and the entry for H.L. Elliot in the *New Zealand Dictionary of Biography*, 3 (Auckland: Auckland University Press, 1996); also G.T. Beilby, *A Handful of Grain: The Centenary History of the Baptist Union of N.Z.*, 3 (Wellington: N.Z. B.H.S., 1984), 96-98.
[3] *NZB* (November 1920): 164.
[4] J.J. North, *Protestant...and Why*, (Wellington: 1938), 92.
[5] Cited by E.W. Batts & A.H. MacLeod, *J.J. North: The Story of a Great New Zealander* (Wellington: N.Z.B.H.S. 1965), 49. See also North's book *Protestant...and Why* (Wellington: Baptist Union of New Zealand, n.d.).
[6] Oral account of J.J. North as teacher by Rev. Royston Brown to Martin Sutherland, January 1988.

coercion of the mind. Baptists were for him a community of contrast, not by virtue of mere nonconformity, negatively defined by others, but as radical Protestants. Nevertheless he favoured strong leadership and an efficient organisation. He was not alone in this, and the decades of his ascendancy (1900-1940) mark a period in which New Zealand Baptists made a profound shift to order and structure.

This was evident from the beginning of the new century. Calls in England for a stronger connection between Congregationalists were noted and taken up in the pages of *The N.Z. Baptist*. The very assumptions of Baptist polity came under scrutiny. In 1900 Rev. A.V.G. Chandler spoke on 'The Weakness of Our Baptist Church Polity' at an Auxiliary meeting in Oamaru, urging 'that, while our denomination is, like the Colony, young and progressive, some endeavour be made to cement our churches in closer bonds'.[7] Picking up on this theme, J.J. North, made an even more direct challenge.

> As a denomination, we are resolved to spread our principles through the colony; for we believe that the health of the Catholic Church requires the triumph of the truths which we maintain. But nothing is more obvious than that our church is managed in a shocking fashion. Our intense Congregationalism hampers our free development at every turn. There are few, perhaps none of us, who make a conscience of our Congregationalism. We should find, I apprehend, no insuperable difficulty in the Presbyterian system of church government, or in a modified form of Methodism. The doctrine of Believers' Baptism is only accidentally joined to a Congregational form of church government. Many of us are thoroughly convinced that the wedding is a mistake, and that there must be a divorce, if we are to overtake our opportunities in this colony.[8]

This was throwing down the gauntlet, in a manner J.J. North knew would provoke. He would later admit 'I deliberately used strong language

---

[7] *NZB* (June 1900): 90-92, 92. Chandler had trained at Spurgeon's Pastors College. After a London ministry he came to the Caversham church in Dunedin in 1899. His call was for a 'United Baptist church'. *NZB* (October 1901): 148). In April 1902 he contributed an article on "Why I am a Baptist' with a strong affirmation of the position on Baptism. He resigned the Caversham church in 1904 to take up journalism but by 1907 was applying for admission to Presbyterian ministry. He was accepted in 1908 after satisfying the Presbyterian Assembly as to his change of views. See *NZB* (February 1908): 40 and (December 1908): 224.

[8] *NZB* (August 1901): 115.

in the first article, because I thought the pot would hardly boil without it'.⁹ It also put him at odds with his father. If the denomination was 'managed in a shocking fashion.' then Alfred North, the perennial committee member, would have to be one of those most culpable. Moreover J.J. North's stance on congregationalism clearly was not shared by Alfred. North junior's close friend Harold Peters warned 'I think you mistaken when you say "perhaps none of us make a conscience of our Congregationalism" - Your father e.g. most certainly does. And I don't think he was by any manner of means alone - though no doubt the mass of our younger folk do not.'¹⁰ North senior would publish *A Primer on Baptist Principles* in 1904 which contain a spirited defence of the theological necessity of congregational polity. The matter was subject of a number of exchanges in *The N.Z. Baptist* through the year 1901. It led to little immediate change but signaled the attitude of the rising generation. They wanted a system which would facilitate efficient mission, and in particular, better oversight and management of the ministry.

It was concerns over the ministry which lay behind J.J. North's questioning of congregationalism. To the Conference of 1901 he brought a telling motion: 'that the Assembly affirms its conviction that the true policy for the denomination in this colony is the education of colonial students for the ministry of the Gospel.'¹¹ This reveals the difference felt by colonials and their dissatisfaction with an imported ministry. Peters expressed it to North explicitly

> For instance it is awkward for you or me to say what yet must be said, that the most thorough-going, and probably only really satisfactory scheme for supplying our pulpits is to raise and thoroughly train Colonial men. These will have a 'stake in the country' - ties that will bind them to us - and what is even more important - will *not* have those Home grown notions that render it almost impossible for an imported man to rest content in our little struggling causes.¹²

Such thoughts would be crucial to the eventual shaping of the Baptist College. In 1924, before he was appointed to be its first Principal, J.J. North was adamant that local training was needed.

---

⁹ *NZB* (November 1901): 162
¹⁰ Letter, Harold Peters to J.J. North, 31 August 1901. NZBA, J.J. North Papers.
¹¹ *NZB* (December 1901): 188.
¹² Letter, Harold Peters to J.J. North, 7 October 1901. NZBA , J.J. North Papers.

> The thing we lack is essential to us. It is not an extra. We have no adequate scheme for training our ministers. We want to focus the attention of our whole membership on this problem. In time past we have relied a good deal on importations.... But...the need of 90 per cent. of our churches cannot be met by importations. The best men are kept at Home, and have far more attractive spheres than this Dominion can offer them. Even if our smaller churches could find the heavy travelling charges, they cannot rely on getting the sort of man they want. It is a very fine sort of man who is needed in our smaller towns and churches. Any one will not do. We must train men racy of our soil.[13]

The march to order may have been the most obvious trend among New Zealand Baptists in the first half of the century, but there was a lot else going on besides. Since the departure of Thomas Spurgeon doctrinal conservatives had temporarily been eclipsed. However, a prominent champion arrived in 1920. Joseph Kemp came (symbolically to Thomas Spurgeon's church, the Auckland Tabernacle) after a notable ministry at Charlotte Chapel, Edinburgh and a less successful period in New York. Greatly influenced by American fundamentalism, Kemp was, like J.J. North, a charismatic, at times domineering personality. Moral propriety was an essential of his creed - dancing and cinema-going were anathema. His greatest battle however was against 'modernism'. On the face of it this might have put Kemp in direct conflict with North. The relationship between Kemp and North is examined more fully in chapter nine. Strong characters both, they might have split the denomination. That they didn't is testimony to their tact and skill. Not everyone would be as successful. As we shall see, their respective successors - Luke Jenkins as Principal of the College, Alexander Hodge at the Tabernacle – were each at the centre of controversies which did threaten the union.

For the first sixty years of the twentieth century J.J. North's *mana* and legacy was greater in the denomination as a whole. Kemp's influence in Baptist affairs was primarily in Auckland, but he was also the key figure in trans-denominational conservative Christianity. He set up the Bible Training Institute in 1922, an interdenominational college which for decades provided a virtual rite of passage for young fundamentalists, especially those interested in overseas mission. The impact of this approach on the question of Baptist identity has been immense. Evangelism and biblical purity were the central themes of Kemp's preaching and the Bible

---

[13] *NZB* (August 1924): 170.

Training Institute's teaching. Traditional denominational distinctives were played down. It was thus possible for his followers to understand themselves as conservative evangelicals first, Baptists second. Kemp's was a lay training institute. North, on the other hand, trained a generation of ministers. 'North's men' were the leaders of organised Baptist life for forty years but Kemp would leave a massive imprint on conservative lay people. For decades Kemp's stream had little obvious institutional impact on denominational affairs. It was a subterranean movement which would surface periodically as issues demanded. It would find a powerful new form in the charismatic movement of the 1970s. For now, the approach exemplified by North – freedom of conscience within a strongly ordered structure – would hold sway.

As the twentieth century unfolded, the shortcomings of the national organisations - first the Missionary society, then the Union - became obvious and the need for change became pressing. The building of central structures became increasingly important from the 1920s onwards. But a subtle change was taking place. J.J. North's vigorous championing of freedom of conscience was overtaken by a drive for order and respectability. As a third generation emerged, the sense of being a contrast community was relegated. A 'centripetal' or centre-seeking movement was taking over. Church life was in this sense following a similar path to that of political and economic developments. Initiative would increasingly lie with the centre. In keeping with this more ordered approach it was natural that Baptists would make a pitch for the mainstream, to join the Anglicans, Presbyterians and Methodists with a claim to a seat at the Protestant table. For such a tiny group it was in many ways an absurd ambition, but it was attempted with energy and some success. Conservatives were occupied in battling modernism; the sterner sectarian advocates for freedom were growing old. The way ahead seemed clear. In mid-century New Zealand Baptists must play, and look, their part in wider church life.

The symbol of this new era of increased focus on organisation and structure was the Baptist Union Incorporation Act of 1923. The roots of this statutory statement of Baptist respectability lay in the passing of the first generation of property trustees and the practical difficulties encountered in transferring assets when trustees were either dead or no longer to be found. More broadly, however, it was the supreme product of the desire to direct and to organize better. J.J. North's stinging 1901 indictment that the denomination was 'managed in a shocking fashion' was not forgotten.

The concept of incorporation had been brought to the 1917 Conference. Its time had come. A.S. Adams, R.S. Gray and M.W.P. Lascelles were the key architects of a more centralized, organized and efficient post-war Baptist Union. Adams, a prominent lawyer and later Supreme Court Justice, led discussions on the proposed Act at the 1919 and 1920 Conferences. The key moment was in 1920, when a creedal statement for the Bill was sought. This in itself was a massive step, though one surprisingly rapidly achieved. The reporter on the Conference exhibited the bemused ambivalence of the denomination over such a move.

It hardly needs to be said here that we Baptists have no creed other than the Testament itself. We have an historic repugnance to creeds. We know what fetters man-made creeds have been. We know how conscience has been strained, and how prevarication has been made easy by creeds. And so we have never had so much as a rag of a creed, until this 1920 Conference came along. But a creed became suddenly essential. We want to be incorporated, so that our property, and money willed to us, may be properly handled. We cannot be incorporated without stating the creed of our Church. Was ever such a fix?[14]

The minimalist creed which still forms the framework for the Union was speedily drafted by a committee convened by J.J. North and adopted unanimously, without debate. The reporter assured all readers that 'these statements are as brief and as essential as an Act of Parliament requires.'

Adams also promoted the need for a full-time General Secretary. Gray was appointed to this role in 1919 and so steered most of the preparations for the Private Bill. On Gray's untimely death in 1922, Lascelles succeeded to the role. As President 1918-19, Lascelles had promoted and secured a Sustenation Fund to support struggling causes. In his first full report as General Secretary, he noted the advantages of the Act and urged churches 'to place their properties in trust forthwith'.[15]

The Incorporation Act was the most public outcome of the shift to centralisation which had begun with the new century but which picked up pace considerably following the World War. In the next decades a raft of committees were set up to more efficiently manage the work of the denomination. There were committees on literature, to govern the Jubilee

---

[14] *NZB* (November 1920): 164.
[15] *NZB* (November 1924): 247. Lascelles had encouraged his own church in Napier to do so as soon as it became possible. This action set the context for the disputes at Napier a decade later.

fund, the College, and church extension. There was the broadcasting committee, the fire insurance committee, the home committee, the architectural committee and so on. In 1915 the annual assembly had appointed six committees; in 1945 it appointed twenty-three.[16]

The expansion of the role and reach of the Union was a sign that the imperative for connection would be fundamental to the New Zealand way of being Baptist in this era. Building a strong denominational body with a growing bureaucracy was, however, primarily the men's story. Women, too, were agents of connection. Effectively excluded from Union leadership, they built other, semi-independent organisations. In a story so relentlessly dominated by men, it is instructive to examine the roles and aspirations of two of these: the Baptist Ministers Wives Union (B.M.W.U.) and the Baptist Women's Missionary Union (with the confusingly similar initials B.W.M.U.)

Ministers' Wives

At the 1918 Assembly ten ministers wives gathered and formed a Union with the motto 'Labourers together with God' (I Cor. 3:9). The first President was Florence Lascelles, wife of M.W.P. Lascelles.[17] Branches were to be set up across the country. This quickly happened in Auckland and Wellington, although it took a few years to gather momentum in the South Island. The objects of the new body were 'to promote a spirit of friendliness and comradeship, to encourage any who might have special difficulties, and to help each other by prayer, by correspondence, and by occasional meetings.'[18]

The early minutes closely reflect those aims. In 1921 it was reported that Auckland had held two meetings and a picnic. Wellington had also held two meetings and enjoyed 'much loving fellowship'. At Dunedin, meetings were quarterly, being 'in the nature of a talk, closing with prayer.' The Canterbury branch did not commence meeting until March 1923.

Generally annual meetings included an inspirational or informative speaker on such topics as 'The Ideal Minister's Wife' (1943). Letters of sympathy, congratulation, or welcome to new members were assiduously

---

[16] Beilby, *A Handful of Grain*, 30-32.
[17] *NZB* (November 1918): 161
[18] This and the summary which follows of the history of the B.M.W.U. are drawn from the Dominion Minute Books of the organisation, NZBA, M26/1&2.

recorded. At the 1925 meeting 'Miss Batts, the prospective bride of one of our ministers, was specially welcomed.' Letters of greeting were also sent to 'absent members'. This practice was challenged at the tenth meeting in 1927. The Canterbury Branch proposed that the letters 'be cut out as being tedious and time-wasting'. Their preference was that the meetings be purely social in nature. There was 'considerable discussion', though no decision - other than to write to inform absent members of the debate!

Canterbury was also concerned to increase missionary membership. This too was debated in 1927 under the question of 'whom...other than actual ministers' wives be invited to the meetings.' Again, there was no resolution. Not until 1943 was the full name of the Union quietly extended to include missionaries. The issue of membership was a frequent agenda item. In the 1960s Deaconesses were recognised. There appears to have been a growing reluctance to appear exclusive. The meeting of 1971 at Lower Hutt discussed possible extension to include social workers, or even (though apparently reluctantly) to the Baptist Women's League President!

Not all concerns were internal. For several decades contact was maintained with similar organisations in Australia and Britain. Outside events forced their way in. In 1942 the AGM resolved to write to the Prime Minister, proposing the appointment of special women constables 'for the protection of girls at night' and calling for the strict enforcement of the licensing laws.

For two generations of manse women the B.M.W.U. enabled communication and support. But times change and perceived needs with them. The 1964 meeting decided to keep 'formalities and programme to a minimum' and the annual gatherings grew progressively less structured. In the 1970s a greater interest in combined meetings with the Ministers is evident. (Once again the Canterbury branch led the change - arranging for the 1979 meeting to join the men for an afternoon of seminars.) By the 1980s the desire for 'tight' structures, indeed the imperative for denominational connection itself, was not so obvious. The raison d'être of the organisation was lost to the collective memory. A full and evidently highly entertaining meeting was held at the centennial Assembly in 1982, but it was the last.

Women's Missionary Union

New Zealand Baptists have never lacked for strong women. They were often key players in the formation of churches and were outstanding among the earliest missionaries. Yet, despite the involvement and commitment of many Baptists, men and women, in the suffrage movement, there was, as we have seen, only very slow movement towards equal opportunity and representation of women in leadership, both locally and in denominational affairs. After various attempts to secure a place for women at the Annual Assembly, a compromise was agreed in 1897. Women could attend Assembly as 'personal' members of the Union. This individual form of membership had been open for some time but carried much less voting power than a delegate from a church. It was an unsatisfactory outcome and the issue continued to be raised. It would not be until 1908 that women were finally accepted as full delegates.

It was in this context of limited opportunity for women to exercise official leadership that the suggestion arose for the formation of the women's missionary union. In a letter published in *The N.Z. Baptist* in October 1903, Mrs S.B. Bennett, of the Kaikorai church, Dunedin proposed 'a union whose object, naturally, would be the promotion of missionary zeal amongst the women of our churches.' This was far from a radical expression of first wave feminism. Mrs Bennett sought a close alignment with the New Zealand Baptist Missionary Society and proposed a guiding principle 'that we do nothing contrary to the wish of our Foreign Mission Society.' She clearly felt the value of a male endorsement citing in support for her suggestion that the missionary, 'Rev. John Takle, thinks that such a union would be a good thing.'[19] The proposal was brought to the meetings of the Missionary Society at the next Conference and the new organisation was formed.

Here, then, was a new forum, a vehicle for the talents and commitment of Baptist women. It was not immediately welcomed. Indeed, the men of the denomination were a bit bemused by this female activism. 'Wrox', the wry commentator on Assembly proceedings, reported startling events on missionary day, 1905.

> For the first time in the history of the society two ladies spoke to the adoption of the report. Mrs Driver got in a word on behalf of the now famous B.W.M.U. These mystic letters mean, not as I heard one ungallant delegate suggest, 'Baptist Working Man Undone' but the 'Baptist Women's Missionary Union'. And with all a woman's winsome witchery and wickedness she closed her speech by exclaiming defiantly:

---

[19] *NZB* (November 1903): 172-3.

'And in spite of all the prejudice against women speakers, we mean to go on and on!'[20]

A year later, 'The Rambler' commented on the annual meeting of the new organisation in similarly mocking tones. 'No male foot might tread the sacred precincts of the shrine wherein the priestesses of the cult wearing the mystic initials B.W.M.U. met in solemn conclave.'[21]

Along with the emerging Young Women's Bible Class Unions, Ministers' Wives association and other local initiatives, the B.W.M.U. was one of a range of outlets for women which opened up in the first decades of the twentieth century. The importance of these opportunities cannot be over-emphasised. The denomination remained overwhelmingly male-led. Even after the belated admission of female delegates to the Conference in 1908, there was the recognition in some quarters that much greater progress was needed. In 1910 Rev. F.H. Radford of Mosgiel noted

> How delightfully illogical we are. We allow a woman to grace the Throne of this mighty Empire, and forbid her a seat in our legislative halls. We make her pastor in all but name of our most difficult charges in India, and shudder at the bare suggestion of the Rev. Mrs Smith being pastor of Hanover Street, Dunedin!
>
> The day is surely coming when in every department of life the limit will be set - not by sex or fancied inferiority – but by efficiency.[22]

Radford, nevertheless, retained the view that 'woman's true welfare is ever bound up with the welfare of the home'. Mrs Bennett would have largely agreed. After prayer, she saw as a major benefit of local meetings, the communication of news and missionary enthusiasm to the home, so that 'children, the future church, would have a missionary atmosphere constantly surrounding them.' The 'diffusion of missionary information' would be among the first objectives of the new body.

In the early years, branches were formed in a number of churches. Numbers were not large. In 1911, Epsom (six), Richmond (seven) and North-East Valley (also seven) headed the list of average monthly attendances. Yet the minute books of these local groups reveal a surprisingly full curriculum of crafts, discussions, book studies and fundraising activities. A remarkable thirst for information was met by visiting missionaries, sometimes aided by illuminated addresses, and what

---

[20] *NZB* (November 1905): 175.
[21] *NZB* (November 1906): 26.
[22] *NZB* (July 1910): 130-33.

became a key tradition of missionary letters and journals. Emma Beckingsale, medical missionary in India, kept up a record of her activities for some thirty years in journal form. These volumes were sent home for circulation among interested branches.

Yet there could be a more radical edge. This is especially evident in the first half of the century. On at least one occasion the B.W.M.U. took on the leadership of the Baptist Union. The key figure in this was Emily Gainsford. Miss Gainsford embodied the limited but nonetheless real opportunities for Baptist women in the first half of the century. She was a missionary with N.Z.B.M.S. for sixteen years. On her return she quickly established a place in both the B.W.M.U. and the Young Women's Baptist Bible Class Union, serving as secretary of the B.W.M.U. for a total of 25 years.

In the 1920s the executive power of the denomination was very firmly in men's hands. In this same period the B.W.M.U. turned its attention to prospects for home evangelisation. This was a notable expansion of its original vision. Through the decade it lobbied for the appointment of an itinerant woman missioner who could travel around the 'back-blocks' areas of New Zealand spreading the Gospel and providing contact for isolated women. No action was taken, even though various women's groups were undertaking to fund the work. The women did not give up and in 1929 mooted a more specific scheme. It was argued that two women might be commissioned to set up a mission among Maori along the then relatively remote Wanganui river. In 1930 a commission (of men) from the central executive somewhat grudgingly investigated, then rejected this proposal. Their reasons for not proceeding were indicative of the thinking at this time. Firstly, the proposal needed money at a time of deepening depression. Such resources as were available were deemed necessary to preserve for existing structures. Secondly, there was already an Anglican mission among Maori in the area and it was felt to be impolitic to appear to be competing. Any 'Maori work' should only proceed by cooperation with (and preferably under the auspices of) another denomination.[23]

The fate of the Wanganui River proposal highlights divergent priorities. For the B.W.M.U. women the imperative to evangelism was obvious and paramount. For the men of the executive, order and church diplomacy suggested a more cautious approach. Not until the more affluent 1950s

---

[23] See the *New Zealand Baptist Handbook 1930-1931* (Wellington, BUNZ, 1930), 44 and the correspondence relating to the Wanganui proposal in the NZBA.

would Baptist women gain formal recognition for Home Mission purposes with the introduction of Deaconesses, and a Baptist Maori Mission begin.[24] The incident nonetheless demonstrates the opportunity the B.W.M.U. accorded activist women to come up with their own visions and initiatives.

An undoubted financial clout was also emerging. The B.W.M.U. proved itself adept at micro-fundraising – small amounts at a time, but frequently and from a large membership. In 1912 it contributed 13 percent of the Missionary Society income; in the 1930s it regularly exceeded 30 percent. By the end of the 1950s this figure had dropped to a still substantial 20 percent. This slide continued as the Missionary Society expanded its funding base and the membership of the B.W.M.U. declined in the 1970s. In 1980 the contribution was approximately 11 percent; by 2000 it was less than 5 percent.

There was much more going on in the B.W.M.U. than merely providing a platform in an otherwise male-dominated denomination. By far the greater bulk of activities reflected the interaction of women with other women of similar commitments and spiritualities. Here it is again worthwhile to recall the vision of Mrs Bennett in 1903. She spoke of promoting missionary interest through prayer, information and sewing for the field. These objectives were reflected in the aims of the organisation when it was constituted, with the only real addition being fundraising, 'especially…to benefit the women of the districts occupied by the Society'.

In 1909, just six years into the life of the organisation, but when already 33 branches had been formed, the national secretary, B. Spedding noted the importance of the regular gatherings.

> Many beautiful adjectives are used to describe the branch meetings – bright, happy, helpful, enjoyable, stimulating, profitable, interesting being amongst them. For this we cannot be sufficiently thankful. We believe a spirit of earnest supplication pervades our meetings, and these results are largely brought about by the reading of our missionaries' letters. One Secretary writes me 'I could feel the atmosphere warming as I read.'[25]

---

[24] There had been a brief attempt to establish a mission among Maori in the 1880s. On the formation of the twentieth century work see C.D. Jones, 'The Long, Painful Birth of Baptist Maori Ministry' *N.Z.J.B.R.* Vol. 1, Oct. 1996, 47-65.
[25] *NZBU Handbook* 1909-10, 90.

Such interests and sentiments are further demonstrated in the minutes of the various branches. Epsom's annual report in 1912 is an early example.[26]

> There does not seem anything very special to report this year. As a band of women we have got to know one another better, and though we are small in numbers, we have felt the Master's presence with us at each meeting.
>
> At present we are studying Mr Takle's[27] Book 'The Bible in 'Baria' & as our reading are taking Paul's Missionary Journeys.
>
> A 'Missionary At Home' was given to the ladies of the Congregation, at which 'Missionary Lotto' was introduced & all the games our Missionary had in hand were sold. We feel that the interest of those who are not members of our Branch was deepened, & three friends have since signified their intention of joining us as the result of this special effort.
>
> Mrs Smeeton took charge of our August meeting & gave us a most helpful & interesting address.
>
> As a contribution towards Miss Wilkinson's outfit, we are giving her some towels and to Nurse Cowles we sent a Dressing Gown.
>
> We are each subscribing a small sum towards an American Magazine called 'Motherhood' with the idea of passing it round to each member. This magazine was brought under our notice by a friend from Nelson & we think it will be most helpful to parents as well as to Sunday School Teachers.
>
> Number of Members – nine   Average – five
>
> Total contributions 2/-/-

The importance of these regular gatherings, where women were able to express to one another their understanding of the divine plan and the mission of the church is immense. Particularly in the early decades, when women's voices were not often heard in main services other than in song, these meetings and others like them facilitated a Baptist women's

---

[26] 'Copy of Report sent to Miss Spedding, Secretary of Auckland Union 8/9/12', NZBA, E.2/70.
[27] Rev. John Takle, N.Z.B.M.S. missionary 1896-1925, who wrote extensively on Christianity and Islam.

spirituality which developed its own style. Much more study is needed in this area but some features stand out.

The first is the role of craft. Mrs Bennett envisaged sewing clothes for use among the poor on the field. Much more common was work done for fundraising sales. As seen, in material terms the B.W.M.U. was an outstanding success in this. But there is wider significance in such work. The devoted creativity found in women's craft is barely appreciated in Baptist history. When the most prosaic item of sewing or knitting is understood as a gift to God it takes on new meaning. Baptists, heirs to a radical reformation suspicion of distraction and idolatry, were cautious about colour and display as part of worship. Only relatively recently have craft skills been freed to enhance churches with banners, pennants and cushions in vibrant colours and patterns. Before this became acceptable, the work tables and sewing circles of generations of B.W.M.U. women provided a rich outlet for the expression of devotion to Christ.

The outstanding element of B.W.M.U. spirituality was plainly prayer. This is testified over and again in reports and reminiscences. This was a praying body. In the nature of things, the full quality of this central act is difficult to describe. However, it is clear that there was a particular character about B.W.M.U. prayer. It was neither mystical nor private, and yet only rarely would it be fully corporate, in the sense of prayers read in unison. Rather, the typical form lay between types. B.W.M.U. was prayer spoken by individuals as part of a group. The group thus shared and often affirmed the prayers of its members, but the prayers themselves would be individual and extempore. Extempore, but informed. This was the point of all that information, discussion and letter reading. These Baptist women prayed with outcomes in mind and expecting results. B.W.M.U. prayer was activist. It was not generally contemplative or general but intercessory and specific. Such prayer is understood by its participants in terms of its effect. It was undertaken as a natural and crucial part of their commitment to support the missionaries on the field. Yet the impact of this regular form of shared intercession on the Christian lives of the members of the branches must not be discounted. Prayer meetings were a doubly significant contribution of B.W.M.U. to wider Baptist life. They provided a reliable and often genuinely relational connection between home base and the missionaries on the field. Yet there was more. The same acts of prayer and support, replicated locally, regionally and nationally, formed the Christian spirituality of generations of Baptist women.

In an era when wider roles remained stereotyped and restricted, women's own organisations represented a primary, often the sole opportunity to demonstrate leadership, short of the mission field itself. This would change gradually after the Second World War, with its loosening of gender roles. The massive reordering of society and roles from the 1960s meant the uniqueness of the opportunities provided by women's organisations would fade. For Baptists the landscape changed rather quickly. The Baptist Women's League, with a New Zealand rather than overseas missions focus, was formed in 1952. Seen by some as an alternative to B.W.M.U., the B.W.L. absorbed much of the energy for local initiatives. Baptists would introduce training for Deaconesses in the 1950s and, eventually, congregational leadership would become an option (at least in theory). As these developments unfolded, the B.W.M.U. continued its core functions but became less obviously the main forum for women's leadership.

Strong male leaders like J.J. North and W.P. Lascelles managed to craft a robust denominational framework, with enough gravity to draw all elements of Baptist life towards itself. They had the advantage of the coercive power of rules. The women did not lack for strong-willed individuals – ask anyone who dealt with Annie Driver or Emily Gainsford – but theirs were voluntary organisations, established and held together quite differently from the Union's structures. What the B.W.M.U. in particular showed was that a deep and lasting connectivity could be built along relational, as well as constitutional lines. This was not a unique case. Indeed, relational connections have been a crucial factor in establishing a New Zealand Baptist identity. As we shall see, the denominational magazine functioned (sometimes splutteringly) in a similar way. The ministerial training scheme began as a tight creature of rules and became a key constitutional element of the denomination when the college was formed in the mid-1920s. Yet it would come to be seen that the best work of the college, too, as with the women's organisations, was found in the strength of the relationships formed between students and (as importantly) with their Principal.

Chapter Eight: *The N.Z. Baptist* as an agent of identity

The N.Z. Baptist is the oldest continuously running religious periodical in New Zealand. Its place in the history and development of denominational life is profound. This chapter traces the impact and editorial policies of the newspaper from its beginnings in a scattered, sparsely populated colony to its role in an increasingly confident Baptist community following the Second World War. In this time it established itself as a key arbiter of Baptist identity. By the end of the period this was changing, with the New Zealand Baptist becoming more a mirror to the denomination than a window into its world.

When the New Zealand Baptist Union was formed in 1882 it consisted of a mere 25 churches. Not only was the group small but it was scattered across a barely developing colony. Only seven churches exceeded 100 members and these were in five different towns. Roads were poor and the rail network was rudimentary. Most Baptists had in common their English heritage and most of their ministers had trained in English colleges. But New Zealand was not England. It was a new religious, economic and social environment which would require fresh approaches to building denominational identity and unity. This was one of the fledgling Union's ambitions. A key element in that mission was the decision to take responsibility for an existing Baptist paper.

The N.Z. Baptist was to be a vehicle for Baptist identity. However, it was a long time before it truly began to serve this function. Successive editors took different approaches. It was not until the long (1915-1948) tenure of J.J. North that an overt, hard driving, partisan tone sealed New Zealand Baptists' view of themselves. At the same time, the paper and its editors reflected back what congregations were already thinking on a range of questions. The history of the periodical thus provides a unique record of the development of the denomination.

Establishment

The N.Z. Baptist began as a regional effort, designed to support the work of the Canterbury Baptist Association, which had been formed in 1874. This group immediately appointed an evangelist to further what it took to be its principal purpose. Its second initiative was to publish a magazine which, in its various names over the next years would symbolize not only the motivations of the founders but also a gradual shift in focus.

The first issue of the *Canterbury Evangelist* appeared in August 1876. The editor (Robert Morton, pastor at the Hereford Street church in Christchurch) eschewed sectarian bias.

> Though issuing from a Baptist source, we do not wish to incur the idea that it will be a strictly denominational magazine....
>
> It is the intention of the promoters of the Magazine to make it of some utility amongst all evangelical denominations, meeting the wants of both saint and sinner. We do not by any means propose to represent the Baptist denomination as a whole, and therefore we are not responsible for any outside the Association, whilst, at the same time, we will gladly work with all who will work with us.[1]

This apparent openness reflected the 'loose' Baptist ethos already noted among key Canterbury leaders. Individuals like J.W. Sawle and William Pole may have been convinced Baptists but evangelical fervour was more significant to them than building a denomination. A change in the tone began, however, almost immediately. The second issue (November 1876) opened with the first of a two-part apology by J. Upton Davis on 'Believer's Baptism' which concluded unequivocally that 'the proper subjects [for baptism] can neither be infants nor unbelievers.'[2] The magazine soon began a process by which it became a principal means of establishing identity amongst scattered Baptist groups and individuals. With the May 1877 issue the name underwent the first of series of changes, to *The Canterbury Baptist*. In explanation, the editorial talked of preserving truth 'sadly neglected by other denominations'.[3] This was the voice of a new editor. Charles Dallaston (1852-1934) was now at the helm. Dallaston had just arrived as pastor of the Hereford Street church, the only large congregation in the province. A young man, trained at Spurgeon's Pastors' College, he would soon show himself to prefer more classically Baptist approaches than those of earlier Canterbury leaders. Fifty years later he recalled that it was decided to change the name and 'to make the magazine

---

[1] *The Canterbury Evangelist* (August 1876): 1-2.
[2] J. Upton Davis 'Believers' Baptism', *The Canterbury Evangelist* (November 1876): 25-28 (see also February 1877: 49-51). Davis was Minister at the Dunedin church and would chair the first Union Conference in 1880.
[3] *The Canterbury Baptist* (May 1877): 1.

more distinctly denominational.'[4] The magazine henceforth increasingly displayed this 'tight' approach. It would be a Baptist magazine first, and it would increase its role by moving beyond its immediate region. An August 1878 editorial made 'no apology, either for declaring ourselves denominationalists, or for introducing the subject in our *Magazine*.'[5] In January 1880 'Canterbury' was dropped from the title and the major feature in the renamed journal was an 1876 sermon by Rev. A.W. Webb which argued that Baptist denominational existence was 'a necessity'.[6] By July the title had reached its final state: *The New Zealand Baptist*. In September 1880 another new editor, William Spencer, was secretary to the conference which resolved to form a colony-wide Union.

The magazine came under the control of the Union in 1883. Charles Bright, one of a number of ministers who had careers in both Australia and New Zealand, served as editor for two years, followed by Alfred North (1884-1887) and Lewis Shackleford (1887-1889). With such a run of short term editors, it is not surprising that no consistent character attached itself to the publication. North, a keen Union supporter, used his editorial control to push for greater centralization and particularly for the formation of a N.Z. Baptist Missionary Society. He would play a significant role in both denominational and mission affairs until his death in 1924. Shackleford was, like North, a graduate of Rawdon College. He was also a controversialist who led the charge against the perceived heresies of Rev. Charles Brown.

These editors and their successors would struggle to build a sustainable subscriber base. As its initial focus had been local, *The N.Z. Baptist* had a lot of work to do to achieve a colony-wide readership. Limited distribution meant limited capacity to be an agent for building corporate identity. A desire to increase subscriptions, to get a copy in every Baptist household, was regularly expressed but a major sticking point seems to have been the cost. Low print runs meant high unit cost, creating consumer resistance. In December 1885, a correspondent from Thames wrote of frustration at the price of 4d per copy.

> I think it is a *great mistake* not to have reduced the price long before this. I believe the paper would soon double its circulation and you

---

[4] *NZB* (October 1926): 263.
[5] [Charles Dallaston] 'Denominationalism', *The Canterbury Baptist* (August 1878): 56-59, 56.
[6] A. W. Webb, 'The Baptists: Their Denominational Existence a Necessity', *The Baptist* (January 1880): 3-12.

would reach those who won't buy now, for the simple reason that you can get more for your money....Other papers of similar size are twopence and threepence, and why should not the BAPTIST be published at such a price, so that *every family* belonging to our churches would buy it?[7]

The price did not come down – and the circulation did not go up. This problem was noted by the supporters of the N.Z. Baptist Missionary Society which had been formed in 1885. They were in no doubt that widespread support for the new Society was crucial and that *The N.Z. Baptist* was at that point an inadequate vehicle for promoting this support. The solution was to commence a dedicated newsletter, the first number of which appeared in June 1886. Comprising of (generally) four pages of news from the pages of *The N.Z. Baptist* itself, *The Missionary Messenger* made no pretence about its *raison d'être*: to reach Society subscribers and to raise funds. Tellingly, it was distributed free. The hope was that it might (in the way that *The N.Z. Baptist* did not) 'enter every Baptist home in the land, and to awaken in every Baptist heart a response to our appeal for generous aid.'[8]

The N.Z. Baptist meanwhile continued to pursue its mission, however falteringly. From the outset the magazine included 'News of the churches' - reports from individual congregations. These would become a feature of the publication. Though for many years only one page of sixteen was given to such accounts, their significance cannot be overestimated. In these are the names and activities of ordinary Baptists who otherwise would not be noticed and who certainly would have been unlikely ever to have left a published account of their lives. It is, moreover, in these short notices that the experience of 'being Baptist' in New Zealand is truly encountered. Social gatherings, controversies, deaths, births, baptisms, visiting speakers, these small moments add up to a rounded vision of Baptist life. News of them also, crucially, encouraged groups to identify with congregations in other parts of the colony.

In May 1889 Lewis Shackleford left for Australia. His replacement was Arthur Dewdney. Dewdney had trained at Spurgeon's Pastors' College. Like his predecessor he was not averse to controversy. In an early editorial (critical of F.W. Walker, a Baptist minister at Nelson who had 'seceded to

---

[7] M. Whitehead 'The Price of 'The Baptist': To the Editor', *NZB* (January 1886): 10 (emphasis original).
[8] *The Missionary Messenger* (June 1886): 1

the Anglican church') he protested 'surely truth and principle are of more value than ease and popularity.'[9] Dewdney was quite prepared to use the pages of *The N.Z. Baptist* for Christian activism, though his would be the activism of individual piety, typical of English Baptists at the end of the nineteenth century.

> The race is not to be uplifted *en masse* by any social schemes, however well devised and carefully guarded.

> The new mission is the old: the old mission is the new. 'Into all the world and preach the gospel.' The regeneration of the individual man by the power of the Holy Spirit through the grace of God and the love of Christ.[10]

In these years *The N.Z. Baptist* typically consisted of 16 pages of foolscap. It carried advertisements, largely from Baptist businesses, and much of its content was reprinted material from overseas, especially English sources. The Union Annual Report for 1888 noted with satisfaction that the paper was showing a small surplus of income over expenditure.[11] By 1890 however the publication was in slight deficit and it was suggested that 'another 60 subscribers would enable the paper to be published without loss.'[12] A year later, a proposal that the paper move to weekly publication was seriously considered. Ultimately no change was deemed feasible.[13] By now it was increasingly acknowledged that the publication 'constitutes a bond of union between the widely scattered churches' and in 1893 the Union was prepared to subsidise the paper by £10.[14] In the Annual Report of 1896 it was noted with some satisfaction that 'the *Baptist* is now, as far as we can learn, the oldest religious periodical in the Colony.'[15] In late 1897 it was signaled that new procedures and layout would be adopted to speed publication and appeal to a wider range of Baptists, particularly the young. However, little, if any, change to the format resulted.

---

[9] *NZB* (August 1889): 120.
[10] *NZB* (February 1892): 17. See also Dewdney's comment on 'Christians and Social Reform', *NZB* (November 1893): 168-9.
[11] Supplement to *NZB* (January 1889): 4.
[12] *NZB* (December 1890): 183.
[13] *NZB* (December 1891): 183. See also *NZB* (December 1892): 184.
[14] Supplement to *NZB* (January 1892): 4; (January 1894): 5.
[15] Supplement to *NZB* (January 1897): 5.

In June 1899 Dewdney, on taking up a new ministry at Thames, concluded his ten years as editor of *The N.Z. Baptist*. Reflecting on his contribution he concluded

> this much may be said: that our churches know more about each other, and are more deeply interested in each other's welfare than before, while the bonds that unite us have been drawn closer, and we are beginning, at any rate, to be aroused to the wider interests of our denominational life.[16]

Preservation

Dewdney was succeeded by a very different personality. Frank W. Boreham was already well on his way to international recognition as a Christian writer. His most successful work appeared outside the pages of *The N.Z. Baptist*. However, a lighter tone entered the paper during his seven-year term. Editorial pages began to be appear with headlines such as 'Scribblings by the Seaside' and 'The Moral Significance of Cricket' and a regular feature of 'Bits for Preachers and Teachers' featured the often quaint anecdotes for which Boreham would be famous.[17]

In at least one case, Boreham's ironic style led to more serious debate than he might have anticipated. In the early years of the new century, denominational amalgamation on a number of levels was much debated. In May 1901 Boreham noted that the religious weekly *The Outlook*, which already represented both Presbyterians and Congregationalists, had recently added a Methodist connection. 'We congratulate our excellent contemporary upon its marvelous performance; but we counsel it, with friendly, and perhaps nervous, entreaty, not to try to swallow anything else.' Sparring further with his competing editor, Boreham suggested a month later that, as Methodists now had only to subscribe to one periodical, they might feel compelled to expend the saved subscription on a monthly copy of *The N.Z. Baptist*.[18] Perhaps to Boreham's surprise, Harold Peters, a former business manager of *The N.Z. Baptist*, suggested that a merger of the papers was in fact worth considering. Peters' central argument was one of scale, or the lack of it.

---

[16] *NZB* (June 1899): 88.
[17] *NZB* (March 1901): 33; (September 1901): 129.
[18] *NZB* (May 1901): 73; (June 1901): 89. On the *Outlook* see E.W. Hames *Out of the Common Way: The European church in the Colonial Era 1840-1913* (Auckland: Wesley Historical Society, 1972), 134-5.

That we should lose some present advantages is certain. The question is whether we should not gain others of more value. One outstanding feature of the suggested arrangement that must commend itself is that our people would have a weekly instead of a monthly paper. It would be far better for us to have a journal of some thirty pages of reading come into our homes once a week than one of sixteen pages once a month.[19]

Over the next three issues the question was debated, with the correspondence overwhelmingly against Peters' proposal. Nevertheless a concern that did emerge in a number of letters concerned the price of *The N.Z. Baptist*, which, at 4s. 6d. per annum, posted (unchanged for two decades), was still seen to be a brake on subscription growth.[20]

The expansion of *The Outlook* and the debate engendered by Peters caused a fresh look at the impact of *The N.Z. Baptist*. The annual report of the paper pointed out that the distribution had been slowly rising but that nonetheless only 630 copies were paid for each month. 'Does this not seem a very small number, when it is considered that there are 16,035 Baptists in the Colony, according to the latest census?'[21] The Conference agreed and a committee was set up, charged with identifying ways of increasing the paying readership. A year later the situation had worsened. Fully a third of subscriptions were in arrears and the printer was owed the substantial sum of £55. The enterprise was technically insolvent, as liabilities exceeded assets. The printer (T.E. Fraser of Christchurch) had in effect been carrying the paper for several years. Something had to be done and a series of bold steps were taken immediately. A tinted cover to carry advertisements was added and an advertising manager appointed. Most significantly the price was reduced to 2s. 6d. per annum, in the conviction that this would result in a significant lift in subscriptions.[22] The risk met with reward. By November 1905 subscriptions had doubled and in 1906 the size was increased to twenty pages.[23]

Boreham, however, was by then about to move on. In June 1906 he departed to take up a new ministry in Hobart. R.S. Gray of Christchurch took over as interim editor until, at the November Conference, H.H. Driver was appointed to the permanent role.

---

[19] *NZB* (August 1901): 118.
[20] *NZB* (September 1901): 131-32; (October 1901):148-49; (November 1901): 164.
[21] Supplement to *NZB* (January 1902): 8.
[22] Supplement to *NZB* (January 1903): 7, 11, 13.
[23] *NZB* (November 1905): 171-2.

Driver, like Boreham, had studied at Pastors' College. He was, however, a very a different personality, with a much less lively style. His own preaching ministry had been cut short by problems with his throat and he had begun a new career as a bookseller. He was thus a literate, well read figure, but he lacked Boreham's verve and spark. It is hard to argue with Ayson Clifford's assessment that 'his attempts at humour were seldom successful.'[24] Driver claimed 'no feigned humility' in taking up the post 'with no little self-distrust and anxiety'.[25] Nevertheless, he did manage and produce his paper efficiently. It continued to achieve its aim of adding to the cohesion of a still scattered Baptist community and better technology allowed the increasing use of photographs and other illustrations.

Like Dewdney, like Boreham, Driver was a conservative. He was critical of the unions in the Shipping strike of 1913.[26] In September 1914 (the first issue which responded to the outbreak of World War One) the editorial material unequivocally took the part of the British Empire. 'To Arms!' was Driver's first sub-heading and the willing response of potential combatants across the empire was celebrated. 'This spontaneous outburst of patriotism is of priceless worth....While Britain commands such universal and fervid patriotism her supremacy and perpetuity are assured.'[27] But running a monthly newspaper under wartime conditions was never going to be easy and the pressure seems to have told on Driver. He chose to retire from the editorship in 1915. A popular figure, he was given a warm and generous send-off at the 1915 conference.[28] His departure, however, had created a big problem for the denominational leadership. Finding a suitable replacement was in one sense easy - there was an outstanding potential candidate – but would he want the job?

J.J. North as Editor

J.J. North was by 1915 already the leading figure in the denomination. He was minister of the Oxford Terrace church in Christchurch, one of the 'big four' central city churches along with Wellington (which North had already served as Pastor) the Auckland Tabernacle and Hanover St in Dunedin. He had served on every major body of the Union and Missionary Society,

---

[24] J. Ayson Clifford, *A Handful of Grain: The Centenary History of The Baptist Union of N.Z.* Vol 2., 1882-1914. (Wellington: Baptist Union of NZ, 1982), 95.
[25] *NZB* (November 1906): 21.
[26] *NZB* (December 1913): 225-6.
[27] *NZB* (September 1914): 171-173.
[28] *NZB* (November 1915): 209-10.

had been a regular contributor to *The N.Z. Baptist* for twenty years and, never shy of controversy, was building a reputation as a public figure. In many ways a new task was the last thing he needed. 'I have undertaken, beginning with the next issue, the Editorship of the paper. I have added this to my many pressing engagements at the urgent request of the Executive.' Nonetheless, he immediately announced measures to increase the number of contributions, including two book prizes per month for the best writing.[29]

Underlying these measures was the usual anxiety to generate an increase in subscriptions. Progress was not spectacular on this front. In 1917 the figure was 1800, a slight lift, but by 1920 it had dropped back to 1700. The business manager, W.H. Hinton, noted in frustration that, although prizes had been offered for the boy and girl who brought in the greatest number of new subscribers, only one child had even entered the competition![30] The publication was hamstrung by production difficulties. The war had led to a shortage of paper. Expected supplies did not always turn up.[31] This seems to have continued in the period after the war. In December 1920, the printers were changed and the format was altered from foolscap to the smaller quarto. At the same time pages were reduced from sixteen to just twelve. This was, however, just a temporary setback. As times improved so did the size of the newspaper. By 1923 issues were 20 pages long; 26 by the end of 1924; 28 by 1929 and 36 in 1930, before the economic depression of the 1930s forced a reduction back to 32. By now circulation had nudged above 2000, where it would plateau for a decade before gradually rising again during the 1940s.

In part this seems to have been the result of North's energetic editorship. He carried the editorial duties largely alone until October 1922, when, in anticipation of a year's travel, he stepped down temporarily from the post. North was replaced for the year by W.S. Rollings who handled the 'editorial' material. He was assisted by Samuel Morris, who, in the new role of Sub-Editor, received the 'news' items, such as reports from camps, meetings and churches. North picked up the reins again from Rollings in November 1923 but Morris continued in the Sub-Editing role until his death in October 1925. L.B.J. Smith filled in until April 1926. He was followed by Eric Evans (1926-28), Stanley Jenkin (1928-32), H.R. Turner

---

[29] *NZB* (November 1915): 210.
[30] *Annual Report of the N.Z. Baptist Union, 1920*, 35.
[31] *Annual Report of the N.Z. Baptist Union, 1917*, 32-33.

(1933-41), W.J. Gibbs for five months in 1941, then J.T. Crozier who, in November 1941, began a near thirty-year stint. All these men were based in Dunedin, where *The N.Z. Baptist* was printed from December 1921. With North first in Christchurch and then in Auckland, the major part of seeing the paper through production lay with the Sub-Editor.

The division in the editorship soon proved essential. In 1926 North began as founding Principal of the new Baptist College. For the next two decades he thus filled two crucial opinion-forming roles in the denomination.

Though a prodigious writer and commentator, North was no social radical. *The N.Z. Baptist* did not suddenly become an anti-war or pro-labour publication on his appointment. Yet in a manner unimaginable from Driver, North would think outside the square, often tackling the nuances of issues with gusto. An example is his position on conscientious objection. In 1916, though eschewing the very notion of neutrality, he nonetheless avowed

> we are winning this war. We can win it without surrendering the precious gains of the past....Conscientious objectors can be given tasks more useful to the Nation than martyrdom. They can be retained at peaceful, yet essential tasks, and can be regarded as the prophets of the golden year which we earnestly hope is 'at the door'.[32]

When the war ended he warned against vindictive demands on Germany.

> We confess to great anxiety as to the terms that shall be imposed on the fallen Fatherland. The problems of victory are not going to be easy of solution. We know perfectly well that it is only too possible to impose such a peace as shall be an immediate incentive to the next war....We want to see peace terms that contain no seed of future wars.[33]

North would be editor for over thirty years. Although he would regularly comment on public affairs, it was vigorous engagement with religious and denominational controversy which marked his editorship. Increasingly *The N.Z. Baptist* became a vehicle for debate and argument in which correspondents would at times take umbrage at North's positions and would receive a riposte in similar tone.

---

[32] *NZB* (August 1916): 150-52.
[33] *NZB* (December 1918): 177-8.

At times this pugnacious approach could land North in hot water. As will be seen in chapter eleven North nearly derailed the Union's settlement with Napier's Machattie in 1935. A threat of legal action was avoided in that case, but a few years later North was forced into court. In 1942 the Baptist Union was taking its first practical steps in ecumenical cooperation. As a member of the newly formed National Council of Churches (N.C.C.) Baptists joined the 'Campaign for Christian Order'. This was an ambitious venture aimed at Christian social reconstruction.[34] The name, it seems, was not covered by copyright. In the December *N.Z. Baptist,* editor J.J. North excoriated a group that had appropriated the name for very different ends.

> In times like these prophets of the impudent type pop up....A brazen Auckland group, seizing piratically on the term 'Campaign for Christian Order,' advertised in the 'Herald' that the Lord Jesus Christ is coming to take up his kingdom on 17 July 1944,' – a little less than two years from now. They have offices in Exchange Lane and invite dupes to call or write to them. We say 'dupes' advisedly....What are all such dates but defiance of our Lord's word?[35]

The strength of this denunciation was not unusual from North. However, the group concerned took severe umbrage and sued the Baptist Union for libel. The case was heard in May 1943 and was a minor sensation, not least for the unusual nature of the evidence for the plaintiffs, who represented themselves. The first, G.E. Hyde, gave his occupation as 'a Prophet of the Lord God of Israel' and described in detail how he has been inspired to write his poetry and proclamations concerning the imminent return of Christ. The plaintiffs agreed in their evidence that God had specifically instructed them to use the disputed term in order 'to irritate the churches'.[36] For the defence, expert evidence was given by retired Anglican Archbishop A.W. Averill, the Auckland Coordinator of the N.C.C. campaign Presbyterian Rev. J.D. Smith, and Baptists N.R. Wood and E.M. Blaiklock. The burden of the defence case was to discredit the writings of the plaintiffs and, thence, their claims to be 'prophets'. Blaiklock described the publications as 'the disconnected utterance of a

---

[34] On the campaign see A.K. Davidson, *Christianity in Aotearoa: A History of church and Society in New Zealand* (Wellington: Education for Ministry, 1991), 121.
[35] *NZB* (December 1942): 321.
[36] See notes and papers relating to *Hyde & Ors vs the Baptist Union of N.Z.* (Supreme Court, Auckland Registry A. 20/43), NZBA B.1/81, fol. 19.

form of mental delusion'.[37] Apparently agreeing, the jury found for the defence.

In the midst of war news the case achieved some notoriety, with daily papers reporting the details of the 'strange libel action'. It was crucial that the Union should win, and not merely because of the £500 damages sought. None of the other denominations in the N.C.C. felt the need to criticize the group in the public manner that North had.[38] Baptists, with a forceful anti-modernist wing, were perhaps the most exposed to bizarre theological schemas.[39] A united front was required. The moderate and conservative streams of Baptist life were thus both represented at the hearing, in the persons of Wood and Blaiklock respectively.

For North, the need to dissociate from such 'impudent prophets' was paramount, and not just because of his personal distaste for their views. At this point in their history Baptists could not afford to be regarded as on the 'fringe', lunatic or otherwise. They had gained a place at the main table and they wanted to stay there. The desired result was achieved. Not only had the legal case been won, but Baptists could take comfort in the support they had received for their stand. Reviewing the outcome of the case in the July 1943 *N.Z. Baptist*, North noted with satisfaction that 'the general view, voiced by Archbishop Averill, was that the N.Z.B. had done a notable service to church and State. For that we are very glad. We want to be useful.'[40]

The core of Baptist identity

The primary function of the newspaper, however, remained the building of cohesion within the denomination. Reports from churches and from missionaries continued as a principal feature of each issue. To this building

---

[37] *Hyde & Ors vs the Baptist Union*, fol. 62.
[38] The Associated Churches of Christ took the next most public action but this consisted merely of reprinting North's condemnation in its publication of February 1943. From the official campaign, Rev. J.D. Smith approached the group in person.
[39] For instance, the excesses of 'Brethrenism' had been of concern on the edge of Baptist life since early days in the colony. J.J. North was particularly suspicious of Plymouth Brethren (see e.g. *N.Z. Baptist* (December 1942): 322). For the impact of the Brethren on Baptist life in Nelson, Canterbury and Wellington see P. Tonson *A Handful of Grain: The Centenary History of the Baptist Union of N.Z.*, Vol. 1 (Wellington: NZBRHS, 1982), 34-5, 47, 88; and G.H. Scholefield, (ed.), *The Richmond Atkinson Papers*, Vol. 2 (Wellington: Govt. Print, 1960), 31.
[40] *NZB* (July 1943): 150.

and maintenance of identity North made a profound contribution. His commitment to a strong Baptist stance is evidenced in the evolution of the mastheads used during his editorship. In their position at the top of the first page of each issue they sent a powerful party signal. Where, under Driver, it was merely noted that the periodical was 'Published under the Auspices of the New Zealand Baptist Union' under North this was changed to a description of the paper as 'The Organ of the Baptist Union'. North went much further, however, than this closer association with the organisation. He introduced a doctrinal declaration which itself underwent a series of telling changes, each sharpening and strengthening the sectarian points of difference.

The first of these statements first appeared in North's fourth issue, March 1916, and read as follows:

> The Baptist church, which has an enrolled membership of upwards of 7,000,000 holds the Evangelical Faith. It believes that Infant Baptism is unscriptural and an impediment to the Gospel. It teaches that Baptism is 'the good confession' which follows Faith.

In 1923 North was overseas for some months. A highlight of his trip was his attendance at the July Baptist World Alliance Congress in Stockholm, Sweden, where he chaired a session. This appears to have been a very significant experience. In the first issue he edited on his return (December 1923) the masthead statement was shifted up a gear.

> Churches which have no distinctive message have no right to exist. The Baptist church separates from other churches on matters of the first moment. There are to-day 9,000,000 enrolled members in Baptist churches in 30 different countries, and there is a total community of 20,000,000. They all say this one thing – salvation is by faith in Christ alone. No sacrament can save. Baptism is the confession of faith when faith is reached. Infant baptism has no place in the Gospel of Christ.

A month later, North was more pointed still.

SETTLE WHAT BAPTISM IS AND YOU SETTLE MOST OF THE QUESTIONS VEXING CHRISTENDOM

Baptism is inseparably connected in the Testament with conversion and the second birth. What is the connection? Two explanations are offered. The Catholic, which declares that Baptism causes second birth; and the Baptist, which declares that Baptism proclaims it. No other theory has any connection with Scripture. The Catholic theory makes Salvation depend upon a ceremony and so is not ethical. The reflection it makes on the character of God is unbearable. The Baptist theory makes Baptism the most radiant thing in the world. It is the first act of a new convert.

This was the final form of the masthead that North would use for the next twenty years. It represents a profound development in his own thinking. In 1901, when calling for radical change in what he called a 'shockingly managed' denomination he was less inclined to magnify the significance of Baptist distinctives.

Now, the words 'bigoted' and 'exaggerated' confess a truth, while they denounce an error. Congregationalism is true, but, like other little truths, is liable to become false when it is unduly insisted on. There are bigoted Baptists. Any man who talks as though the doctrine of Believer's Baptism were the supreme thing in Christian Doctrine is guilty of turning a truth into a destructive error.[41]

In 1924 Baptism may not have been elevated to 'the supreme thing in Christian Doctrine', but if it could 'settle most of the questions vexing Christendom' it was coming close.

It was not until January 1944 that the new masthead ceased to appear. By then, North's editorship was approaching its end. The denominational leadership was moving in a new, ecumenical direction which made such provocative sectarian positions unattractive. However, every month for a generation, New Zealand Baptists were reminded that they had the key to the church's problems.

---

[41] *NZB* (November 1901): 162.

Chapter Nine: from training scheme to college

The early conflicts in New Zealand Baptist churches were often a reflection on the character of the minister. Men such as Thornton, Birch and Morton were extreme examples, but many ministers found the going tough and lasted only a few years in the colony. J.J. North's rueful comment in 1901 on the quality of those willing to come to the other side of the world highlighted the need to find a way to strengthen training with an indigenous model. A quarter of a century would pass before this became a solid reality. The process of establishing the Baptist College, which commenced its first sessions in 1926, illustrates many of the challenges and power dynamics facing Baptists as they sought to better organize themselves. On the face of it, it was all about constitutions and committees. In fact, both in the set-up and in the operation of the college, relationships proved paramount.

Baptists had of course been training students for some years. In response to concerns over the shortage of qualified ministers, the 1887 Conference unanimously resolved

> That provision be made forthwith for assisting students for our ministry & directing their studies, & that a Committee be appointed to draw up a scheme for carrying the resolution into effect & instructed to submit such scheme to the Assembly on the last day of meeting.[1]

This proposal was unanimously endorsed. As the new remit had signalled, there were three major elements to the plan: a) support of students, b) direction of their studies and c) a committee to oversee these commitments. For the small Baptist Union, just five years old, the financial commitment was significant. Up to £75 per student might be expended, including costs of board and lodging. Recognising the particular challenges of colonial Baptist life, the scheme aimed at maximum flexibility. There was no one place of study or curriculum implied. Each student was to be dealt with on the specifics of their case.

---

[1] Baptist Union of New Zealand Students' Committee Minutes, 1887-1949(SCM), November 1887. B15/67; B15/104.

Just three students were accepted in the first five years of the scheme: J Farquarson Jones in 1887, Harold Peters in 1889 and J.J. North in 1892.[2] All were from Dunedin and each was closely linked to Alfred North. Formal teaching was provided through an arrangement with the Presbyterian Knox Theological Hall. Two further students joined in 1896 and another in 1897, making six in the first decade.

As the new century opened the Committee was presented with a growing number of requests for tailor-made courses of study – sometimes for preparation for a full studentship, but increasingly as a complete package, to facilitate later application for recognition as a minister. The number of candidates for the original scheme (of close supervision in Dunedin and academic study at Knox Hall) stayed low, but more and more were requesting recognition as a special case.

For many years the Union had been recognising individuals as 'Home Missionaries'. These were those appointed to pastoral leadership positions by an Auxiliary or by the 'Board of Introduction and Advice'. In 1900 this practice was given greater impetus with a new Home Missions policy. From 1901 Home Missionaries were listed as a category of accredited ministers. Many of these men had little formal training and they entered the committee's discussions. Prospective Home Missionaries began seeking courses to prepare them specifically for this role. Some, already in placements, requested training programmes to assist them in their calling. Others 'expressed their willingness to serve a year on Home Mission in the back blocks if called upon by the Committee' as a means of supporting their applications for standard training. The programme lacked cohesion and new rules were finally adopted in 1907, with the course placed formally under the Students' Committee.

The new arrangement achieved only a slight improvement. An example of the potential difficulty in managing the course is found in the relationship with the committee of Oswald Machattie, who bumped along down a rocky path for years and would become a particular thorn in the denomination's flesh in the 1930s (see chapter eleven). In August 1906 Machattie, then in Gisborne, sought advice about a course of reading. The following year he indicated he would eventually seek a full studentship but would in the interim take up Home Mission work. After 'a series of communications' he notified that he was now working in Otahuhu and Richmond, Auckland. He was advised to begin the newly standardised

---

[2] SCM Memoranda 1892.

course. Machattie appears to have wanted additional courses arranged. This was declined. In October 1908 he tried again, this time seeking logic and ethics to be added. He was advised to arrange these himself through the University. Now it was Machattie's turn to decline a suggestion. During 1909 he advised he would withdraw from the course and seek entry to Regent's Park College in London. He spent a period from 1911, serving with the Y.M.C.A. in Britain but reappeared in the Home Mission course in 1916, this time in Gore. Unsatisfactory exam results led to his case being 'carefully and earnestly considered'. It was decided that he take further exams the next year. This would delay his application for ministerial status but was required in the hope that 'the discipline of concentrated study and steady application…would…strengthen his undoubted ability and energy in other directions.' Machattie agreed to this plan and finally passed from the Students' Committee's supervision in 1917, eleven years after first entering its books.[3]

The standard denominational programme continued to struggle for students. In 1908 only one student, H.B. Hughes, was in training. A year later it was reported that four applications had been received. However, none of these ultimately translated into students in the scheme. By 1911 only one further ministerial student, Ray Ambury had entered. The report that year concluded somberly, 'again your Committee would impress upon the Assembly, the churches and the ministers the serious dearth of suitable men offering for the ministerial office.'[4] The Home Missions course, too, was floundering. The committee felt it necessary to recommend that the course be made compulsory for all individuals appointed as Home Missionaries.[5]

The war caused significant disruption. Some students resigned, others sought permission to train in England. Under this pressure both schemes for training ministers began to fray. The armistice brought little relief. In particular the committee found itself unable to apply any consistency to home mission training. Every meeting was forced to consider various applications for waiver or variation of parts of the set programme. Special circumstances such as return from war service, age or marital status, or just plain refusal to submit to the discipline of the course made any claim to uniformity of training standards untenable. By 1920 it was becoming

---

[3] See SCM Memoranda 1907-7; October 1907; October 1908; October 1916, 4-5; October 1917, 9.
[4] *NZBU Baptist Handbook* 1911-12, 34.
[5] *NZBU Baptist Handbook* 1912-13, 34.

obvious that a fresh approach was needed. J.J. North called for a thorough reexamination of the training scheme.[6] The underlying issues were broader than the individual circumstances of students. Perhaps the most fundamental factor was a shift in the Denomination's centre of gravity from the South to the North. In 1887 the North Island had only 40% of the total Baptist membership. By 1920 the balance had shifted so that some 55% were in the North. Power was shifting too. Alfred North no longer dominated. He had left Dunedin for a brief Pastorate in Calcutta, India in 1900. When he returned in 1902 it was to positions in Auckland. J.J. North was in Wellington from 1904-1914 and then Christchurch. Joseph Kemp arrived in Auckland in 1920 and immediately established an influential presence at the Auckland Tabernacle. In 1922 he formed the Bible Training Institute which, although not intended as a college for training ministers, nevertheless provided a new, evangelical location for Biblical studies.

John Hiddlestone was the last of the Baptist students to complete the main academic elements of his training in Dunedin. J.J. North developed plans to travel overseas during 1922. In anticipation of this, it was suggested at the October 1921 meeting that the three current ministerial students might transfer for study at 'the new Bible School in Auckland'. In the event it was agreed that Hiddlestone would compete his studies in Dunedin but that the others would be based in Christchurch. There they took courses at both the University College and the Anglican College House. However, this was not regarded as satisfactory, particularly as 'a special Bible course' was not available to them. It was briefly considered whether they might be sent to the Baptist College at Melbourne for 1923. This was deemed too costly and the two instead transferred further north, to Wellington and the tutelage of F.E. Harry.[7]

It was now being recognised that such *ad hoc* arrangements could not continue. At the 1923 Assembly in Wellington, the Auckland Auxiliary put up four resolutions reflecting the growing concern that the existing process was not serving the denomination's needs. Of these the first sought a tighter application process, the third and fourth called for a probationary system of at least two years following training. However, it was the second remit that focused on the method of training itself. It proposed

---

[6] SCM, 7 October 1920, 21.
[7] SCM, October 12 1922, f. 28.

that the matter of student training be again carefully considered and that our students be placed in some recognised College such as the Baptist College in Melbourne, with possibly a brief preliminary course at the Bible Training Institute in Auckland.[8]

If adopted, this proposal would have had profound implications. Although it begins by suggesting that training be 'carefully considered', in fact it called for specific outcomes. These in turn had their own problems. The practicality of sending students to Melbourne had been rejected once already and was certainly questionable. If adopted, the result may have been that the B.T.I. would have become the *de facto* centre of ministerial training.

These difficulties were quickly spotted. Alfred North, attending his last Assembly, proposed that the present arrangements continue for a further year but that a committee review the entire question 'and bring up to the next Assembly a report with definite and detailed recommendations.' A year later four resolutions had been framed. These called for the founding of a Baptist College in Auckland and for special fundraising measures to pay for its operation and a property.

The session readily agreed to the first element, passing unanimously the resolution 'that it is desirable that a Baptist College should be established in the Dominion at the earliest possible date.' However, there was vigorous debate on the other matters, with particular concern expressed about the cost and the location. There were a number of issues at stake. For a denomination focused to this point further south, the establishment of a college in Auckland would represent a major shift. More fundamentally, it would represent a move of the centre of gravity away from the relatively moderate churches of the south and towards the more theologically conservative Baptists of Auckland. It appears that the location issue was key, and that Wellington was put forward as an alternative. The committee was asked to reconsider the issues over the weekend.

Training thus had become a focus of key questions of Baptist identity. Would the denomination be characterized by the anti-modernism of Kemp? Were the churches truly ready to understand themselves as part of a national body? The establishment of a single college would secure the already powerful move to centralization. Could it be done?

---

[8] S*CM*, October 1923, f. 44.

When the committee came together on the Saturday, it was faced, then, with having to meet concerns over expense, location and theological balance. Some imagination was required, and it was provided by Joseph Kemp. Kemp offered a series of suggestions which cut through the concerns in one brilliant package. He proposed, first, that the Auckland Tabernacle be asked to supply facilities until a College building could be purchased. This neatly tied up the shift to Auckland, whilst meeting objections over cost, at least in the short term. Theological tensions were potentially more difficult to address. Here too, Kemp decisively cut through a knot which might have strangled the project. The matter of Principal had not publicly been addressed to this point. To allay any fears that he himself might exercise undue influence, Kemp proposed that J.J. North be invited to become the Principal. To reinforce his point he offered the possibility that North 'might share in the teaching ministry of the Tabernacle church in such ways and to such extent as may be mutually arranged between him and the Tabernacle minister.'[9]

The committee immediately recognised that Kemp had provided a way forward, one remarkably generous in its tone. The proposals were brought back to the Assembly on Monday 13 October. J.K. Archer, who had moved the first clause and now seconded the further elements of the proposal, noted in his speech that at the heart of the proposal was the fact that both North and Kemp would play ongoing roles in the work of training. The revised plan was overwhelmingly endorsed. It was a big call, a fact not lost on the gathered delegates. Indeed the decision to found a Baptist College was the most significant move by the denomination since the founding of the Missionary Society in 1885. New Zealand Baptists, with a mere 6821 members in some 60 odd churches, would now fully train their own ministers.

Significant questions remained. When would the college commence? Would it have a Principal? Nobody, it seems, had checked with J.J. North, who declined to accept the offer immediately. Whilst a powerful thinker and speaker and a prominent leader, he was not a scholar. His own training had been under the previous scheme and he had no formal qualifications. He had never lived in Auckland and, at 53 years of age, was not at all sure that he wanted to start again in such a pioneering role. He immediately notified his father. Alfred North was now in failing health, but this did not prevent him from replying in pungent style.

---

[9] *SCM*, 11 October 1924, f. 46.

> The news not only interested me. It startled me. I did not imagine that our men would have enterprise enough to ask you, though we all know you are the fittest for the post!
>
> You do not ask my advice. If you had, I could give you no counsel. Your present work is so big and successful that the quitting of it would involve very serious responsibility. If you do link up with Kemp, it will be necessary that the lines of co-operation should be most strictly defined. The element of control or direction must be excluded.[10]

J.J. North knew that the relationship with Kemp would be crucial. Indeed, the entire scheme would depend upon the ability of these two strong personalities to work together. He raised a series of issues with Kemp in a letter of 8 November, 1924. Kemp's response was direct, clarifying the proposed nature of their cooperation.

> I would not have you think for a moment that all our Office Bearers are overwhelmingly enthusiastic over the idea. If they were living in Dunedin I should be inclined to think they were smitten with a good deal of Scottish caution. Some of them see rocks ahead, while others are keen for the College. There is, of course absolutely no thought of any official connection between you and the Tabernacle and on the other hand it is just as clear that there is no official connection between the College and myself, the two are held distinct and must remain so. We are coming with a recommendation to the church that the request of the Conference for the facilities of the Tabernacle for College purposes be acceded to and also that the Tabernacle assume some measure of responsibility.
>
> I feel sure you will be led aright and that your decision once made will be found the mind of the Lord. In the event of your coming to Auckland I am sure that whenever opportunity offered we shall be able to work together most harmoniously. The work of the pulpit would be as it usually is between two ministers and not a mutual arrangement.[11]

The deal was now all but sealed. In April 1925, North and others met at the Tabernacle and negotiated with Kemp and the officers for the use of specified rooms and times.

In all this, Kemp had been a pivotal figure. It would be absurd to suggest that the formation of the Baptist College was in any way uniquely

---

[10] Letter, Alfred North to J.J. North, 16 October 1924. NZBA, J.J. North Papers.
[11] Letter, Joseph Kemp to J.J. North, 11 November 1924. NZBA, J.J. North Papers.

his initiative. But what must be acknowledged is that without him, it may very well not have been set up at all. He seems to have had a clear distinction in his mind between the B.T.I. and the Baptist College. In 1926, at the stone-laying ceremony for its new building, he stressed the interdenominational nature of the B.T.I. and readily conceded,

> The Institute did not pretend to turn out students with the academic and intellectual training required in a minister of religion, but aimed at giving young people such knowledge of the Bible as would equip them for Christian work generally.[12]

He would maintain a differentiation of this type through to the end. Indeed it is clear that, although not trained in this way himself, Kemp was as committed to theological training for ministers as he was to Bible training. The college, he declared, 'should be the normal door of entrance into the Baptist ministry of this country', and ministerial students 'should be urged to secure degrees and become as efficient as possible for the great service to which God has called them.'[13] (In this, ironically, he was more open than North, who resisted formal qualifications as part of the training.)

Kemp's support was noteworthy. On more than one occasion Kemp encouraged students to move on to the Baptist College. He was a member of the Baptist College board from its inception until his death. He spoke regularly at college functions and promoted its interests. The Tabernacle church featured prominently throughout this period in support of the Baptist College. However, the most outstanding aspect of the eight years of Kemp's continuing involvement was the relationship he established with J.J. North.

The myth among New Zealand Baptists is that North and Kemp were foes. Both certainly inspired fierce loyalty and equally definite opponents. This polarizing effect has led to some surprise that the two men should have been able to work together. As noted, Kemp was on North's board. North in turn became an elder at the Tabernacle. The two regularly shared platforms and gave each other public compliments. There was nothing forced about this. They were in fact much closer than has been recognised. Both were supremely convinced of the correctness of their positions. For Kemp, the focus of his dogmatism was biblical authority and conservative morality. North's activism was focused on his take on Baptist principles. He felt free to contrast Baptist respect for the individual with what he saw

---

[12] *NZB* (January 1927): 5.
[13] *NZB* (April 1928): 113; (November 1927): 330.

as the authoritarianisms of other traditions. Regular servings against Roman Catholics were one thing, but as North was not averse to extending his criticism to Presbyterians and Plymouth Brethren[14] he was never likely to be the coalition builder that Kemp proved to be. The differences between the two men were, however, more of emphasis than substance. Kemp was a Baptist 'by conviction',[15] but his energies were directed elsewhere. North, conversely, was committed to biblical authority, although he sought to acknowledge 'many unsolved problems'.[16] Their interests and their constituencies were different, but their motivations were similar, and both men saw it. They provide a powerful example of the creative interplay between conflict and connection.

A Baptist Manifesto

On Wednesday 3 March, 1926 the Baptist College of New Zealand was officially inaugurated at a service and a public meeting at the Auckland Tabernacle. It was, as are all such occasions, an opportunity for celebration and congratulation. The leaders of the denomination were present in force and there were greetings from Presbyterian Congregational and Methodist colleagues as well as from the new Bible College, until recently itself based in the Tabernacle buildings. Telegrams from supporters throughout New Zealand were read, prayers were offered and the first group of students was proudly photographed by the steps at the side entrance to the Tabernacle.

Amidst all the ceremony the key figure was J.J. North. He avowed that listening to the effusive welcomes had been 'one of the most embarrassing hours of his life'.[17] Yet the opportunity to make his stamp on the new venture was not to be passed up. His address was reprinted in the Baptist under the heading 'A Baptist Manifesto'. It is an important insight into North and the dreams he harboured for the fledgling college.

North's first assertion was the need for local training. This was a concern he had been expressing for a quarter of a century. Imported ministers would never meet the needs of New Zealand Baptists as 'they are not racy of the soil.' The official training scheme had not proved adequate and to rely on the untrained was not satisfactory. Citing St Paul, Augustine and Martin Luther as evidence, North justified his cause. 'Let those who

---

[14] See e.g. *NZB* (October 1927): 302-4; (September 1933): 270-1.
[15] *NZB* (October 1929): 293.
[16] *NZB* (December 1942): 322.
[17] *NZB* April 1926: 87.

suspect college as homes of dullness and criticism reflect on the history of the past....He who rails at knowledge rails at God. No man is reverent unless he cultivates all his faculties. The imperative need of an educated minister is beyond challenge.'

This was doubly true for Baptists. In a pointed analysis North argued that unlike other denominations, Baptists could not rely on national identity or tradition to attract followers. 'The Baptist church stands four-square on a 'case',' and an effective preacher must 'both know Christ and know the thought currents that flow through his age.' The college, accordingly 'will be Baptist to the core'. There is a Baptist outlook, there are Baptist principles that run through the whole realm of theological thought. These will be emphasised. 'We have not founded a colourless College.' The principles turn on the Baptist respect for 'the sacredness of the individual'. There can therefore be no coercion into faith, in particular no choosing on behalf of children, 'for forced faith is heretical, though it be formally orthodox.' Along with their preaching, Baptists thus also fight for liberty of conscience and for better social conditions, both of which create the circumstances for 'true choice'. As far as students were concerned, North wanted whole people. He wanted 'to develop personality, and not simply furnish expert sermon-makers.'

The college, then, must reflect all these values.

> The dream is of an institution, presently to be properly housed, which pulses with light and life and love, an institution to which the most chivalrous of the youth of our churches will be drawn, that they may adventure for Christ in the high places of that field which is the world.[18]

The new venture faced a number of serious challenges. North had earlier pointed this out to the readers of *The N.Z. Baptist*. 'The New Zealand Baptist College has at present no capital and no income. It does not possess so much as an office chair.' Premises and a library were yet to be secured and income of £1000 would be necessary.[19] It is perhaps a measure of the enthusiasm of the denomination for this bold project that none of these challenges would prove insurmountable, but would enough students of high calibre present themselves for training? The waning of the earlier official scheme had in part reflected a reluctance of students to commit to full-time training in Dunedin. Would the momentum of a new

---

[18] For North's address see *NZB* April 1926:96-97, cf 87.
[19] *NZB* February 1925:29

model and a new location be enough to attract the 'chivalrous youth' North sought?

The first students

Visitors to the Carey Baptist College site in Penrose today are immediately confronted with a near life-size picture of the first college students, taken at the inauguration in March 1926. The composition of this group is interesting and reflects many of the themes which surround the early years of the college.

The most striking figure in the photograph is also the most surprising. At first glance the presence of a woman among the foundation students at the theological college of an essentially conservative denomination is unexpected. The reality is a little less revolutionary. Thelma Gandy came from Wellington and was admitted to the college with a view to training for the mission field. There is no suggestion in the records that she might be a minister in New Zealand Baptist churches. Later in 1926, prospective missionary nurse, Margaret Livingstone would also study at the college before leaving for India. The studentships of these two women forced consideration of the question of 'Lady students'. In February 1927 the Committee recorded that 'some doubt having been expressed concerning the wisdom of mixed classes in our college, it was decided to consider each case on its merits.'[20] This masterful decision not to decide typifies the college's approach to the question. On the one hand, there would never be a bar placed on women students; on the other, it would be nearly 30 years before the next woman student officially entered. It remained, as Thelma Gandy later reflected, 'essentially a man's world'.[21] Gandy completed her theological course but, largely for health reasons, did not proceed to the field. She became a teacher and continued to support college students until shortly before her death in 1997.

Among the men a range of backgrounds, interests and subsequent histories is found. B.N. ('Bun') Eade and E.W. (Eddie) Grigg were both missionary students who had begun studies under the old scheme. Vic Hudson was from Palmerston North and, like Eade and Grigg, was presenting himself for missionary training. He was in his first year of study but would withdraw at the end of 1927 due to personal circumstances which made continuance impossible. Also coming in as a missionary

---

[20] College Committee Minutes (CCM), 22 February 1927, f. 91. NZBA B15/104.
[21] Letter, Thelma Gandy to R.J. Thompson, 18 February 1976, NZBA.B15 /54

student was Eric Batts. Batts, a member of Kemp's Auckland Tabernacle, had spent a year at the Bible Training Institute. He would later relate his discussions with Kemp about transferring to the Baptist college.

> We sought the advice of our pastor again, fully expecting disapproval and insistence upon the completion of the Institute course. But no....He foresaw the possibilities and probabilities, the increased opportunities, the larger scope, and urged change.[22]

Batts too, apparently saw new possibilities and turned his attention to Pastoral Ministry, going on to serve in a number of churches in New Zealand.

J.T. (Jim) Crozier came from Invercargill but had spent a year at the Bible Training Institute. Apparently a determined individualist, Crozier was accepted with the proviso that he be counseled 'regarding the ideals of student discipline and relationship'.[23] B.M. (Barney) Wilson, son of the Pastor at Grange Rd, Auckland, was a third to come from a year at the B.T.I.. He would not complete the full course but would later have a ministry in Australia. R.L. (Len) Fursdon of Morrinsville completed two years at the college, followed by a further two-year extra-mural programme of study. J.E. (Ewen) Simpson had begun study under the old scheme. Initially accepted for missionary work he, like Batts, Fursdon and Crozier, would have an important ministry in New Zealand.

North sought to integrate this group, with their widely differing training stages and needs, by means of almost individual attention in the first year. Importantly, of the nine foundation students, six were (at least initially) in preparation for overseas missionary service. As valued as this aim clearly was by the denomination, the proportion was a sign of the fragility of the new venture. The college was commencing with just three students, one third, focused on Pastoral Ministry training. It was a sign that North would face an uphill battle as he sought to realise his vision.

The odour of modernism

Students would not be the only measure of North's challenge. The late 1920s were a time of great theological controversy among Christians worldwide. 'Modernism' was matched by the rise, particularly in the United States, of 'Fundamentalism'. The effects would soon be felt in New

---

[22] *NZB* (October 1933): 298
[23] BCM ff 64-5.

Zealand. Joseph Kemp, who had encountered the tension first hand in his American ministry, was a determined anti-modernist. North was temperamentally unable to stay away from vigorous debate and as editor of the denominational newspaper he could hardly avoid comment. During 1926 he made a number of references to the controversy. In June, describing it as 'the bitter fight of the day', he criticised the attitudes of both sides. However, he made it plain that he felt that new discoveries in science, including 'the light on human origins...have one way or another to be accommodated to the indestructible faith of Christ.'[24] This sent disturbing signals to some of his correspondents, who sought a more definite denunciation of modernist error.[25] When North declared his approval of theistic evolution, lingering doubts as to his soundness hardened into outright suspicion.[26]

In January 1927, emboldened by the promise of a new college site, North re-stated his vision for the college in terms not likely to allay fears of conservative critics.

> The new college must be Baptist to the core, because it must be Christian to the core. We want to make men conversant with the great things of the Faith and we want that faith in its whole extent applied to the whole life of the whole man, and to the whole community. With windows open to all the light which comes from every quarter, and with a fine chivalry, and with an unaffected belief in the sincerity of men who differ from us, we want to see our College fulfill its mission.[27]

North could be as determined a 'valiant for truth' as anyone. He was especially hard on any weakness in preaching, lambasting on one occasion 'the 'this is how it seems to me' heresy'.[28] This was not enough to remove the aura of modernism which would stay with him. Matters seem to have come to surface towards the end of 1927. At the Annual Conference in October, a powerful ally found it necessary to come to North's defence. The report of the college debate features an endorsement from Joseph Kemp.

> Rev. Joseph W. Kemp made a speech that stirred the conference very deeply. He resented very deeply aspersions that had been made against

---

[24] *NZB* (June 1926):152. See also *NZB* (December 1926): 336-337.
[25] See *NZB* (July 1926):189 and (August 1926): 200.
[26] *NZB* (August 1928): 208-209.
[27] *NZB* (January 1927): 2
[28] *NZB* (March 1927): 80-81.

the 'soundness' of Principal North. He declared that if North was a modernist, so in the same sense was he. He did not always agree in details with his friend, but they stood together for the great evangelical verities, and he would not hesitate to place anyone for whom he cared under the Principal for theological training.[29]

This boost from such an impeccably conservative source seems only to have blunted objections briefly. During 1928 North was again defending his position in the face of 'problems of college'.

> We do not believe in a college in which men are taught to repeat the shibboleths of their tutors, and of their sect. We do not believe that orthodoxy can be administered in tabloid forms, and secured with smart little catch cries....We do not allow that the Christian faith is open to serious revision. It is a firm foundation, and it stands sure. We do feel in every fibre of our being the urgent need of relating Christ and the implications of his Gospel to the thoughts and problems of our age.[30]

This was as clear a statement of his approach as North could make. Yet neither it nor Kemp's backing would ease the minds of those who saw modernism in anything not aggressively fundamentalist. North would never lose the confidence of the denominational leadership. As he grew older, he would become almost universally acknowledged and respected as a senior figure. The college, however, would have to endure a fluctuating but never disappearing reputation for unsoundness. This is evident in the comments made to Ayson Clifford when in 1933 he announced to his friends that he would be going to the Baptist College in the following year. One, a student at Kemp's Bible Training Institute, whilst encouraging Clifford to attend a revivalist mission being held in Dunedin at the time, added

> I can imagine you getting so much on fire that you may even find that your place is in the 'B.T.I.' instead of the 'Bible Banging College'. I say, 'Come out from among them' & that applies not only to churches where Modernists preside but also to _all_ places where they have any authority at all.[31]

Bible 'banging' clearly meant something like Bible 'knocking' to this writer. Perceptions like this would have a profound effect on the college's

---

[29] *NZB* (November 1927): 330.
[30] *NZB* (December 1928): 354-5. See also (June 1929): 172-3.
[31] Letter, 'Bert' to Ayson Clifford 25 June 1933, f. 4. NZBA, Clifford Correspondence.

history. Clifford was clearly cautious and later reported his first impressions of North's theology to his confidants.[32]

Curriculum and Teaching

The shaping of the students was more than a function of their proximity to the Principal. A number of the features of the training at Knox (the model with which North was most familiar) were replicated in the new Baptist college. Most obvious was the expectation that most students would undertake studies at the Auckland College of the University of New Zealand during their four year programme at the Baptist College. E.W. Grigg came to the college with a B.A. and managed to complete a Master of Arts by the end of his first year as a Baptist student. North noted in his first report that 'all the students have done University work'. He had a particular commitment to political economy but was not too impressed with the classes the three first-year men had taken in psychology and logic. The college itself provided the more theological topics. New Testament Greek was a major focus for the senior students, with English Bible study in 1926 focusing on Luke and 'a typical O.T. Prophet.' A particular interest at this time for North was systematic theology, or what he described as 'the philosophy of the Faith.' The text for this subject was to be A.H. Strong (apparently chosen as a less controversial option to W.N. Clarke's more 'liberal' work).[33]

In his 1926 report North also gave an insight into his approach to teaching. 'Students have worked steadily at the major doctrines. The method of a prescribed text book, open conversation round each point, and final test of comprehension in examination has been followed.'[34] Writing in a tribute volume in 1944, D.H. Stewart recalled glowingly

> Our Principal believed that the surest way to deepen the impressions made by contact with truth and knowledge was by each man being given opportunity to express what he had learned. And the discussion

---

[32] See Letter E.C. Wright to Ayson Clifford, 27 April 1934. NZBA, Clifford Correspondence.

[33] J. E. Simpson, 'John J. North, D.D.' in 'New Zealand Baptist Theological College: Sixtieth Jubilee Essays 1986', (unpublished collection, N.Z. Baptist Theological College, 1986: 8.

[34] NZBU *Handbook* 1926-7, 30-33.

group method certainly helped each student to appreciate what he was learning, and made the various subjects absorbingly interesting.[35]

The style was remembered in similar terms by Ewen Simpson.

He allowed his students to argue with him in the course of lectures....There were numerous incidents like that, and they were important in the training process. If he were proved wrong on some point of fact he was quick to admit that he had learned something from a student....When he frankly didn't know something he was ready to have any student provide the information, an attitude which impressed on our minds the importance of truth.[36]

The vigour and directness of North's teaching was not, however, universally appreciated. Even such an admirer as Simpson, could concede that 'not all students throve under North's robust style'.[37]

Students of the college were, as had been the case with the old scheme, very much under the direction of the committee. N.R. Wood's student experience illustrates this well. Nathan Rillstone Wood applied to the College Committee during 1926. He had a background in clerical work and had achieved matriculation. At the Assembly of that year six applications were considered, with only Wood and Cecil Boggis accepted. Wood was notified by telegram and then a letter from the Secretary F.E. Harry. 'You have been accepted as a _probationary_ student of the...college. I emphasize the word 'probationary' that you may fully understand the position.'[1] When the college began in 1927 Wood was twenty. He would complete the typical four year course.

At the end of 1930 Wood's services were sought by Ponsonby in Auckland (where he had been stationed during the year) and Linwood in Christchurch. It is clear that discussions were held with the churches on these placements, often through representatives at the Assembly. On the other hand it appears to have been assumed that the graduating students would be available to go wherever they were sent. Wood was notified that he was going to Christchurch by the Secretary in October 1930 and was in Linwood by the end of January. He was now on a further probation for two years, to be supervised by Rev. J.K. Archer of Sydenham. In 1931 an examination on the Greek text of Hebrews was required. Archer reported

---

[35] *College Magazine* (1944): 21.
[36] Simpson, 3-9, 7.
[37] Simpson, 7.

each year and in 1932 Wood was approved to be given full ministerial recognition.

It is difficult to assess the academic work at the college in these early years but it seems the standard was not onerous. The clear fact is that the college was not intended to be renowned for its academic level. It was its function to produce evangelists, rather than scholars. Beyond the classroom, students were frequently called upon to preach at churches around Auckland. Indeed the meetings of the students' association for the 1926 year were dominated by discussions as to how preaching fees were to be handled.[38] This regular student preaching delighted North, who himself carried a heavy speaking load. From the first year a tradition began whereby students were 'dispersed' to Easter Bible Class Camps. B.N. Eade was at Temuka in 1926, whilst North himself spoke at the northern Young Men's Camp at Henderson. The following year Thelma Gandy was at the Women's camp at Whangarei whilst seven of the male students were with the men at Wanganui.[39] In 1928 all the men attended the South Island camp at Timaru, leading Bible studies and doing the cooking.[40]

The first two years of the college, when it was forced to use rented rooms and there was no residential option, presented difficulties in developing a sense of corporate identity. A Students' Association was formed and a corporate student life of sorts began. Nevertheless North lamented that 'the élan which belongs to community life has been sorely missed.'[41] Despite the occasional clash of wills, student relationships and personal intimacy with North would form the outstanding features of many memories of training. This accelerated with the advent of the residential college. With the students living together, the nature of their community life became a fundamental part of their training. Life on the large hill section which required development meant the organisation of rosters and duties. Planting slopes, tending livestock and shaping the tennis court were the stuff of non-classroom time. The Students' Association was responsible for this detail and for the devotional and recreational life of the students. There was inevitably some tension between these aspects of college life. Daily 'ping-pong' was an early initiative and this was quickly extended to deck tennis and became an opportunity to engage with students at the

---

[38] Minutes of the N.Z. Baptist College Students' Association, 1926-1936, NZBA B15A/1.
[39] *NZB* (June 1927): 163; (May 1928): 143.
[40] *NZB* (May 1928): 143.
[41] NZBU *Handbook* 1926-27: 32.

Bible Training Institute and at Trinity Methodist College. Regular 'fellowship meetings' with these two colleges would be a feature of student life on Mt Hobson. A 1928 proposal to make similar arrangements with Anglican students seemed to languish.[42]

The nature and mood of a community of ten or so rapidly changes with new personnel. From 1929 a more serious tone is evident in the students' meetings. In March 1929 the devotional life of the college was given more definition. 'Loose' behaviour was discouraged. Following the Easter camp of 1930 it was agreed 'that we watch ourselves in regard to slang [and] levity; with a mind to deepening our devotional life.' A further fifteen-minute prayer meeting each evening was commenced. Similar concerns were raised in 1931 and 1932.[43]

The college, especially through its Principal, took a close interest in the entire lives of the students. The emotional and relational impact of this 'Household' model of training cannot be over emphasised. The students, mostly in their early twenties, were younger than the North's own children. As far as was possible with a larger group, they became a second family of the Principal and his wife. North would refer to them as his 'other sons'.[44] Again, this is evident in the recollections of those who were students in this period. Comments on both J.J. and Cecilia North are more than just respectful or affectionate, they are almost filial - more homage to beloved parents than tributes to teachers. North deliberately fostered this type of relationship. He began an annual dinner which he hosted at Assembly for those who had trained under him. Though this tradition grew to be a highlight for many it did not survive the strained atmosphere of the denomination which would coincide with North's retirement.[45]

By the end of 1933 the college was entering a new phase. It had established its patterns and trained two full cycles of students. North had weathered theological suspicion and financial stringency as he struggled to establish the new institution. Indeed, he was attaining new heights. He was completing a year as President of the Baptist Union (his second term). He was concurrently editor of *The N.Z. Baptist* and Principal of the denominational college. The next years would present their own economic,

---

[42] Minutes of the N.Z. Baptist College Students' Association, 11 June, 27 July, 17 October 1928.
[43] Minutes of the N.Z. Baptist College Students' Association 23 April 1930, 1 June 1931, 22 July 1932.
[44] *College Magazine* (1945): 5.
[45] See Simpson, 9.

social and personal difficulties but, as he buried Kemp in September 1933, North had already entered a less troubled period as Principal. The years of his greatest impact as a church leader were arguably behind him, but his *mana* had never been higher. Over the next decade this reputation would become fixed.

The college too would firmly secure its place in denominational life. Its graduates would provide the next generation of leadership. These were 'North's men', they would carry his emphases and methods forward into the 'fifties and 'sixties, reinforcing the tight, confident vision of Baptist life which was emerging. They would need all their confidence. The vision was to be tested severely.

Part III
Harmony and its Challengers

Chapter Ten: forging unity

By the 1920s New Zealand Baptists were finding their feet, gaining a stronger sense of themselves. The legacies of English Baptist life were being transformed as the dominance of English-formed leaders diminished, to be replaced by the different activism of those shaped by the New Zealand experience. R.S. Gray had shown the possibilities of an organized, more centralized denomination. J.J. North had developed a deep commitment to positive principles. Identity could be defined with less resort to what Baptists were not and more for the insights they brought to the Christian table. New Zealand Baptists need not be defined first as Dissent or Nonconformity. They had their own story to tell. But if this meant a more local identity, no longer directly governed by the attitudes of the past, there were costs. The political edge of Baptist life was blunted. J.K. Archer recognised this and chose to focus his energies instead in party politics. Under the powerful influence of North, social issues could not be ignored, but neither could they be at the centre. The Union looked to its own affairs, bringing property and constitutional matters under an Act of Parliament. The college was formed and national organizations took up the intuitive for building unity and a common mind. Baptists may be a peculiar branch of the wider church, but they expected to be taken seriously.

It would not prove quite so easy. In the two following chapters we shall see that taming an unruly ministry and independently minded churches would require more than the stroke of a legislative pen. It was difficult to escape the fallout of those colonial conflicts. Had Baptists grown beyond the antics of the likes of Thornton and Birch? The events of the next decades would suggest not. Arguments and scandals would threaten the reputation and stability of the denomination. If the edifice was not to crumble, these would need to be managed.

New Zealand Baptists had some experience in damage control. The case of Robert Morton is an example. For five years in the 1870s, Morton had had a successful ministry at the Christchurch church. He was an effective evangelist and proved his leadership skills by unifying hitherto disparate groups in the fellowship. He was instrumental in the formation of the Canterbury Association and was first editor of what became the denominational magazine. Yet, in May 1876, Morton's ministry came to a sudden halt. He abandoned his family for the wife of a local Presbyterian minister, resigned his position and fled to the United States.[1]

Such events have a profound and continuing effect on church life. In the aftermath of the scandal, the Christchurch church addressed the matter squarely and provided financial support to Mrs Morton. Yet, over the next decades, Morton himself was progressively expunged from the record. His photograph was not hung among other former ministers. In 1921 his ministry could still somewhat uncomfortably enter the official history, but ten years later the 'Diamond Jubilee Souvenir' merely moralized about 'union without purity' and did not mention Morton by name. Not until 1961 did he reenter the history.

Morton's case was not untypical of the ways in which New Zealand Baptists responded to shame and disgrace, both immediately and in subsequent memory. Whilst incidents as stark as Morton's were not common, episodes which caused real or potential embarrassment arose in a number of ways. Two are considered here for what they reveal about the evolving image Baptists had of themselves - or, at least, the way in which they wanted to be perceived. The first occurred just as the First World War was beginning and had some similarities to Morton's demise, although the moral lapse was more public and involved a conviction and imprisonment. The second spanned fifty years, bracketed by events on the mission field in 1899 and efforts to suppress details of those events following World War Two. Other controversies are addressed in the following chapters. These cases rattled the doubtful harmony and self-perception of New Zealand Baptists. The Union survived - even a façade of unity was preserved – but it was a near run thing.

A.T. Brainsby at Wellington and Christchurch, 1914

No-one can know what was Rev A. T. Brainsby's state of mind as he traveled to Christchurch in September 1914. He had come to New Zealand in 1913, called to Vivian St, Wellington. This was one of the most socially active and (situated as it was in the heart of the capital city) most strategically placed Baptist churches in the country. As he made his way south, Brainsby could reflect that he had made already made his mark, as an evangelist and in supporting the position of the 'Red Feds' during the 1913 General Strike. Now he was briefly exchanging pulpits with his

---

[1] The fullest account of Morton's ministry is in A. Macleod *Oxford Terrace Baptist church: Centennial History 1863-1963* (Christchurch: 1963), 23-27.

predecessor at Vivian St, J.J. North. This was no small honour. North was the bright star of Baptist leadership. To be treated as his equal was a significant recognition for a newcomer. The prospects for notable, respected ministry must have seemed bright. But within four days Brainsby would be in prison, convicted of a serious crime, his career in tatters. He would be determinedly forgotten. As happened to Morton, his name would be silently dropped from the record.

Brainsby had had a flamboyant ministry in England before arriving in South Australia in 1911 to take up the pulpit at the North Adelaide Baptist church. To a church community concerned at the dropping male interest in religion he presented an attractive prospect. He was described as 'hearty, virile, eager, impetuous... in the best sense a manly man, vigorous in body, mind and soul.' Brainsby's 'fine physique' and delight in 'manly sports' were also noted.[2] He portrayed a noble model of Christianity, declaring that 'every man who builds up a steadfast Christian character is helping to build a Christian state'.[3] Such boosting of course merely highlights the tragedy of what transpired in New Zealand, where Brainsby transferred in 1913.

After a successful members' meeting in Wellington on Wednesday, 9 September 1914, during which the church's response to the pressing denominational question of ministerial placement was defined, Brainsby left for Christchurch. The journey and its occasion were not uncommon in New Zealand Baptist life. The four principal city churches - the Auckland Tabernacle, Brainsby's church in Wellington, Oxford Terrace in Christchurch and Hanover Street in Dunedin - were the 'big pulpits' of the denomination. Auckland developed its own identity, but there was regular traffic between the other three. Vivian Street and Oxford Terrace were particularly close, with a number of ministers serving consecutively at both in the first half of the twentieth century. The exchange between J.J. North and Brainsby was part of that emerging pattern. It signaled Brainsby's acceptance into an intimate denominational inner circle.

Brainsby preached at Oxford Terrace services on Sunday 13 September and was scheduled to deliver a 'popular lecture' on the ensuing Tuesday

---

[2] *Southern Baptist* [Adelaide S.A.] (6 July 1911): 439.
[3] A.T. Brainsby (ed.), *Christian Outlook: A Monthly Calendar and Record of Christian Work and Outlook at the Baptist church, North Adelaide, South Australia*, March 1913, 4. For more on Brainsby's context in South Australia see John Walker, 'Duties of Manhood': South Australian Baptists and Manly Character circa 1880-1940, PJBR 5:1 (April 2009): 5-26.

evening. The address was never given. As *The Press* newspaper reported, on the morning of the planned lecture 'a man, who gave his name as Arthur Todd, was charged with having the previous evening indecently exposed himself...and also with having used obscene language.' 'Arthur Todd' was soon revealed to be Brainsby, who protested his innocence but, having elected to be dealt with summarily, was nonetheless convicted and sentenced to six months imprisonment with hard labour.[4]

Not surprisingly, the report of the offence and conviction sent shock waves through the Vivian St church. The Deacons met on the evening of Wednesday 16 September to address the crisis. At that early juncture, and given the speed of the conviction and sentence, they were prepared to consider the possibility that an injustice had occurred. They resolved to continue Brainsby's salary (seven pounds per week) for a month and thereafter pledged two pounds per week to Mrs Brainsby for the duration of the prison sentence. They then gratefully accepted J.J. North's offer to draft a statement to the members.[5]

This cautiously sympathetic approach continued at a special members' meeting on 1 October. Not surprisingly the meeting was well attended, with some 120 members present, compared with an average of 28 at the three previous meetings. By now the facts were soberingly clear. J.J. North's statement combined concern for Brainsby with realism.

> We cannot pretend that lapses from right life are impossible. We are very loath to believe that such a lapse occurred in this case. The facts with which we are confronted are that Mr Brainsby tells one tale and does not waver from it.... The difficulty is, that on the sworn evidence of three people, his story is contradicted in certain essential details. The possibility of upsetting this evidence has been abandoned by the lawyers.... Mr Brainsby is opposed to any reopening of the case. He regards his life as a public man absolutely at an end. His only desire is to leave this country as quickly as he may, and start life again quietly somewhere else. We will be meeting his wishes most by furthering this desire of his.

---

[4] *The Press*, Christchurch, Wednesday, 16 September, 1914.
[5] Minutes of the Deacons' Meetings, Wellington Baptist church (Alexander Turnbull Library, Wellington, New Zealand, MSY1151), 16 & 23 September 1914, 245-248. The payments to Mrs Brainsby were continued until the end of February 1915, whereupon she rejoined her now released husband in Christchurch. The cost of her fare south was also met by the church.

The church unanimously received this statement and endorsed initiatives to support Mrs Brainsby. On 14 October the Deacons recommended the acceptance of Brainsby's resignation as both pastor and member. The church accepted only the first. The resignations from membership of both Mr and Mrs Brainsby as members were not accepted until 17 February 1915 and then with the assurance of 'the love and esteem of the members of the church and good wishes for their future welfare'.[6] An attempt was made to raise funds to assist the Brainsby's to commence farming in New Zealand.[7]

It is hard to imagine a more measured and compassionate response to what must have been a grievous disappointment for the church. The members made no move to expel Brainsby as a member and responsibility was accepted for his clearly wounded wife. A similar quality is found in the wider denomination where a note of concerned empathy for Vivian St is evident. By the meeting of 1 October several messages of condolence from other Baptist churches had arrived. More would follow. The official response too was careful and supportive, taking pains to protect Brainsby if possible. The October issue of *The N.Z. Baptist* gave the brief facts of the incident but suspended judgment until an investigation was made. The Secretary of the Union, R.S. Gray, the eminent solicitor A.S. Adams and J.J. North met in Christchurch to interview Brainsby and review the case, primarily to ensure justice had been done. In the next issue the reluctant decision to remove Brainsby's name from the ministerial list was reported.[8]

It is probable that not all churches would have responded as generously as Vivian Street to their minister's fall. Nevertheless, the pain of this event was shared by the wider body. Importantly, at both local church and denominational level the facts were acknowledged and appropriate action outlined. New Zealand Baptists were a small, scattered group in 1914, but they seem, at least on this occasion, to have functioned along relational

---

[6] Minutes of the Wellington Baptist church, 1902-1924 (Turnbull MSY1146), 1 October & 14 October 1914, 358-362; 17 February 1915, 375-76. The Deacons seem to have been more enthusiastic than the members about Brainsby's resignation from membership. They presented the matter again in December 1914, as a virtual ultimatum. The resignation was accepted at that juncture but that action was rescinded in February, when it became clear that Brainsby had not intended resignation at that point. The same meeting then proceeded to accept the now proffered resignations of both Brainsbys. See Deacons Minutes, Wellington Baptist church, 14 December 1914, 264.
[7] Deacons Minutes, Wellington Baptist church, 10 February 1915, 269.
[8] See *NZB* (October 1914): 191 and (November 1914): 212.

lines, as a genuine community. The hard work of connection, which had gathered pace in the previous decade, was paying off.

However, that same connectedness, that concern for and exercise of unity had a less impressive payoff. The frankness with which both congregation and denomination addressed Brainsby's tragedy in 1914 was not matched in subsequent decades. In 1928 the Wellington church celebrated its Jubilee. The short history prepared for the occasion noted Brainsby's brief pastorate but made no mention of his demise other than a cryptic reference to 1915 as 'the most critical period of [the church's] history'. No photograph of Brainsby was included.[9] The denial had become complete by the time seventy-five years were marked in 1953. So thoroughly was the record cleansed that the list of ministers printed in the commemorative publication omits Brainsby altogether. The tenures of his predecessor (J.J. North) and his successor (J.K. Archer) are listed without comment on the two year gap between them.[10] Silence had descended over the matter.

Missionary Crisis and Cover-up, 1899-1949

The New Zealand Baptist Missionary Society was set up in 1885. Never as independent as its English counterpart, the N.Z.B.M.S. was effectively an arm of the Union. The annually elected President of the Union was also head of the Society. The early decades were not easy. By the late 1890s the N.Z.B.M.S. was struggling. Begun with great enthusiasm, it had sent a number of women missionaries to East Bengal but had been unable to provide the on-field structures and support necessary for their care. Two had died. In 1896 a fresh start was made. For the first time a team approach was attempted. At its head was a young Englishman named George Hughes. Joining him over the next few years were eight missionaries, four men and four women, who were intended to form a coordinated body, avoiding the isolation which had contributed to the deaths of Rosalie Macgeorge in 1891 and Hopestill Pillow in 1895. The experiment failed badly. In 1899 the Society was forced to acknowledge its

---

[9] Anon, *Vivian Street Baptist Church Wellington N.Z. Jubilee Souvenir* (Wellington: 1928), 11.
[10] See the list of ministers in the *Programme of the Seventy-fifth Anniversary Celebrations*, (Wellington: 1953), 3. (Turnbull MS 1890-17/4/24). In the 1978 centennial history, a much fuller treatment, Brainsby's imprisonment for 'a grave moral charge' is noted and a photograph included as well as other details of his pastorate. See G.T. Beilby, *Central Story* (Wellington: 1978) 34-36.

'gravest crisis'. There had been a complete break-down of the team on the field. Deeply concerned at the reports it had been receiving, the New Zealand Society commissioned the English B.M.S. to investigate. In response to the commissioned report and the 'voluminous' documents which accompanied it, drastic action was taken. Hughes' resignation was accepted and he and his wife transferred to an English B.M.S. field.[11] Two other missionaries, John Ings and Walter Barry were dismissed. The ripples spread wider. John Ings' sister Letitia, also on the field, resigned, as did Annie Bacon who in 1899 had married Walter Barry. The final tally was the devastating loss of six missionaries from a company of twelve.

The matter was brought to the 1899 Conference and debated at some length in a closed session. Both Ings and Barry were connected to prominent Baptist families and churches and there was considerable disquiet at the action that had been taken against them. There does not seem to have been any attempt to hide the basic facts of the case. That there had been a serious personal clash seems clear. However, the major catalyst for the action of the governing committee of the Society was the unsatisfactory administration of a language examination for Ings and Barry. Put simply there had been a conspiracy to cheat the exam. This dishonesty hinged on Hughes, who was supposed to be supervising the examination. It seems he supplied Ings, Barry and the other examinees the answer to a crucial exercise. This unexpected provision was mutely accepted. When it emerged, the incident stiffened the official response to the wider problem of the disunity on the field. The Missionary Committee, led by Alfred North, held that, in addition to Hughes, the positions of Ings and Barry were also untenable and they were asked to resign.[12]

On the face of it, the Baptists had responded forthrightly to a sad if somewhat petty case of dishonesty. However, the dismissal of Ings and Barry was hotly debated at the 1899 Conference. Although the reporter of the conference, 'Wrox', identified the cheating as the principal offence, it was clear in the reports of the Society printed at the time that the failure of relationships on the field was the more serious matter. Both issues were publicly acknowledged in the pages of the denominational newspaper.

---

[11] See Brian Stanley, *The History of the Baptist Missionary Society 1792-1992* (Edinburgh: T & T Clark, 1992), 271.
[12] See the report of the action in *NZB* (August 1899): 122. See also the *Missionary Messenger* (December 1899): 1 and *NZB* (February 1900): 10. Ings went to the Australian B.M.S.. He struck further trouble there, being dismissed after a dubious enquiry in 1906. See correspondence in NZBA N2/18.

With the benefit of hindsight other factors emerged as underlying causes of the crisis. Walter Barry, in a report of the events written fifty years later to assist the research of E.P.Y. Simpson, insisted that the cheating incident was merely the most concrete of a series of unacceptable behaviours by Hughes. By this account (according to Simpson verified by other eyewitnesses) Ings and Barry declared a lack of confidence in Hughes' leadership, a challenge which led to the collapse of trust within the team. When Charles North, son of Alfred North and a medical Doctor, encountered this dysfunctional situation on his arrival on the field in 1898, he tendered his own resignation (later withdrawn), setting in train the investigation and subsequent events.[13]

E.P.Y. Simpson was an astute historian who went on to an academic career in the United States. In 1947-48, whilst still in New Zealand, he wrote a history of the N.Z.B.M.S. as part of an M.A. degree at the University of Canterbury. He set the affair in a wider context, finding that the crisis of 1899 was the direct result of poor planning by the Society's Committee. The large group of new missionaries sent out in 1896 was faced with poor accommodation and erratic leadership by Hughes. Most importantly, Simpson concluded that the reaction by Alfred North in dismissing the junior missionaries was precipitate, damaging and unjust.

Without any doubt it was Alfred North who dictated the course of the history of the Baptist Union and Missionary Society in those formative years. The folly of the Committee in regard to the Missionary policy was North's folly.[14]

The affair proved to be a watershed for the Society. Indeed it was the catalyst for a shift of power to a new generation. In January 1900 Alfred North resigned from the Committee and took up the Pastorate of the Circular Rd Baptist church, Calcutta. In this, his elder son may have played a role. By 1902 J.J. North was in the crucial position of Secretary to the Society, with his friend R.S. Gray as President.

As with the Brainsby affair, the focus of our interest is less on the facts of the affair than on the manner in which it was handled and recorded. In this case we are fortunate in that there were no less than five histories of the N.Z.B.M.S. written in the period under review - in 1914, 1927, 1935,

---

[13] Letter, W. Barry to E.P.Y. Simpson, 8 November 1948, NZBA B2/157.
[14] E.P.Y. Simpson, 'Additional Confidential Statement Regarding Crisis on East Bengal Field, 1896-99, and Accompanying Events in New Zealand' [1949]. NZBA B2/157, 4.

1948 and 1960. Each is revealing of different aspects of the affair and its aftermath.

The first review of the mission was written by H.H. Driver (1858-1943), founding Secretary of the Society, whose tenure in that office included the 1899 crisis. Driver wrote two histories of the N.Z.B.M.S.: the first in 1914 and the second, a revision and expansion of the first, in 1927. Both are largely conventional narratives of the growth of the mission. However, for the purposes of this study, they are notable for two features. Firstly, Driver plays down the role of Alfred North in the Society's affairs. All other treatment of the origins of the N.Z.B.M.S. identify North as the driving force in its inception. Driver barely mentions him. Instead it is Charles Carter, a respected former missionary to Ceylon who seconded the motion to form the New Zealand society in 1885, who is singled out for especial praise.[15] The pattern continues through both of Driver's books, which contain only passing references to Alfred North. The second feature is the change in the manner with which the 1899 affair is dealt. In the first edition the mention is very brief, with no implication of blame. None of the specific issues or incidents are mentioned, merely that 'circumstances arose...which resulted in the retirement of Mr Barry and Mr Ings.'[16] However, in 1927 three further paragraphs were added, in which Driver goes on to describe their work in other missions, lamenting

> it was cause for deep regret that our young Society was deprived of the services of these devoted volunteers...but we have watched their career since with keen interest...and complimented them warmly on the success they have achieved.[17]

Driver's was the recollection of a party implicated in what he clearly came to regard as an unfortunate set of events. Reticent about details, he nonetheless acknowledged the trauma of the incident. Ten years later, in his Jubilee history, Rev. W.S. Rollings was not under the same burden.[18] In this account Alfred North appears more prominently, especially in the formation of the Society. The affair of 1899 is hardly addressed at all.

---

[15] H.H. Driver, *Our Work for God in India: A Brief History of the N.Z.B.M.S.* (Dunedin: 1914), 9-10; *These Forty Years: A Brief History of the N.Z.B.M.S.* (Dunedin: 1927), 7-10.
[16] Driver, *Our Work for God in India*, 42.
[17] Driver, *These Forty Years*, 43-4.
[18] W.S. Rollings, *A Story of Faith and Adventure: Jubilee Souvenir of the New Zealand Baptist Missionary Society, 1885-1935* (Wellington: N.Z.B.M.S., 1935).

Rollings merely adopts Driver's 1914 phrase, relating that 'circumstances arose' which led to the transfer of the missionaries to other societies.[19]

A decade further on again, E.P.Y. Simpson attempted the first critical analysis of the Society's history. Simpson was pastor at Greendale, a rural church near Christchurch in the South Island. With the capacity and opportunity for further study he completed a B.A. at the University of Canterbury and in 1946 commenced an M.A. programme. He was attracted to the idea of a study of the N.Z.B.M.S. when he noticed Kenneth Scott Latourette's near silence on the New Zealand Baptist effort in his mammoth *History of the Expansion of Christianity*. Isolated from the Union and Missionary Society's headquarters in Wellington, he wrote to the General Secretary, Percy Lanyon, seeking access to minute books and reports. Lanyon's delay, partly due to his own illness, led to the postponement of the research.[20] Simpson was from the outset aware that such an investigation could prove controversial. He acknowledged that that the final thesis 'may contain material and views unacceptable to the Missionary Council.'[21] He asked that the very fact that he was undertaking the research not be made public. By January 1947 he warned Lanyon that he could see 'trouble looming ahead'.

> There will be a lot of people who will be annoyed if I tell the truth about the management of the Society in its first fifteen to twenty years....I find that I am unearthing a hornet's nest – and some of the victims of the trouble are still alive. The ramifications of that matter will have to be discussed with you some day in the future.[22]

Lanyon, too, was aware of the potential for controversy. In September 1948, Simpson suggested placing his treatment of the affair in an appendix which 'could well be omitted' in the event of publication.[23] For Lanyon, even this was not discrete enough.

> I should say that it would be better to ignore the past altogether. You will never be able to tell the whole story, and in any case, what is official cannot be altered unless it were brought up anew. Including yourself,

---

[19] Rollings, 27.
[20] Simpson made his first requests in February 1945 and a year later was having to spell out his need again, for the same documents. See the correspondence between Simpson and Lanyon NZBA B2/157, esp. Simpson to Lanyon, 11 February 1945; 26 February 1945; 9 July 1945; 31 January 1946.
[21] Simpson to Lanyon 26 February 1945.
[22] Simpson to Lanyon, 31 January 1947, 1.
[23] Simpson to Lanyon 7 September 1948, 2, NZBA B.2/157.

possibly not half a dozen people know anything very much about it all....Personally, I do not see why the whole thing needs to be brought up even in an appendix to a thesis.[24]

This counsel to silence was reinforced by J.J. North who concurred that Simpson was 'wise to refrain from publicity on such a dead and incurable issue'.[25] By then, Simpson had taken Lanyon's advice. No appendectomy would be required. The solution was to locate the crisis firmly in the failure of the expansionist policy which prevailed through the 1890s, a zeal engendered by 'light-hearted optimism'. The thesis thereby avoided the need to provide any detail of events and made only tangential criticism of Alfred North.[26]

Any potential embarrassment to individuals or to the Baptist community was thus averted. There was, however, one further precaution taken. Simpson had obtained a written account of events from Walter Barry, one of the dismissed missionaries of 1899 and in 1948 living in retirement in Sydney, Australia. This crucial document gave details of the various incidents which led to the action of the committee and included harsh criticism of Hughes, Alfred North and Driver. Simpson was in no doubt as to the veracity of the Barry account. In an 'additional confidential statement' on the affair, he confirmed that 'it tallies exactly' with what he had heard from other involved parties. Most importantly, Simpson asserted that 'a deliberate endeavour has been made to suppress the story' by Lanyon and others.[27] That no such statements reached the thesis suggests that the suppression was effected, with Simpson's compliance. In a final measure to contain the story, the correspondence and written evidence he had gathered was filed 'under seal' with the recently formed New Zealand Baptist Historical Society. Simpson's stated hope was that the material would in the future assist 'some qualified person' to write a full history.[28]

Albeit reluctantly, Simpson had acceded to the desire of the Baptist leadership to keep the facts of the 1899 affair quiet. Not until 1960, when George Beilby wrote yet another history of the N.Z.B.M.S. was it felt that 'we are now far enough removed to admit the facts'. Even so, only the

---

[24] Lanyon to Simpson 16 September 1948, NZBA B.2/157.
[25] Letter, J.J. North to E.P.Y. Simpson, 30 November 1948. NZBA B.2/157.
[26] E.P.Y. Simpson 'A History of the New Zealand Baptist Missionary Society 1885-1947' Unpublished Thesis, University of Canterbury, 1948, 65-81.
[27] Simpson 'Additional Confidential Statement', 1.
[28] E.P.Y. Simpson, cover note on envelope of 'Additional confidential documents concerning the crisis ...on the field in 1899', NZBA B.2/157.

breakdown in field relationships was acknowledged. Beilby makes no mention of exam irregularity or Alfred North's role. Even Simpson's important findings on policy were ignored.[29] The cone of silence was largely preserved.

These cases demonstrate a growing concern to contain, even deny embarrassing incidents. In 1899 and 1914 the presenting issues were dealt with directly and remarkably openly. As the twentieth century progressed, however, a concern clearly grew to avoid reference to such distasteful episodes. As the momentum for control gathered pace, Brainsby disappeared from the record and reference to the missionary troubles was censored. What were the reasons for such determined concealment?

It must first be recognised that a desire to keep skeletons firmly 'in the closet' was not unusual in the middle decades of the century. New Zealand was a secretive society. This reflects what James Belich has identified as a 'great tightening', a trend by which a remarkably conformist society emerged from the less structured colonial past.[30] The disruptive experience of World War Two began a long process of unraveling, but authoritarianism and control continued well into the 1960s. Approved social mores were rigorously enforced. The maintenance of limited horizons for women is a poignant example. A recent study has shown that most women, though 'emancipated' into previously barred occupations during the war, settled back into more traditional roles as the men returned from military service. Moreover, this return to domesticity was rarely resisted. The pattern was expected and generally accepted.[31] With tight control comes an increased anxiety about potentially disruptive developments. In 1954 the New Zealand Government commissioned an enquiry into the sexual habits of teenagers. It was headed by a Baptist, O.C. Mazengarb, senior partner in the Baptist Union's official firm of solicitors. Mazengarb's conservative report led to a number of legislative measures designed to shore up public morality. Official concern at the possible corrosion of standards was so great that a copy of the report was sent to every home in the country.[32]

---

[29] G. Beilby, *Bread on the Waters: The Story of the First Seventy-Five Years of the New Zealand Baptist Missionary Society* (Wellington: N.Z. Baptist Union, 1960), 33.
[30] James Belich, *Paradise Reforged: A History of the New Zealanders from the 1880s to the year 2000* (Auckland: Penguin, 2001), 121-124.
[31] D. Montgomerie, *The Women's War: New Zealand Women 1939-1945* (Auckland: Auckland University Press, 2001) esp. ch. 8.
[32] Belich, 504-507.

Baptists shared in this general move to structure and control. From the 1920s, pioneers of indigenous literature had identified, as a pervasive feature in New Zealand society, a 'Puritanism' which mirrors Belich's 'tightness'. One, Frank Sargeson, described two versions of this ethos, represented in his parents: the one based on genuine religious and moral commitment; the other more a matter of appearance.[33] Institutionally, Baptists came to exhibit both versions. Theological motivation for moral purity never flagged, but the need to 'look the part' of a sensible, trustworthy denomination grew. Baptists wanted to project stability and propriety. The sectarian belligerence of such as J.J. North was passing and a more urbane, moderate position was sought in the Protestant spectrum. This was not an easy transition. As I have already signaled, the 'thirties and 'forties saw Baptist claims to stability threatened by a series of very public disputes. If the leaders of the denomination were to hold their course through those storms they could do without embarrassing reminders of earlier ones. Past scandals were best ignored. An appearance of unity, forged if necessary, must be preserved.

---

[33] F. Sargeson, *Sargeson* (Auckland: Penguin, 1981) 94. The importance of 'puritanism' for 20th century N.Z. literature is discussed in a lengthy entry for the concept in R. Robinson and N. Wattie (eds) *The Oxford Companion to New Zealand Literature* (Auckland: Oxford, 1998).

Chapter Eleven: Machattie and the Baptist Union

On 3 February 1931 a magnitude 7.9 earthquake rocked Hawkes Bay on the North Island's East Coast. In terms of loss of life, this remains New Zealand's worst natural disaster. The centre of the town of Napier was destroyed by the 'quake and the ensuing massive fire. For a country struggling, as was the rest of the world, with the implications of the Great Depression, this was a severe blow.

Destruction and death, appalling as they are in such events, are not the only impacts of disaster. Much is made of solidarity and camaraderie at such times but increased stresses and tensions are just as evident. Often latent before the event, these can be exposed and rubbed raw by the extreme circumstances, with serious implications for families and communities.

And for churches. Already on the watch list, Napier Baptist church would become the epicentre of the denomination for disruption and dispute in the years following the earthquake. A combination of personalities, money, litigation and ambition created a crisis which would threaten the determined march to centralisation which had picked up pace since the end of the World War.

The key protagonists in the Napier disputes each brought to the affair a curious mixture of personal interests.

M.W.P. Lascelles had come into the ministry later in life after a successful business career. His first church was at Petone (1914-16). In 1917 he took leave from his second church (Timaru) to serve as Y.M.C.A. Commissioner in France. From 1920-23 he was pastor at Napier. Napier was in fact his home town. He had been in business there in real estate and then as Public Trustee. Property and trusteeship were thus his meat and drink. Lascelles was General Secretary of the Union from 1923-1938. He was the principal architect of the constitutional strengthening of the denomination.[1]

John Ings had been one of the N.Z.B.M.S. missionaries disciplined in 1899. Ings succeeded Lascelles as minister at Napier in 1923. He developed

---

[1] See *NZB* (October 1939): 309; *NZB* (November 1939): 334.

a close relationship with the chief benefactress of the church Amelia Randall and was appointed one of the Trustees to her estate on her death in 1930. Ings' ministry at Napier had been steady, but unspectacular. In November 1928 the Deacons called the church's attention to a stubborn deficit in the accounts of some £10/-/-. Concluding that there was no other obvious way out of that financial hole, Ings resigned in February 1929.[2] He would return to the church as pastor in 1935.

After a short interregnum Oswald Machattie took up the Napier pastorate in June 1929. Machattie had served in a number of churches and fellowships as a Home Missionary. Like Lascelles, for a time during the war he too had worked with the Y.M.C.A., in his case in London. For much of the 1920s Machattie was out of ministry and for a period held the role of Town Clerk in Timaru. In an experience which undoubtedly contributed to his reaction to events in Napier, he was summarily dismissed from this post in November 1928. The reasons for this are not clear but they involve a breakdown of relationships with key officials. Machattie felt a deep sense of injustice over the manner in which this sacking occurred. He made an unsuccessful attempt to contest his dismissal before moving briefly to Christchurch then on to Napier.[3]

There is no record in the minutes of the Napier Deacons' or Members' meetings of a call being issued to Machattie. Indeed, there are no Members' minutes between February 1929, when the pastorate was vacant and 9 July 1929, when Machattie is in the Chair as pastor. Nevertheless he appears to have been well received.[4] Reports from the church in the denominational magazine maintained the typically upbeat character of such notices. Tensions, however, appear to have emerged early over the leadership of the choir and music ministries in general, with Machattie exerting considerable control as Pastor. The well respected secretary, Frank Rice resigned in February 1930 although he was immediately appointed life elder on Machattie's motion.[5] Replacements for vacated positions were found, however, and the minutes indicate a confident church, planning a range of activities including an evangelistic mission involving Joseph Kemp

---

[2] See Napier Members' Minutes (NMM) 20 November 1928. February 1929 and Napier Deacons' Minutes (NDM) 27 November 1928
[3] See *Timaru Herald* (7 November 1928): 8; (13 November 1928): 6; - cf. (30 October 1928): 6. For an extensive account of the affair see *N.Z. Truth* (24 January 1929): 5.
[4] *NZB* (July 1929): 220.
[5] NMM 11 February 1930. See in particular the detailed rules for the Choir which extend to three typewritten pages.

from the Auckland Tabernacle. Nonetheless, Rice's resignation was a signal of growing disquiet in the leadership. Treasurer Martin resigned as a Deacon in March and as Treasurer in July. In May, H.W. Milner (later a prominent leader in the denomination) raised concerns as to the state of the finances, only to be criticised for this action by Machattie at a members' meeting. Machattie was forced to apologise - admitting that he had 'caused Mr Milner to come under a cloud so as to speak' – but the incident was a portent of things to come.[6]

Even as Machattie was storing up trouble within the church, alarm bells were beginning to sound at the Baptist Union. Funds for a new manse needed to be brought together from various trusts, held by the Union under its still relatively new (1923) *Act of Incorporation*. Lascelles, an ardent advocate for centralised modernisation of the denomination had in the final months of his own pastorate at Napier placed all trusts and properties in the name of the Union. His successor Ings had continued the practice. Strict rules, requiring detailed resolutions of properly convened meetings of members were required for any alteration to be made. The manse venture necessitated a mortgage secured over the church property from the ever-generous Mrs Randall. Lascelles required precise authorisations before enabling this transaction.[7] Such requirements would dog Machattie over the next two years and would contribute to his undoing.

In October 1930 Mrs Randall died. Amelia Mary Randall (1844-1930) was a remarkable Baptist business woman. Widowed and destitute she came to Hawke's Bay at the age twenty-nine to be companion to her uncle, a wealthy landowner. When he died in 1896 he left a substantial part of his estate to her, including a large orchard at Greenmeadows. A keen member of the Napier Baptist church, Amelia worked in and supported financially a number of social initiatives in the region. A successful manager, Mrs Randall left an estate of land and mortgages (massive by N.Z. Baptist standards) valued at £54,000, much of which she left to Baptist causes. Among other grants, the will designated £1500 for the Napier Baptist Manse Fund and £4500 for a new church building on the Tennyson Ave site. Crucially, all funds were held in trust by the Baptist Union. Whatever the complications, this was clearly a huge windfall for the Napier church. The building of the manse could proceed on a larger scale and immediate

---

[6] Special NMM 26 June 1930.
[7] See letters, Machattie to Baptist Union, 11 August 1930; M.R. Grant (solicitor) to Baptist Union, 26 August 1930; M.W.P Lascelles to Grant, 13 August 1930. NZBA N2/17.

consideration was given to possibilities for the new church building. As Machattie went away on holiday in late January 1931 he must have been anticipating the coming year with relish.

Shaken

The biggest of unanticipated events changed the outlook irretrievably. The earthquake devastated the city. People taking communion at the Anglican Cathedral died when it collapsed on them and then got caught up in the fire. No-one in the region - few indeed in the country - were unaffected, if only by association. There were not any fatalities among the Baptists, but the church building and its contents were completely lost.[8]

Once the initial shock to the membership passed, it quickly became clear that the church was in an extremely fragile state. In theory it had ample capital – a central site and trust funds for rebuilding – but both were now problematic. The Tennyson Ave site bordered Clive Square which was designated the location of the temporary post-quake business district whilst the old centre was rebuilt. The hastily constructed 'tin-town' would operate for several years. The Baptists felt duty bound to add their site to the plan. The insurance on their destroyed building was used to erect several shops. This left the church with no place of its own to meet but with a stream of income from the shops. The destination and use of this rental income would become one of the bones of contention between the church and the Union.

As no-one could tell how long Tennyson Ave would be required for business purposes, another new site was sought and eventually located just south of the CBD, in Nelson Crescent. However, construction was not a simple matter of spending the Randall bequest. The earthquake had rocked this financial windfall as severely as it has shaken the town. The Randall estate consisted largely of farm properties in the region. The ability of the trustees to realise these assets was compromised by the economic impact of the local earthquake and the world-wide slump. By May, Ings was warning Lascelles that 'no-one must build on receiving their portion for some considerable time'.[9]

Napier Baptists were thus potentially asset rich, but in reality could gain benefit from none of these assets in the immediate future. Only the new manse had escaped the various effects of the disaster. Moreover, although

---

[8] See the reports on the earthquake in the March 1931 issue of *NZB*.
[9] Letter, Ings to Lascelles 29 May 1931. NZBA N2/17.

none of the members was killed in the 'quake, many were materially affected and a number left the district, some permanently. On 12 February representatives from the Union and the Central and Auckland Auxiliaries met with the Napier Deacons and pledged support in the following terms: 'that the central Auxiliary are willing to stand behind the Napier church for three months as far as finance is concerned. The position to be reconsidered at the end of that period.' The Auxiliary agreed, in addition, to fund a Marquee for church meetings until Randall or insurance money became available.[10] A nationwide relief fund appeal was set up with the aim of raising £500. New Zealand Baptists responded well, with the fund being oversubscribed by November 1931.[11]

It appears that Machattie interpreted this assurance of support in impossibly optimistic terms. Indeed he seems to have seen it as a total solution to the cash-flow problems facing his church. As far as he was concerned, the Auxiliary had undertaken to meet any monthly deficit figure which arose. As the denominational relief fund was higher than first anticipated he assumed the arrangement would continue until funds were exhausted. On 16 March he held the first post-quake meeting of members to begin implementing plans to obtain the new site. This was approved, but the wider issue of 'the future policy of the church' was adjourned for a fortnight to be considered further by the Deacons.

It is clear that key officers had an assessment of their circumstances very different from Machattie's view. One, W. Larrington, who had replaced Rice as secretary less than a year earlier, resigned. On 27 March Rice and Milner proposed a questionnaire to members seeking feedback on a number of issues regarding the future of the church. The first three questions proposed were:

- Are we determined to carry on as a Baptist church in Napier?
- Do we wish to continue with a Pastor
- Do we desire the resignation of the Pastor?

Pointedly, the Deacons resolved to make 'a very strong recommendation in the affirmative' on the first question. No comment was to be offered on the next two.[12]

---

[10] NDM 12 February 1931.
[11] *NZB* (November 1931): 346.
[12] NDM 27 March 1931.

Machattie was having none of this. Three days later, at the adjourned meeting of members, he sprang a surprise motion from the chair in an effort to finesse his opponents.

> That this adjourned meeting....wholeheartedly regrets the unwarranted inquiries and insidious rumours concerning our minister the Rev O. Machattie and assures him and Mrs Machattie of our continued love and respect and trust that in spite of the recent earthquake disaster it may yet be possible for them to continue among us and that should they see their way to do so we assure them of our continued loyalty and cooperation....

This resolution was carried. Further, it was resolved to delete 'all questions as to the present ministry' from the Deacons' questionnaire. To top it off, Machattie himself was appointed to replace Larrington as Secretary 'during the period of reconstruction.'[13]

This was audacious in the extreme. Machattie was not going to endure another humiliation such as he had suffered at Timaru. As the position of Secretary was the key lay constitutional role he was in uncharted territory as far as New Zealand Baptists were concerned. W. Carey, at the meeting representing the Central Auxiliary, was dumbfounded. Rice resigned the diaconate and at the Members' Meeting of 21 April seconded a motion of no confidence in the Pastor. The motion failed and further expressions of loyalty and esteem were passed by Machattie's supporters.[14] At subsequent meetings it was resolved that nothing 'of an unpleasant nature' should be brought to members' meetings unless all attempts to resolve matters within the Deacons had failed.[15] Effectively, all discussion of the pastorate was thus denied.

In response to an increasingly dysfunctional situation, the Auxiliary proposed a meeting with members to explore all the issues and attempt 'to come to some amicable arrangements'.[16] This overture Machattie and most of his remaining Deacons rejected outright as interference in local church government.[17] Machattie now sought legal opinion as to the limits of denominational authority and the possibility of removing all properties

---

[13] NMM 30 March 1931.
[14] NMM 21 April 1931.
[15] NMM 10 June 1931.
[16] Letter, Ernest Nees to Napier Baptist Church 5 May 1931. See NDM 12 May 1931.
[17] NDM 12 May 1931. The one dissenting voice to this resolution was Milner's.

from the trusteeship of the Union. His letters to the Union demanding various funds become more strident and aggressive from this point.

In May 1931 John Ings wrote in anguished tones to Lascelles.

During…recent visits to Napier, I could not avoid hearing the Napier church affairs discussed. OUTSIDERS and INSIDERS spoke freely to me. What my ears heard made my heart sick. The whole position is extremely grave and something should be done _immediately_ if the church is to be saved from disgrace and ruin.[18]

The most remarkable aspect of this period is that the church managed to get a new hall and worship space built and opened by 6 September, just over seven months after the earthquake.[19] Although this was a public moment of triumph for Machattie he seemed temporarily to lose the initiative. The financial equations were becoming hopelessly complicated and intractable. At a carefully prepared meeting of Deacons and elders on 19 October the finances were reviewed and a wearied Machattie 'requested that he should be relieved of all the financial business'. This was actioned with alacrity. It was next resolved 'that it be a recommendation to the church that Mr Machattie be asked to resign'.[20]

The officers then arranged a meeting with Union representatives to attempt to resolve all matters at issue. But they had underestimated Machattie. His apparently submissive tone merely disarmed his opponents.[21] In the spirit of understanding, key monies were released. Now better resourced and emboldened, Machattie turned almost immediately to move formally against those who were disaffected with his leadership. At a Members' Meeting of 25 November he named his opponents as cases in which 'in the real interests of the church discipline had to be exercised'. The positions held on the diaconate by three of these were declared vacant.[22] On 9 December the church met again and passed a resolution suspending the meeting and voting rights of 16 members, including most of the key officers over the previous two years. At this same meeting Machattie reported his now winnowed Deacons' proposal that he be given a contract of at least three years 'to secure tenure of his office and to relieve his anxiety against those who are insidiously attempting to oust him from

---

[18] Letter, John Ings to M.W.P. Lascelles, 29 May 1931. NZBA N.2/14.
[19] See the account in *NZB* (October 1931): 295.
[20] NDM 19 Oct. 1931.
[21] NMM 28 Oct. 1931.
[22] NMM 25 November 1931.

his ministry by way of insidious statements[23] but who would not come out into the open but secretly poison the minds of the membership.' In order further to shore up Machattie's defences it was also resolved that 'any member proved to have slandered the minister of this church ...shall be deemed guilty of disorderly conduct.'[24] Notice was given of proposals for constitutional change which would strengthen disciplinary actions against dissenting members.

This brash grab for absolute power was clearly not going to be taken lightly by Machattie's opponents. Matters came to open conflict at a special meeting of members on 23 December. The meeting was called by Machattie in order to challenge certain 'malicious and slanderous statements' circulating about him, apparently including allegations relating to his Timaru troubles. A number of those who had been excluded were present at the meeting but were denied a voice. It was stated from the chair that a decision to remain in the meeting would result in their names being struck from the roll. The meeting broke up in confusion.[25]

Stirred

With the affairs of the church now clearly in crisis forty-six members petitioned the Baptist Union to initiate an enquiry 'regarding the Pastoral methods, the Ministry and the general affairs of the Napier Baptist Church.' The Union Executive immediately recognised that it was on new ground. Just where did its authority lie, if anywhere? Could it act at all without violating congregational principles? Ings, by now a constant watcher of the situation suggested a Commission focussed not on the church, but on Machattie himself.

> It was the Union that recognized Machattie as a minister and if a minister of the Union mishaves himself the Union is well within its rights to deal with him as minister of the UNION.[26]

A Commission was set up, though it seems with widespread misgivings. On 9 February Lascelles acknowledged that

---

[23] 'insidious statements' is a later correction. The clause originally read 'slander and persecution'.
[24] NMM 9 December 1931. The logic behind the proposal for a new contract lay in the fact noted above that no record of a decision to call Machattie exists in the minutes. See NDM 3 December 1931.
[25] NMM 23 December 1931.
[26] Letter, Ings to Lascelles, 20 January 1932.

with reference to a Commission, opinions differ so much among the Executive that I was in a quandary how to act....The whole position is bristling with difficulties and unless great tact is exhibited Mr Machattie will outwit our efforts.[27]

Machattie certainly tried. His response mirrored that given earlier to the proposed Auxiliary visitation. The Union, in his view, had no standing regarding internal affairs of the church.[28] He countered with a proposal for a different Commission, to investigate slanderous statements allegedly made about him by Union and Auxiliary officers.[29]

The Commission visited Napier in February 1932. Its terms of reference were specific: 'to enquire into the affairs of the Napier Baptist Church'. Thus, a broad mandate was assumed, rather than the narrower focus on the minister suggested by Ings. Evidence was heard, mostly from Machattie's opponents (the minister and many of his supporters boycotted the proceedings). It found that Machattie had acted irregularly on a number of matters and recommended that he be called upon to resign. Should he fail to do so, his name should be removed from the Union's ministerial list.[30]

Machattie ignored the directions. By May 1932 so many members had been removed that it was deemed necessary to rewrite the Membership Roll.[31] At a special meeting with Union officers present on 17 May the matter of trusteeship of assets was addressed. Over the pleas of the denominational leaders, a resolution was passed to transfer all trusts from the Union to local control.[32]

The first of many lawsuits now commenced. A number of excluded members applied to the Supreme Court for an order for their reinstatement. The Union Executive was clearly in support of this action, which was filed by leading Baptist solicitors Horner and North, of Hawera.

---

[27] Letter, Lascelles to Ings, 9 February, 1932.
[28] See formal response to the proposal for a Commission, NMM 17 February 1932.
[29] NMM 2 March 1932.
[30] See the Commission's findings (NZBRHS N.2/17) and also North's report of the Commission's findings *NZB* (May 1932): 138. In a later report North was at pains to assure his readers that 'the Commission was exceedingly guarded in its procedure lest the rights of any section of the church should be jeopardised. The Commission did not claim executive authority, and did not infringe the congregational rights of the church.' – *NZB* (September 1932): 262.
[31] NMM 11 May 1932.
[32] NMM 17 May 1931.

This action proved to be the manoeuvre which broke Machattie's grip on the pastorate. With this still in process the Union made another attempt at reconciliation. Under the chairmanship of Rev. J.K. Archer (Minister at Sydenham and recently Mayor of Christchurch) proposals were considered for reconciling the excluded members and the rest of the church. A peculiarly balkanised arrangement was suggested. There would be two groups in the church, the Nelson Crescent Group (Machattie's supporters) and the Tennyson Street Group (excluded members). Each group would have its own roll, the combined rolls constituting the church. A complex income and property sharing formula was devised. A further Union Commission was to investigate all matters. It was agreed that Machattie would resign if the Commission found against him. Intriguingly, the members, no doubt fatigued beyond measure, directed that 'any references whatever to the past unhappiness be ruled out' and that their recent trouble was 'to be as tho it had never been'.[33] This was a serious error. The members might have wished to forget, but Machattie would not.

Nevertheless, a measure of Machattie's apparent capitulation at this point is found in the final entry in his handwriting in the members' minute book.

'Here Endeth'

Mr Wakely having been appointed Secretary, commenced new minute books in the hope that with a new beginning these old records of dissention may never again be referred to.

I hereby record for my successors my heart's desire before my Lord to preserve peace and follow the will of Christ.

O Machattie, 28/6/32.

Matters moved very quickly. On 29 July agreement was reached for Judgment by Consent in favour of the plaintiffs in the Supreme Court action. Machattie and his officers conceded all major points, including the restoration of excluded names and the admission that as a result all church decisions since 1 November 1931 were null and void. A meeting of the restored membership was to take place to consider the pastorate.[34] This settlement effectively superseded the two-group reconciliation proposal, returning the church to its previous unitary (if not united) state.

---

[33] NMM 21 June 1932.
[34] NMM 2 August 1932.

The reconstituted membership met on 2 August and endorsed the terms of the judgement. This meeting had been set up 'to hear a statement of the case against the pastor by the ex-members and Mr Machattie's reply.'[35] The minutes indeed read like a record of trial evidence, with accusatory questions being levelled at Machattie by a number of key members. It had already been arranged that Machattie would tender his resignation. This was accepted immediately.[36]

There was thus to be no second Union Commission to make further enquiry. The restored leadership of the church took the view that Machattie's decision to resign at this point was taken to avoid such a full investigation. Financial audits revealed that the church had been in a serious operating deficit over the 29 months of Machattie's pastorate - averaging over £9/-/- per month.[37] This was a considerable sum, especially in the light of Ing's conclusion in 1928 that a total accumulated deficit of £10 was too high to sustain his ministry.

In October the officers were concerned that Machattie was gathering signatures 'with the object of pushing himself back on the church and using coercion so to do.'[38] This nightmare scenario did not immediately eventuate. Indeed, although anxiety about an attempted come-back by Machattie persisted, the issue of the pastorate now seemed resolved. Early in 1933, after an interim ministry from Keith Ewen, Rev C.W. Duncumb was called to the church. This added a further personal twist. Duncumb had been minister at Timaru, a church Lascelles had also served and of which Machattie had been a member and Deacon when he was Town Clerk. Perhaps because of his knowledge of his predecessor Duncumb would express considerable nervousness over Machattie's threats and allegations. He knew his man.

Machattie certainly was not finished. In the 1860s James Thornton would pursue his interests and attempt to defend his reputation publicly through the pages of the newspapers. Machattie's preferred method was litigation. In July 1932 Machattie had drafted 24 notices of motion about the Napier controversy for the consideration of the Annual Baptist Assembly, set for October that year. These were sent to every church in the country. The Union suddenly found itself exposed. Its problems traced

---

[35] NDM 29 July 1932.
[36] NMM 2 August 1932.
[37] NDM 5 August 1932.
[38] NDM 3 October 1932.

back to executive actions taken in the aftermath of the February Commission of Enquiry. Anticipating (correctly, as it turned out) that Machattie would refuse to comply with its recommendation that he resign, the report made a further recommendation that his name should be struck from the Union's official list of ministerial members. This advice was followed. Machattie's name was removed from the official list, though by questionable procedure. The action was taken on the decision of the Union Executive, without reference to Assembly.

Machattie's solicitors had identified this and other actions as unconstitutional. The trouble at Napier was now a challenge to the increasingly centralised power structures of the Union. Far from preventing a localized embarrassment the Executive's intervention had created a national sensation. This was doubly distressing, as 1932 was the Jubilee year of the Union and special celebrations had been planned for the Assembly. The Honoured guest was J.H. Rushbrooke, General Secretary of the Baptist World Alliance. This was someone to impress, not expose to bitter wrangles.[39]

Machattie spoke in his own defence at a closed session which took up a whole afternoon at the Jubilee Assembly.[40] He did not succeed in his motions but the matter dragged on for another two years.

Sued

It would flare into life again in January 1934. Machattie had resigned as minister, though not as a member, of the church at Napier. In December 1933 he demanded of the Napier Church Secretary (Rice) to see the membership roll. Noting the extraordinary omission that the names ordered reinstated by the Judgment of 29 July 1932 had not been added back on to the roll he devised a plan to seize back the initiative. By letter of 6 January, when Duncumb was out of town on holiday, he called a special meeting (giving only two days notice) of the members whose names *were* on the roll (excluding thereby most of his opponents). To this meeting he put resolutions dismissing Duncumb from the pastorate and installing himself in Duncumb's place. By letter of 9 January he triumphantly

---

[39] Machattie sought, but failed, to enlist Rushbrooke to investigate his case. The importance of the 1932 Assembly is reflected in the lavish programme and history of the denomination prepared for the occasion.
[40] Minutes of the Baptist Assembly, 10 October 1932, NZBRHS B.1/122, 102.

reported this extraordinary action to Lascelles as a *fait accompli*.[41] Lascelles, staggered at the audacity of the move, was just as astounded 'that Mr Duncumb and the officers acted so carelessly about the Minute Book and church Roll.'[42] Duncumb speedily returned and the officers resolved on 15 January to give effect to the Supreme Court order by formally replacing the names. Machattie's response was to issue Writs, first against Rice, then, withdrawing that action, against Duncumb, seeking their compliance with his meeting's decisions. This writ too was ultimately withdrawn.

Machattie next turned his attention to the Union. He filed for a Writ of *mandamus*, ordering his restoration to the ministerial list and/or for a rehearing of his appeal to the 1932 Assembly. At stake were the validity of the Commission, the decision of the Executive to follow its recommendations, and the conduct of Machattie's appeal to the 1932 Assembly. The Union was exposed on all these fronts. The solicitor for the Union, nervous as to the strength of the defence and anticipating that the Supreme Court Judge would expect the parties to negotiate a settlement requested 'the usual authority to act as he thinks best'. This was granted by the majority of the Union Council although some demurred if it meant granting another hearing at the Assembly.

The solicitors were right to be concerned. The court hearing revealed the fragility of the Union position. Justice Blair expressed disdain for the 1923 *Act of Incorporation*.

> It is the most extraordinary bit of draughtsmanship....I spent a lot of time trying to interpret it, and I could not make head or tail of it. I ask you [Mr Hay, Counsel for the Union] how one becomes a Baptist minister, and you don't even know that.

The judge focussed on the effect of removal from the denominational list on Machattie's ability to officiate at weddings. He was critical of the Union's treatment of the issue.

> I thought it was a case to try according to church rules, now I find there are no rules and the matter must be considered according to the principles of natural justice.[43]

The truth is, the Union too was uncertain of its position. J.J. North pointed out that

---

[41] Letter Machattie to Lascelles, 9 January 1934. NZBA N2/14.
[42] Letter, Lascelles to J.J. North 24 January 1934. NZBA N2/14.
[43] *Evening Post* (4 September 1934): 11.

a great deal depends on the question What does ministerial recognition mean? Since it does not mean that a man cannot be a minister without it, and since withdrawal does not mean 'unfrocking' the case is simplified. What was done was that MacH does not carry a recommendation from the Union to any church he seek to serve.[44]

Lascelles took a different view.

The fact of a Minister not being on the Ministerial list of the Union is a serious matter. While it is true that any unaided church is at liberty to call him, it is unlikely that any church which holds the Union in respect would do so. Further, the fact of a Minister not being on the Union's list would in a great measure prevent his getting a church outside the Dominion.[45]

Reluctant to make a finding amid such confusion Justice Blair strongly advised the parties to settle. Chastened, the Union was thus forced into a back-down in December 1934. Machattie was returned to the official list and the Union's copies of the 1932 Commission's report were to be destroyed.[46]

By this the Union hoped to 'bury the whole matter'. However, even the action of settling with Machattie was problematic. In settling this way the Executive was in effect overturning decisions of Assembly. To the frustration of the Union and its Solicitors the matter was very nearly blown open again by the editorializing of J.J. North. It had been expected by the legal counsel of both sides that the terms of the settlement would be printed without comment in *The N.Z. Baptist*. North, however, was not one for diplomatic silence. As soon as the terms of settlement became clear he indicated his intention.

The right of the N.Z.B. to fully explain the case to our people must be preserved. So far as I can now see, if that right is refused I could not continue to be responsible for the paper. There must be no weakening.[47]

---

[44] Letter, North to Lascelles 3 August 1934. NZBA N2/14.
[45] Letter, Lascelles to North 6 August 1934. NZBA N2/14.
[46] There was also a recommendation that the Commissioners and Executive should be asked to destroy their copies. It seems the Union did not comply, as a copy of the Commission's findings is in the files of correspondence associated with the Machattie case - NZBA N.2/17.
[47] Letter, North to Lascelles, 19 December 1934. NZBA N2/14.

North was exerting the standard claim of the Press to editorial freedom, but for him this was doubly important. To be Baptist was to preserve the right to independent thinking. Coercion of ideas was anathema. For North the push for more centralised authority could never ultimately trump this basic conviction. Lascelles, on the other hand, though he trod a careful line with his editor, would have preferred that there be no additional comment. Drafts of the editorial comment were supplied to the Union's solicitors but not shared with the solicitor for Machattie. North's lengthy preface was added to the official statement when it appeared in the February 1935 *Baptist*. It provoked further threats from Machattie. Lascelles, passing these on to North, wearily noted that 'this man's business is slow in dying.'[48] Fortunately for the Union, the protests were not pursued further.[49]

The Union leadership cast the restoration of Machattie's ministerial status as an act of forbearance and Christian grace but, however they explained it, the whole affair was an embarrassing setback. It made the denomination look disparate and confused – as indeed it was. Moves towards greater centralised direction of the denomination were still in their early stages and the Napier case had exposed weaknesses. The Executive would ensure it would not be caught in the same way again. As will be seen, a remarkably similar case would arise in 1942 with regard to the Auckland Tabernacle. This was a far more significant church than Napier and the risks were correspondingly greater, but by then the Union executive was more influential and constitutionally secure. In the case of Dr Hodge and the Tabernacle the Union would endure the process and obtain at least a legal victory. They would need all the gains they could win. The troubles at Napier and the Tabernacle were not to be the only challenges faced by the Union. The remainder of the 1930s was relatively peaceful, but the heightened tensions of war years made the 1940s the Union's most difficult decade.

---

[48] Letter, Lascelles to North, 8 February 1935. NZBA N2/14.
[49] See *NZB* (February 1935): 49 and correspondence leading up to it in NZBA N.2/14.

Chapter Twelve: the roaring 40s.

In 1940 the Baptist Union of New Zealand issued a brief, self-congratulatory profile.[1] Themes of continuity and security dominated. The long unbroken publication of the denominational newspaper, the steady growth 'in churches, membership and institutions' and the international affiliation of the Union with the Baptist World Alliance sent reassuring signals of dependability and virtue. The pamphlet was clearly designed to advance the Union's claims to be taken seriously among the churches. The assurance was given that 'the Baptist church in New Zealand at the present time is vigorous, splendidly organised, and progressive.'

'Splendidly organized' - J.J. North's generation believed they had transformed a denomination which in 1901 they regarded as 'managed in a shocking fashion'. Yet, in the long decade which followed, New Zealand Baptists were beset with controversy and crisis. The Union effectively lost its largest church and was forced to mount a running defence of its involvement with the World Council of Churches. The period culminated with the forced resignation of the Theological College Principal. These were the most disrupted years in the denomination's history.

Links between these controversies are not immediately obvious. Complex, sometimes sordid, personal idiosyncrasies played a part. The post-war environment presented unanticipated problems, particularly for the college. Theological differences lurked in the wings in some cases but in others strode dramatically to centre stage. There was, however, a broader context in which the various disputes of the period must be placed. In the middle decades of the twentieth century the Baptist Union of New Zealand was characterised by a centripetal drive to greater coordination and control. Behind this was the desire of denominational leaders to position Baptists nearer the mainstream of religious life – to shed as much as possible the fringe, sectarian image with which previous generations had been more comfortable. In a naturally conservative society, Baptists were to become

---

[1] *The Baptist Churches in New Zealand 1851-1940* (Wellington: Baptist Union of N.Z., 1940). In New Zealand in 1940 there were numerous publications surveying or celebrating progress in the 100 years since the signing of the treaty of Waitangi. The Baptist pamphlet was no doubt issued in recognition of the national centenary.

respectable. To do so they must show themselves to be organised, moderate and (particularly in war years) loyal.[2]

In 1940 there were 9305 Baptist members among some eighty-one churches. The distribution was not even: a third of the members were in the northern city of Auckland, 921 of them in the Auckland Baptist Tabernacle. This church had a distinguished history. The remarkable ministry of Thomas Spurgeon in the 1880s had recently been recalled in the equally notable Joseph Kemp (1872-1933), who had commenced at the Tabernacle in 1919 and died whilst still minister.[3] Kemp was a principal figure in the introduction of fundamentalist concerns to New Zealand. A powerful preacher and autocratic leader, he fought a number of battles against the incursion of 'modernist' ideas. Kemp's influence was not, however, merely an example of the intrusion of American debates, foreign to New Zealand. His emphases were in many ways continuous with the conservative Spurgeonic stream of Baptist life which had peaked in the 1880s with the presence of Thomas, the popularity of Charles Spurgeon's publications and the arrival of graduates of Spurgeon's Pastors' College to fill vacant colonial pastorates. As we saw in chapter four, New Zealand Baptists had been more sympathetic to Charles Spurgeon's 'downgrade' concerns than their British counterparts and a strong conservative strand persisted into the twentieth century. Not surprisingly this was particularly evident in Auckland.

Spurgeon/Kemp conservatism was not the only or even the dominant stream of New Zealand Baptist thought in the early twentieth century. A more moderate (though self-consciously Protestant) line was associated with the large city congregations of Hanover Street in Dunedin, Oxford Terrace in Christchurch and Vivian Street in Wellington. J.J North was minister successively at two of these – Vivian Street (1905-1912), Oxford Terrace (1913-1926) - and was the vigorous editor of the denominational newspaper, *The N.Z. Baptist*. Though no modernist, he rejected the fundamentalism of those he termed 'nagging literalists'.[4] In 1926 North moved to Auckland to head the newly formed N.Z. Baptist Theological College. The arrival of this strong but theologically moderate leader in conservative Auckland could have caused unhelpful clashes. It didn't. As we

---

[2] Beginning in 1940 the Assembly passed an annual 'Loyal Resolution', pledging allegiance to the Crown. The practice persisted until 1963.
[3] See W. Kemp, *Joseph W. Kemp* (London: 1949); *Dictionary of New Zealand Biography* Vol. 4 (Auckland: Auckland University Press, 1996), 269-70.
[4] *NZB* (December 1942): 322.

have seen, in the 1920s the personalities and skill of Kemp and North militated against division. In the 1940s a very different mix of personalities collided, with near catastrophic results.

The Hodge Controversy

In the interval following Joseph Kemp's death in 1933, the popular British preacher Graham Scroggie supplied the Auckland Tabernacle Pulpit for a time. In 1934, on Scroggie's recommendation, Dr Alexander Hodge was called as Kemp's successor.[5] Hodge was trained in England and had obtained a Ph.D. from the University of London for a thesis published under the title *Prayer and its Psychology*.[6] He was initially well received. His preaching was appealing and he had considerable personal charm. J.J. North suggested he was 'in the Spurgeon tradition'.[7] Yet Hodge had little of Kemp's militancy against modernism. Though willing to defend the idea of verbal inspiration he was no fundamentalist.[8] In his published thesis, for instance, he abandoned on the basis of anthropological evidence the idea of a fall from a perfect state.[9] For a time his ministry proved successful. Numbers held up, even increased, and the Tabernacle maintained its position as the leading church in the Dominion. But all was not well. Hodge's ministry would catapult the congregation and the Union into a decade of turmoil.

Hodge seems to have been unable to manage dissent. He had a large group of officers and was not able to reconcile the range of views within a very activist body. Disagreement was interpreted as disloyalty. Hodge would settle only for unqualified allegiance. Senior officers were marginalised and members were removed from the list on the disputed basis of poor attendance at communion.[10] This was a disturbing echo of the problems at Napier. Concern at the ongoing disruption led the Union executive to set up a commission of inquiry into Hodge's ministry. The

---

[5] Scroggie (1877-1958) knew Hodge personally, in part at least because Hodge had been one of Scroggie's successors at Bethesda Chapel, Sunderland.
[6] A. Hodge, *Prayer and its Psychology*, (London: SPCK, 1931).
[7] *NZB* (November 1934): 345.
[8] See Hodge's articles in *The Tabernacle Record*, July & August 1935.
[9] Hodge, *Prayer and its Psychology*, 41.
[10] One of the 'evicted' eventually filed a civil writ alleging unlawful exclusion. See the notes relating to *Brookbanks vs Hodge & Ors*, (Supreme Court, Auckland Registry 148/1945) in NZBA A.5/65.

commission met in Auckland in March 1944, taking evidence from nearly forty witnesses. The picture which emerged was murky in the extreme.

In 1939 rumours had begun that Hodge had acted inappropriately with a female staff member. The evidence was flimsy and circumstantial but three of Hodge's officers, already disquieted by their minister's behavior, challenged him with the allegations. The three were Baptists of substance: H.T. Stevens, Samuel Barry and E.M. Blaiklock. Stevens was a long-term Secretary of the Auckland Association. Barry and Blaiklock served as Presidents of the Baptist Union. Blaiklock was Professor of Greek at the University of Auckland and would contribute a substantial body of writing to the evangelical world.

The charges against Hodge were vehemently rejected, but he would not stop with simple denial. He took the mere raising of the issue by his officers to be a slight on his integrity and a challenge to his leadership. Evidence was given to the Commission that he instigated an aggressive response. He later acknowledged that he had gathered a dossier on his opponents, to be used to undermine their credibility. (This, what came to be known as the 'fifty page document,' was later destroyed at the insistence of the Tabernacle officers.)[11] Counter-rumours soon spread of serious, even criminal, moral failure by each of the three men. The Commission found that the stories could be traced back to Hodge himself. Of these, the most serious was ruled blatantly false and another was based on 21-year-old gossip. The third and most minor may have been true but was spread by Hodge in clear breach of pastoral confidentiality. Indeed, Hodge's egregious breach of ministerial ethics was deemed to be the real scandal of the affair.[12]

The commission found against Alexander Hodge on eight grounds.

1. Determination…to dominate the life of the church at all costs.

2. Intolerance…of criticism and difference of opinion; and requiring one hundred percent loyalty to himself.

3. Policy of eliminating from church work and office those who differ from him.

4. Grossly unfair chairmanship and control of church business meetings.

---

[11] A.L. Silcock, 'Summary of evidence against Hodge, presented to the Assembly of the Baptist Union of N.Z. November 8 1944', NZBA A.5/65, fol. 4.

[12] See the evidence taken before the Commission and the copies of correspondence in NZBA A.5/65.

5. Repeated misrepresentation of facts.

6. Vindictiveness toward those who oppose him.

7. Sectional discrimination between members in pastoral relationships.

8. Attempt to remove from church roll members of long and honourable standing in the church, and callous indifference to the spiritual wounds and suffering inflicted thereby.[13]

The 1944 Assembly in Christchurch reviewed the controversy in an atmosphere of great tension. Proceedings were held in committee. L.J.B. Smith reported in *The N.Z. Baptist* that 'it will be many a long day before the happenings of Wednesday, November 8 are effaced from memory. On that day the Baptist Union of New Zealand faced the most painful crisis in its history.'[14] The Commission's findings were presented, along with a summary of the evidence. Hodge was given the right of reply. He vigorously contested the manner of the enquiry and its outcome but concluded by tendering his resignation from the official list of ministers.

Hodge, of course, was not finished. Neither was he without support. In the aftermath of this 'most painful crisis' the Auckland Tabernacle church, offended by the treatment of its minister, notified its withdrawal from the Union. Faced with the deeply wounding prospect of losing what was still its largest congregation, the Union declined to action the withdrawal. Nevertheless, for five years the Auckland Tabernacle was effectively an independent church, its figures frozen at 1944 levels in the Union statistics. In 1949 Hodge left with many members to found 'Haddon Hall', an independent mission church in Auckland. The Tabernacle congregation, by now reduced to half its 1940 size, returned to the Union.

The Hodge controversy was driven by personality, paranoia and power play. The addition of slander, malice and conspiracy made it a sad chapter in N.Z. Baptist history. Some theological questions were also at stake. The obvious matter of church polity was cited by a number of protagonists. There were challenges to Hodge's practice. J.J. North, who himself suffered the indignity of expulsion from membership, condemned Hodge's attempt to introduce governance by elders as 'a transgression of Baptist principle'.[15]

---

[13] Report of the Baptist Union Commission into the Affairs of the Auckland Baptist Tabernacle, NZBA A.5/65.

[14] *NZB* (December 1944): 276.

[15] Evidence of J.J. North to Union Commission – Witness 38, NZBA A.5/65, fol. 22. Where eldership existed in Baptist churches at this time it was largely an honorary role,

The place of the Union too was questioned. In the 1940s the initiative was shifting to a generation dominated by ministers trained under J.J. North at the denomination's theological college. Revs N.R. Wood, L.A. North, A.L. Silcock, and J.E. Simpson, powerfully supported by the denominational Secretary, Rev. P.F. Lanyon, and key laymen like Will Carey and Ernest Nees were establishing a strong national leadership.[16] Hodge and his elders disputed the right of the executive to mount an enquiry into the affairs of a local church and urged members not to attend or recognise it.[17] The case thus presented a serious challenge to centralised authority in a manner similar to the Napier debacle. Yet, the Union had learned a few things since 1932. The Napier Commission had reported to the Union Council, which itself took action against Machattie, thus opening to him an avenue for appeal to the Assembly. In 1944, painful as the process might be, the Commission's findings were received directly by Assembly, removing all doubt about authority at denominational level. Nevertheless, in censuring Alexander Hodge the executive was acutely aware that the nature of the denomination was at stake. It would remain under threat for another eight years.

The World Council of Churches

At the turn of the century, New Zealand Baptists had struggled to find their place among other denominations. Although the legacy of Nonconformity was passing, it retained enough power to generate suspicion of bigger groups, especially the Anglicans. North had helped

---

in recognition of significant service. J.J. North was himself a life elder of the Auckland Tabernacle, a status removed from him under Hodge.

[16] N.R. Wood (1907-1979) was denominational activist who served in a number of churches and was editor of *NZB* 1948-1966. L.A. North (1903-1980) was a nephew of J.J. North and like him was minister at Oxford Terrace and Vivian Street. He was General Secretary of the denomination 1955-1968 and played a prominent part in ecumenical activities from the 1930s. Simpson (1906-1992) and Silcock (1906-1979) each held a number of pastorates and served for many years on Union committees. All four of these ministers were trained under J.J. North. Lanyon (1890-1955), General Secretary of the denomination 1940-1955, was an Australian with a missionary background. His leadership was marked by an irenic concern for unity. Carey and Nees were businessmen in the Wellington region who were stalwarts of denominational committees in the 1940s and 50s. Both served as President of the Union in this period.

[17] Letter to Tabernacle members 25 February 1944, cited in Brookbanks' action. See also Hodge's response to the Commission's findings - Letter, A. Hodge to P.F. Lanyon, 4 April 1944. NZBA A.5/65.

redirect that sectarian suspicion. By the 1940s Baptists were more comfortable among other Protestants. The recruitment of Averill to give supporting evidence in the libel case was a symbol of more relaxed relations. When the National Council of Churches (N.C.C.), which did not include Catholics, was formed, Baptist leaders, in particular J.J. North's nephew L.A. North, gave enthusiastic support. Yet this degree of involvement remained disquieting to some. By no means all Baptists were as sold on ecumenism. As ecumenical involvement broadened, theological and governance issues were to be further disputed.

The formation of the World Council of Churches (W.C.C.) was agreed in 1942 although, due to the disruption of war, the first meeting of the new body was not convened until 1948. The N.Z. Baptist Assembly in 1944 (the same gathering which considered Hodge's case) agreed 'that the Baptist Union of N.Z. apply for affiliation with the World Council of Churches.' The decision appears to have been taken hurriedly, in the final session. There was no advance notice given, no mover, seconder or debate are recorded and there is no mention of the decision in the Assembly reports in *The N.Z. Baptist*. The Union Council had resolved to bring the matter to the Assembly only the week before.[18] Given that in 1944 the new ecumenical body existed only in principle, the gaps in the process are explicable. Moreover, the Assembly had other, more immediate matters distracting it – not only the Tabernacle case but also the retirement of J.J. North as College Principal. Nevertheless, the hasty treatment of the issue would surface later as a significant problem.

Baptists had for some time been in another discussion, with the Associated Churches of Christ, as to the possibility of some form of union of the two denominations. In 1946 N.R. Wood foresaw that this conversation and the Union's increasing ecumenical involvement would eventually strike the reefs of doctrinal difference. He thus initiated the drafting of 'a statement regarding the Baptist position in regard to cooperation with other denominations'.[19] The first draft and comments have been preserved.

The title of the document, which remained unchanged through the process, was somewhat unexpected: 'The Baptist churches and the

---

[18] See Minutes of the 62nd Annual Assembly of the Baptist Union of New Zealand, NZBA B.1/124, ff 46-72; Minutes of the Union Council, 3 November 1944, NZBA B.1/129, f. 286.
[19] Minutes of the Union Council, 26 June 1946, NZBA B.1/124, fol. 311; Letter, N.R. Wood to L.H. Jenkins & J.E. Simpson, 13 July 1946 (copy), NZBA B.1/13.

Evangelising of New Zealand'. Conscious of the need to convince conservative doubters, Wood opted to clothe this statement on ecumenism in the more palatable language of evangelism. Explaining this to his collaborators he conceded that the document thus 'attacks the problem indirectly but I think more effectively than a direct examination would.'[20] Wood's draft began with a summary of the urgent need for evangelism and the obvious benefits of cooperation in that effort. J.E. Simpson proposed a more straightforward tone, replacing this paragraph with one which instead emphasised the 'ecumenical spirit' of the time and therefore the need clearly to state Baptist convictions. Third in line, Luke Jenkins, the new Principal of the College, disliked the defensive tone of both approaches. Defensive that is, not of Baptist principles but of ecumenical activity. 'I think it would be better to reiterate the note that we are prepared to co-operate in all matters on which we can secure reasonable agreement.'[21] In the end Simpson's preferred form largely prevailed. Even with its content camouflaged by its title there seems to have been little enthusiasm for testing the statement on the floor of Assembly. It was instead adopted by the Union Council and merely communicated to the churches.[22]

The denomination would not remain passive. In 1949-50 there was a major challenge to the Union's membership of both the N.C.C. and the W.C.C.. The key protagonist was Rev. D.B. Forde Carlisle. Carlisle had had a rather chequered career in Baptist ministry. A pastor in Baptist churches from 1911, he published a dispensationalist account of salvation history in 1915 and clashed with J.J. North over the inspiration of the scriptures. In 1917 he withdrew from the denomination 'on the basis of doctrinal differences, out of conviction' and for eighteen years led an independent mission in Palmerston North. During this time Carlisle applied to the Union for a letter of credentials for use on an upcoming trip to the United States.[23] The response from denominational Secretary Lascelles was frosty.

> The reflections made by you against some of our prominent men when you withdrew were of such a nature that I do not think any letter which I could give you would help you in any way.[24]

---

[20] Letter, N.R. Wood to L.H. Jenkins & J.E. Simpson, 13 July 1946, NZBA B.1/13
[21] Letter, Luke Jenkins to N.A. Wood, 9 August 1946, NZBA B.1/13.
[22] Baptist Union *Yearbook* 1946-47, 162-164.
[23] Letter, D.B.F. Carlisle to W.M.G. Lascelles, 22 March 1928, NZBA B.1/13.
[24] Letter, W.M.G. Lascelles to D.B.F. Carlisle, 28 March 1928, NZBA B.1/13.

Despite these views of him, Carlisle returned to the official list of ministers in 1935. The themes of his earlier disputes continued and he set up a series of polemical magazines to promote his causes. On the letterhead of one of these, *The Charter of Prophecy: A Herald of the Second Coming*, he wrote to the new editor of *The N.Z. Baptist*, N.R. Wood, in November 1948 requesting space for articles on the 'appalling facts' regarding the W.C.C..[25] Wood was cautious, guaranteeing nothing until work was submitted. Carlisle immediately objected and demanded a clear undertaking to accept his article and publish it without amendment. Although this was not given, Carlisle submitted his piece, which was promptly rejected by Wood without explanation. Incensed at what he regarded as a 'curt note,' Carlisle warned of a growing opposition to the W.C.C., raised the spectre of 'modernism' and claimed the high ground of Baptist principle. 'Have not I, or any one of our people, the right to expose what to us is an evil thing as anyone else has the right to support or defend? Is the day of Baptist liberty gone?'[26]

The correspondence continued, becoming increasingly acrimonious. In April 1949 Carlisle submitted another long letter to *The N.Z. Baptist* which Wood again rejected. This time he gave extensive reasons, in particular defending the Assembly's authority to affiliate with the wider body. In a 'private and unofficial' note Wood set out his ecclesiological principles, stating clearly his advocacy for central authority and discipline.

> I have followed with much interest the articles in the *Watchman Examiner* on this issue. The doctrine of the church so expounded is, of course, deficient and I am surprised to find you advocating it. It is not as Baptist as it seems....It is in fact that Brethren view of the church which Strong in his Theology right says to be false.
>
> ...[A] gathering of delegates from the local churches CAN RECEIVE GUIDANCE from the Spirit. It only becomes binding on the local church when the local church recognises it as the guidance of the Spirit. But since the Spirit is ONE a very serious situation arises when the local church sets its interpretation up against the larger fellowship....
>
> To be specific – Our assembly acted in this W.C.C. matter. What then can a local church do? It can repudiate its delegates and denounce as unchristian the decision of its sister churches. But if it does so it has cut at the root of the very basis of Union. It has said its interpretation is

---

[25] Letter, D.B.F. Carlisle to N.R. Wood, 20 November 1948, NZBA B.1/13.
[26] Letter, D.B.F. Carlisle to N.R. Wood, 2 February 1949, NZBA B.1/13.

superior and more correct than the guidance given to the larger fellowship. Strong would say that the local church in such circumstances ought to be visited by delegates from the larger fellowship. If no agreement could be reached the law that Christ laid down re disobedient brethren should be applied. The Union should withdraw from fellowship with a church that denies its guidance of the Spirit....

...To be very blunt, has Forde Carlisle the right of veto of all Assembly decisions? Is there not an obligation upon you as a minister in full standing with the Baptist Union of N.Z. to loyally abide by decisions reached openly at Assembly?[27]

This was a remarkably centralised view of authority. Whatever Wood's assertions, it was not founded securely in Baptist precedent. In particular he was placing an extreme interpretation on A.H. Strong, citing him out of context. Strong (1836-1921), the key Northern Baptist theologian of the early twentieth century, allowed for the withdrawal of denominational fellowship, but only for 'manifest departures from the faith or practice of the scriptures'. In any case, the local congregation retained complete control over its affairs.[28]

Carlisle regarded Wood's letter as an 'amazing document' and responded with a detailed critique. The lines of the dispute were no longer drawn simply around the W.C.C.. Wood's argument, Carlisle declared, 'makes the Assembly a church, which it is not.' A struggle for the heart and soul of the denomination threatened.

If what you say...is correct then the Assembly (the larger body) has some authority over the local church, and the autonomy of the local church and its superiority over all simply does not exist....This, I imagine would be a great surprise to many Baptist churches and it occurs to me that the time has arrived for a clear cut definition to be made, so that we may know where we are.[29]

In the next available *Baptist*, Wood used his editorial to set out his position, though in different terms. In this public statement he was more guarded, but nevertheless quite definite. If every local church is to be left free to find for itself the mind of Christ, how will there be any unity in the church? Citing Paul's appeal to the Corinthians 'to consider the custom of

---

[27] Letter, N.R. Wood to D.B.F. Carlisle, 13 April 1949, NZBA B.1/13.
[28] See A.H. Strong, *Systematic Theology*, 8th edition (Philadelphia: Judson Press, 1907), 926-929.
[29] Letter, D.B.F. Carlisle to N.R. Wood, 26 April 1949, NZBA B.1/13.

the other churches,' he concluded 'a church that ignores or refuses to cooperate with others shows its spiritual weakness.'[30]

In addition to Strong, Wood claimed backing for his interdependent, almost confederate model from his own contemporary, Ernest Payne of England. This link is particularly telling, as English Baptists displayed a similar trend towards central organisation and ecumenical engagement in the middle of the 20th century.[31] Carlisle by contrast cited as authorities the Southern Baptists E.Y. Mullins (1860-1928) and B.H. Carroll (1843-1914) along with Francis Wayland (1796-1865), President of Brown University, who stressed absolute congregational autonomy. Two streams of Baptist ecclesiology were thus in tension in this debate. Indeed, Carlisle was clear that two distinct types of theology were exposed. Wood had taken an extreme view on central authority, but, along with many in the denominational leadership favoured the moderate theological stance of the mainstream Baptists in Britain. Carlisle looked to the increasingly fundamentalist American South.[32] These larger movements were, however, merely international parallels of the moderate and conservative traditions already present in New Zealand Baptist life.

The correspondence between Wood and Carlisle degenerated to a stand-off, but they managed to agree on where they disagreed: Baptist membership of the W.C.C. was merely the second question; the first was a dispute over proper 'Union procedure'. Wood and other key leaders envisaged a denomination more tightly coordinated than ever before. This inevitably set them against conservatives like Carlisle who demanded the right to dissent.

Carlisle continued to protest, and managed to bring the W.C.C. issue to the November Assembly. A series of remits were discussed in committee, among them a motion to withdraw from the W.C.C. and instead join the American conservative Carl McIntyre's International Council of Christian churches (I.C.C.C.). But the case of Carlisle and his supporters was inevitably constrained. To insist on a new set of binding resolutions would simply reinforce the power of Assembly. The motions

---

[30] *NZB* (June 1949): 157.
[31] See for instance P. Shepherd, 'The Baptist Union's Ministerial Settlement and Sustentation Scheme: The end of congregational church polity?', *Baptist Quarterly*, Vol. XXXVIII, No. 6 (April 2000): 277-288.
[32] Carlisle was selective in his use of sources. Mullins, though conservative, was no fundamentalist. Ironically, the Southern Baptist Convention was the most connectional of the major Baptist groups in the United States.

were withdrawn and by agreement 'a representative fact-finding committee [was] set up to look into the whole matter of the World Council of Churches and to report to the next Assembly.'[33]

The committee took to its task seriously. An advertisement was placed in *The N.Z. Baptist* inviting submissions and the committee met twelve times. On three occasions meetings were convened to interview key figures in the debate. Carl McIntyre, visiting New Zealand at the time, gave an account of the I.C.C.C. and its objections to the W.C.C.. From another perspective, Presbyterian Alan Brash, the first secretary of the New Zealand N.C.C., answered to questions about Roman Catholic involvement, Communism and Modernism. Forde Carlisle gave his submission in two sessions. His objection was that Baptists could not associate with such an 'inclusivist' body as the W.C.C. and that the Assembly of 1944 had had no jurisdiction to so affiliate the Union. When it was pointed out that the rules of the Union specifically gave power of affiliation to the Assembly Carlisle dismissed this as a technicality, affirming 'that it was unconstitutional for Assembly to join [the] W.C.C. irrespective of any clause in the constitution'.[34] This, of course, was an absurdity. What Carlisle meant was that the move was fundamentally 'unBaptistic' – at least in terms of his autonomous ecclesiology.

The committee presented its report to the 1950 Assembly. It found that the threat of association with Rome was remote, and that the charge of communist bias was not established. The majority concluded that modernist elements in the W.C.C. did not compromise Baptist involvement. On the question of the validity of the 1944 decision the committee found that there was no constitutional breach but that procedures had been poor, especially with regard to a lack of notice to delegates and information to churches. One member dissented on Carlisle's grounds that the entire procedure was 'unBaptistic'.[35] The Assembly endorsed the majority view without protest (though it should be noted that Carlisle declined to attend). This victory for the ecumenical position was more apparent than real. It provided only a temporary respite - the question of membership of the W.C.C. would be raised periodically

---

[33] Minutes of the 67th Annual Assembly of the Baptist Union of N.Z., NZBA B.1/124, f. 173.
[34] 'Brief Resume of Interviews with Rev. D.B. Forde Carlisle', 1 September 1950, fol. 3 – Minutes of the Fact Finding Committee on the W.C.C. – NZBA B.1/14.
[35] 'Addendum to Report, being minority Report of Mr R. Jackman,' 24 October 1950, NZBA B.1/14.

thereafter, as new rumours of outrages emerged.[36] More fundamentally, the fact that an enquiry had been deemed necessary at all represented a challenge to the centralising of authority. The committee's report included a definition of the relationship between Assembly and the churches. Although the Union had the right under its Act to affiliate with other bodies

> this does not mean that the competence of the individual church to govern its own affairs...is infringed. No decision of Assembly is mandatory upon the individual church but rather advisory. It is possible for any church to decline to accept a decision of Assembly on well-considered grounds.[37]

This was a long way from the confederate model promoted by N.R. Wood in his correspondence with Forde Carlisle. Indeed it was an important statement which tempered the drive to central authority and strong denominationalism. Carlisle had scored on a key point. Others were about to be made. The focus of the conservative challenge now shifted to the Principal of the Theological College.

Luke Jenkins and the Theological College

When J.J. North notified his intention to retire to the Assembly of 1944, the denomination was left exposed. There was no obvious successor from among N.Z. Baptists. Ayson Clifford had been appointed tutor only months before and was in any case deemed too young. In the event a decision was reached quite quickly, with the name of Luke Jenkins endorsed at the June 1945 Union Council meeting and ratified at the Assembly in November that year. Jenkins was an interesting choice. He had been trained at Regents Park College in Oxford and had had successful pastorates in England and Wales. At 37 he had no significant experience in theological teaching, but was well-regarded for his academic ability. He had no firsthand knowledge of New Zealand.

---

[36] Carlisle's former church at Te Awamutu would notify its dissociation from the Union's position in 1952. See Minutes of the Union Council 12 March 1952, NZBA B.1/130. For a summary of N.Z. Baptists' ecumenical involvement, see S.L. Edgar, 'New Zealand Baptists and the Ecumenical Movement,' *N.Z. Journal of Baptist Research*, Vol. One (October 1996): 9-25.

[37] Report of Fact Finding Committee on the World Council of Churches, 24 October 1950, NZBA B.1/14, f. 7.

It was immediately recognised that the job of selling Jenkins to the churches would need to be handled carefully. That he was British was little hindrance in itself, although the ever-present example of Alexander Hodge did cast a shadow. Far more important were Jenkins' theological credentials. Notice of the nomination was given in the August 1945 *Baptist*. Jenkins, readers were assured, 'is keenly evangelical, a convinced Baptist, possessed of evident qualities of leadership, and has a brilliant scholastic career'. The listing of 'evangelical' first masked a definite anxiety on the point. There were three potential triggers of opposition. N.R. Wood, secretary of the College Board at the time, wrote a formal letter to Jenkins on 18 June 1945 offering him the nomination. The next day he sent a more pointed, personal letter alerting Jenkins to possible pitfalls. As the one who would have to field questions on the nomination he wanted to be armed with answers. He first needed an assurance of evangelistic zeal. This was readily supplied. More problematic was Jenkins' pacifism.

> We had information *re* your views in connection with war and kept that confidential to the College Cmte. We did not divulge that to the Council and no questions were raised by the Council. One cannot say of course what the Assembly will raise….In N.Z. here we have avoided any trouble in the church by permitting liberty but those of us holding pacifist views are a very small minority.[38]

As the passage suggests, Wood himself was a pacifist, and he was soon satisfied that Jenkins would not push an essentially unpopular view too actively. A month later though, the third and ultimately more significant issue came into focus: the bogey of 'modernism'. Another formal/personal pair of letters ensued. In the official letter, Wood described the situation as a need for clarification.

> A member of the College cmte who is senior lecturer in Classics at the Varsity takes a leading part in the I.V.F..[39] (This man was not present in Wellington when the whole cmte met.) With this as a background you will understand how easy it is to exaggerate or misunderstand the

---

[38] Letter, N.R. Wood to L.H. Jenkins, 19 June 1945, NZBA, Carey Baptist College files.
[39] I.V.F. – Inter-Varsity Fellowship, formed in 1928, in part as a counter to the Student Christian Movement (S.C.M.) which was held by evangelicals to have drifted to liberalism.

reference in your application to the S.C.M.. Some questions have been raised on this point.[40]

The 'senior lecturer in classics' mentioned by Wood was E.M. Blaiklock, a convert of Joseph Kemp and a leading conservative voice on the College Board, whose opposition to Jenkins would grow over subsequent years. In his follow-up, personal letter Wood described the theological scene in some detail. He noted the presence of Kemp-inspired conservatism and the countervailing cautious openness of J.J. North. The tension between 'the two outlooks' was the context of Jenkins' nomination.

> When it came to a decision in the cmte it came ultimately to a question of whether we would ask for a conservative man or one who would be progressive without being iconoclastic. We chose the latter. We believe you will follow on the North tradition of a sane progressiveness without upsetting the conservatives. Now that lies at the bottom of the enquiry about the S.C.M. and if you can give me some assurance on that we should be able to get the whole thing through Assembly.[41]

A degree of 'assurance' was provided and Jenkins' appointment was ratified at the 1945 Assembly. The decision was not, however, unanimous. Some, including Ayson Clifford, felt there was undue pressure to approve the nomination. The meeting was informed that passages for the family had already been booked.[42] A cloud of suspicion lingered.

The new Principal faced a very difficult task. He was succeeding the most respected figure in Baptist life. The student body from 1946 included returned servicemen. These older students chafed at the discipline that Jenkins imposed. Perhaps most important of all was that Jenkins was geographically isolated from his most important supporters in the denominational leadership. Wood, L.A. North and Simpson had each entered friendly correspondence with him before he came to New Zealand, but they were in Wanganui, Wellington and Dunedin respectively. Jenkins had to establish himself in the theologically conservative (and at that time divided) Baptist life of Auckland. By 1949 L.A North was lamenting that 'he has not won his way in it.'[43] Jenkins himself appears to have found aspects of New Zealand life unsophisticated.[44] Conversely the Jenkins

---

[40] Letter, N.R. Wood to L.H. Jenkins, 24 July 1945, NZBA Carey Baptist College files.
[41] Letter, N.R. Wood to L.H. Jenkins, 26 July 1945, NZBA Carey Baptist College files.
[42] J.A. Clifford, unpublished memoirs, file 3, 3.
[43] Letter, L.A. North to N.R. Wood, 9 June 1949, NZBA B.15/33.
[44] Clifford, 4.

family culture, which included Mrs Jenkins' smoking, disturbed the temperance–minded Baptists of Auckland. Conflict with the student body (which shared the same house as the Jenkins family) arose. By 1950 the students were asking the College Board to set up a liaison committee to ease tensions.[45]

In 1949 Jenkins' reappointment was to come before the Assembly. Criticism had been spreading. N.R. Wood continued to offer support, although he noted that 'certain readjustments' were inevitable in regard to 'some differences of custom'.[46] Jenkins wrote to his supporters on the Board in June, responding to personal accusations which were being put about in the churches. A.L. Silcock replied in sympathy, bemoaning 'this scandalising by people who make great pretentions of piety'.[47] In November the College Committee recommended to Union Council that reappointment be for only a three year term as opposed to the standard five years. This was endorsed, though not unanimously. At the Assembly the matter was dealt with in committee, with the significant proviso that College students would not be allowed to vote. After a long and tense debate, the reappointment was made, but with a majority smaller than had been obtained in 1945.[48]

Matters did not improve. Jenkins sought to address the issues publicly early in 1951. N.R. Wood declined to print his comments in *The N.Z. Baptist*, feeling that they would be counterproductive. 'Underneath our differences in the denomination there is a very real unity and that must be conserved.' In a personal postscript he counseled for a different approach to resolving the issues.

---

[45] See the Minutes of the New Zealand Baptist Students' Assn. 1950-1952, NZBA B.15A/2.
[46] Letter, N.R. Wood to L.H. Jenkins, 14 June 1949, NZBA Carey Baptist College files.
[47] Letter, A.L. Silcock to L.H. Jenkins, 22 June 1949, NZBA Carey Baptist College files.
[48] See Minutes of Union Council, 4 November 1949 NZBA B.1/130, fol. 5; Minutes of the 67th Assembly, 8 November 1949, NZBA B.1/124, fol. 177. The voting figures were not recorded in the Assembly minutes but Ayson Clifford remembered the vote against reappointment to be a substantial 36% - Clifford, 15.

If you continue in your refusal to be helped by your friends on the cmte you will jeopardise your whole career in N.Z.. I say that advisedly after being alarmed at Assembly by the strength of the opposition.[49]

This warning was prescient. Early in 1952 Jenkins' supporters on Union Council concluded that reappointment for a third term would be unlikely. Following informal discussions at an Executive meeting in March it was agreed that L.A. North and P.F. Lanyon should visit Jenkins at the College to inform him of the situation. Jenkins responded with frosty indignation. L.A. North, who had enjoyed cordial relations with Jenkins, was deeply affected by the intensity of the reaction. Jenkins was unrepentant. Whilst affirming continued friendship he maintained that

> smooth words do not alter ugly facts. There are some things that cannot be done in fellowship because they are in themselves a breaking of the fellowship of the Spirit Who is a Spirit of righteousness.
>
> I think you are lending yourself to what will be finally disastrous for the College, the Denomination and all that the North name has stood for in our churches.[50]

Jenkins was not alone in regarding the action of the denominational leadership as high-handed. The Auckland administrative committee of the College objected to the intrusion into what they saw as their jurisdiction.[51] In May, Rev. J.T. Crozier, a Dunedin member of the full College Committee, protested to N.R. Wood that the central body did not have the right to pre-empt or even anticipate the decision of Assembly. Crozier, one of the denomination's sharpest minds, identified the key issue of power.

> There have been other occasions when decisions have been arrived at in Executive or Council and then the rank and file of our people have been conditioned into accepting such decisions without being given an opportunity to discuss alternatives in open Assembly. This may be expedient, but I consider it theologically unsound and out of keeping with Baptist polity. Indeed it is an ecclesiastical oligarchy rather than democracy.[52]

---

[49] Letter, N.R. Wood to L.H. Jenkins, 18 February 1950, NZBA Carey Baptist College files.
[50] Letter, Luke Jenkins to L.A. North, 29 April 1952, NZBA Carey Baptist College files.
[51] See Letter, L.A. North to N.R Wood, 28 March 1952, NZBA B.15/33.
[52] Letter, J. Crozier to N.R. Wood, 9 May 1952, NZBA B.15/33.

By then, abandoned by key supporters, Jenkins had lodged his resignation, allowing steps to be taken to secure a successor. He would not go quietly. The tone of the initial reaction continued in correspondence with erstwhile friends on the Union Executive, to be reinforced when Wood, North and Simpson allowed their own names to go forward for the soon-to-be-vacant position.[53] Jenkins now came to view the matter as a self-serving conspiracy to remove him. This sense of betrayal culminated in a sensational speech to the Assembly on 31 October 1952. In a moment of high drama Jenkins used the occasion of his final Principal's report to detail his conspiracy allegation, portray himself as victim of a heresy hunt and successively resign from the Principalship, from Baptist ministry and finally from Baptist membership altogether. He walked out of the meeting, slamming the door behind him. Stunned, the Assembly declined to accept the verbal report or to respond in detail to Jenkins' subsequent press release.[54]

The affair was a humiliating tragedy for the Jenkins family, shattering the structure of their relationships in New Zealand. It cruelly demonstrated the power of whispering campaigns, especially when focused on theological or moral propriety. Fortunately it did not end Jenkins' ministry. Soon after the 1952 Assembly Luke Jenkins began a successful career as a Presbyterian.

The case was also a great embarrassment to the Baptist Union. In particular it was a setback for the activist leaders who had sought to secure a place for the denomination in the Protestant mainstream. Jenkins' press statement called into question the academic integrity of the college and the personal honesty of key leaders. The public nature of the breach made Baptists look, once more, like sectarian obscurantists. The fact Luke Jenkins, after such an acrimonious departure, could be so readily welcomed by the Presbyterians suggests the Baptists had not become as mainstream as they had hoped.

Yet, although the damage was heavy, it was not fatal. The enormous stress of 1952 challenged but did not defeat the denominational structure. The leadership had been prepared to ease Jenkins' departure because they were committed to 'conserving unity' and concerned to avoid a split over

---

[53] The minutes of the Nomination Committee of the College confirm the version of North and Wood that they did not apply for the job but rather were invited to have their names considered. Minutes of the N.Z. Baptist Theological College Board, 24 September 1952, NZBA B.15/105.

[54] Clifford, 25-26.

the Principalship. Fears were soon allayed; the Union did not divide. Jenkins' swingeing condemnation of all parties united the Assembly behind the Executive. Subsequently, in the irenic personality of Edward Roberts-Thomson, the new Principal from Australia, the College community discovered a healing force which enabled it quickly to re-group and progress. Neither was this bought at theological cost to the moderate faction. The denomination was not 'reduced to a sect of Brethrenism' as Jenkins warned it might be.[55] In fact Roberts-Thomson proved to be more open to new theological movements than Jenkins had been.[56]

The long decade of conflict which followed 1940 severely tested the confidence of the new generation of Baptist leadership. They sought to present the Union as a mainstream group, worthy of recognition as a significant Protestant denomination. This status would not come easily. The Executive was able to demonstrate its resolve through the Hodge affair, but the vision held by such as N.R Wood of a centrally driven, connectional Baptist Union was not realized. Wood's reach exceeded the denomination's grasp. The churches were not about to become a church. Nevertheless a genuine commitment to unity was built. The Union quickly recovered from the potentially crippling Jenkins crisis and entered a period of sustained growth. Indeed, under the General Secretaryship of L.A. North (1955-1966), it seemed to fulfill the 1940 promise of a denomination which was 'vigorous, splendidly organised and progressive'. This would prove an evanescent achievement. The societal changes of the 1960s and the rise of the charismatic movement would demand new models. New Zealand Baptists would once more have to seek a fresh view of themselves.

---

[55] Letter, Luke Jenkins to P.F. Lanyon (undated), NZBA B.1/80.
[56] Roberts-Thomson began from a conservative position but appears to have been profoundly influenced by his doctoral research on the ecumenical movement. He eventually moved to a liberal view on a number of theological and ethical points. His tenure (1953-1960) in New Zealand was peaceful but his later principalship of the New South Wales Baptist in Sydney ended amid theological disagreement. As had Jenkins, Roberts-Thomson subsequently entered the Presbyterian ministry.

Part IV
Shifting Sands

Chapter Thirteen: hesitating too long - the college 1952-1974

The nineteen-fifties was a decade of growing prosperity for New Zealand, and for the Baptist denomination. The country, spared destruction of infrastructure during the war, welcomed back its servicemen and women in the expectation of better times. This hope was largely justified. The now famous 'baby boom' began, with the population further augmented by large-scale post-war European immigration. New Zealand's largest market, Britain, was by contrast in need of massive reconstruction and consumed products from its former colonies at a great rate. The result in New Zealand was a new prosperity, which created full employment and an explosion of home building and public works. New suburbs and towns appeared, each a potential site for a new church.

The general buoyancy extended to the denomination and its college. The decade had begun with controversy and upset. Yet the trauma surrounding the resignation of Luke Jenkins in 1952 did little to restrain the growing self-belief. Indeed, ironically, it seems to have accelerated the effect rather than slowed it. It was as if the contrary post-war tides suddenly all abated at once. With the tensions surrounding the college apparently resolved, the more conducive societal environment could be enjoyed. A new Principal would benefit from a relieved enthusiasm for the college and its role in Baptist life. Ministers were in demand. The college periodically came under pressure to release students early or to modify the course. The goodwill of the denomination towards the college enabled the Household model of training at least nominally to be sustained, but this would be its last hurrah.

Despite its initial intention to find a New Zealand appointee to succeed Luke Jenkins, the College Board quickly settled on Australian E.J. (Ted) Roberts-Thomson. As had been the case in 1945, when founding Principal J.J. North had retired, no viable local candidate had a formal theological qualification. Roberts-Thomson had a Melbourne B.D. and came with strong recommendations from Australian Baptist leaders. His appointment was endorsed by a vote of 176 to 1 at the 1952 Assembly. Ayson Clifford, who had been appointed tutor in the last years of North's tenure and had continued in that role somewhat unhappily under Jenkins, was raised from

Tutor to Vice-Principal.[1] It had been anticipated that Jenkins would see out his term of appointment, which did not expire until the end of 1953. When Jenkins decided to conclude a year early the Board considered a range of interim solutions but was saved from implementing any of these by Roberts-Thomson's willingness to commence almost immediately.[2] His terms of appointment were virtually the same as Jenkins' had been, with the key assumption still being that he and his family would live with the students and that Mrs Roberts-Thomson would manage the household. Ayson Clifford, having witnessed at first hand the difficulties of the Jenkins years, questioned whether the live-in requirement was wise.[3] Little heed was taken, although, in an unrelated move, responsibility for the day to day financial affairs of the college was shifted away from the Principal's wife (where it had sat for Mrs Jenkins) and given to Clifford.[4]

Edward (Ted) Roberts-Thomson (1909-1987) had been born in England but was raised in Tasmania. Although from a Brethren background, he trained for ministry at the Baptist College of Victoria (now Whitley) in the 1930s. After a short pastorate in Tasmania he travelled to England to study at Bristol Baptist College, where he completed a B.A. in Theology together with an M.A. at Bristol University. This study began a lifelong interest in ecumenism and resulted in the publication of a book on the potential for cooperation between Baptists and the Disciples of Christ. On his return to Australia in 1940 Roberts-Thomson served in a number of churches and spent time as a military chaplain. He completed a Bachelor of Divinity at Melbourne and in 1952 was serving at the Brunswick Baptist church in Melbourne.

Stung by the almost total collapse of relations with Luke Jenkins, the Board was determined that its next Principal would be a success. In this they were aided by the Roberts-Thomsons. The family arrived in style, by flying boat on the Waitemata harbour. The new Principal and wife immediately took their place in Baptist life. Their easy manner and informality was immediately noted.[5] Indeed the Roberts-Thomsons seemed to have had a talent for cordial relationships. Gwen Roberts-

---

[1] On Clifford's vice-principalship see Baptist College Board Minutes (BM) 1 November 1952. NZBA B15.
[2] BM 1 November 1952, ff. 134-5.
[3] Baptist College Administrative Committee Minutes (Admin. CM) 30 October 1952. NZBA B15/90.
[4] Admin. CM, 27 February 1953.
[5] *NZB* (March 1953): 54.

Thomson was a major part of this winsome combination. She is described by a number who knew her as a 'Queen of the Manse' type who was always able to provide efficient hospitality and encouragement.

Ayson Clifford immediately relaxed under his new Principal. 'He was genial, cheerful and kindly. He had strong opinions but expressed them in a most disarming manner. I soon found he welcomed my input into College life and Administration.'[6] Ted Roberts-Thomson was a personable, gentle figure who nonetheless took a lead in college and denominational affairs. He was known affectionately as 'the Boss' and his students dubbed themselves the 'Teddy-boys'. The new Principal had a keen insight into the Australasian evangelical culture and he was able readily to 'speak the language'. At the same time his interest in ecumenism continued. During his tenure at the college he completed a doctoral thesis on 'Baptists and the Ecumenical Movement' which was later published.

In financial terms at least, the college was becoming more and more tied to the Baptist Union. The Forward Work appeal provided over half the budget in 1960. Moreover, from 1957, an annual grant direct from Union funds became a standard feature of the accounts. Such a grant had been made before, in 1939-40, but it was then a response to difficult economic circumstances left over from the depression and problems with the Randall estate. Now it would be a permanent feature which would come to dominate the accounts.[7]

Ted Roberts-Thomson had experienced a broader preparation for leadership in theological education than either of his predecessors. He had studied in both Australia and England and his Master's thesis began a process of broadening his appreciation of other denominations. He brought to the New Zealand college a clear vision for standards and for the future of the institution. Under his guidance the college expanded and subtly changed its character. North's intellectual agenda was broad and vigorous, but his college was essentially for nurturing the key youth of a small faith community. Luke Jenkins sought to add more recognised academic standards. Roberts-Thomson wanted this and more. The college needed to be larger, better resourced, with a multi-faceted agenda. It is an interesting reflection on his skills and the times that he largely succeeded.

---

[6] Ayson Clifford, Unpublished Memoirs 3.29.
[7] A measure of the integration of College and Union was the move to include the college accounts with those of the Union from 1959. Until that time they had been reported separately.

A symbol of the new mood and opportunity is found in the formal curriculum. Luke Jenkins had met stiff resistance from students when he sought to make the Melbourne College of Divinity's L.Th. the norm. One of Roberts-Thomson's first moves was to make this qualification compulsory – a decision which was accepted without any apparent question.[8] The college year was extended to accommodate the M.C.D. examination period and the college agreed to meet the costs of students. By 1956 there was some concern that the Melbourne curriculum was dominating the programme.[9] The L.Th remained the basis for the college course but in 1958 a shift took place to encourage qualified students into the New Zealand Bachelor of Divinity, which was held to be better integrated with the college programme. At the same time a new proposal, for an ecumenical Bachelor of Arts in Theology, emerged from the Theological Colleges Conference in Christchurch in May 1958. A plan, agreed by all colleges, was developed and discussions were held with the University of New Zealand and the nascent University of Auckland. Talks continued, though with the plan in danger of getting lost in the transition to regional Universities.[10] There was also resolute opposition to theology within the University of Auckland. In 1961 a greatly pared back proposal saw agreement for two Biblical History and Literature papers to be offered within the ordinary B.A. at Auckland.[11]

The Principal's own academic research continued. In 1957 he was awarded a Doctorate in Divinity from the Melbourne College of Divinity for his thesis on Baptists and the Ecumenical movement. The topic followed on from his earlier Master's study. It also fitted with the general thrust of Roberts-Thomson's vision. The college needed to get bigger and have more staff so as to enable higher academic standards through concentration on chosen fields. Both staff and students needed to be exposed to international and ecumenical developments. The college should discover its place in the Christian world, beyond the confines of a small, colonial denomination.

A new, larger site was purchased and with it the inherited training model came under pressure. Life began to change. Through 1954 residential students lived at Mt Hobson whilst taking classes at Victoria

---

[8] Roberts-Thomson, 'Annual Report' November 1953.
[9] See the report of the Board of Studies, Admin.. CM 31 January 1956 and Admin. CM 7 May 1956. NZBA B15/91.
[10] Admin. CM 9 June 1958; 2 May 1960; 1 August 1960. NZBA B15/93.
[11] See Principal's Report, Admin. CM 6 April 1961. NZBA B15/93.

Avenue. The Roberts-Thomsons had moved into the first floor in the new college at the start of that year. The provision of new students' accommodation in the North Wing and completion of the Vice Principal's house brought all of the college together for the first time since the early 1940s. The structure of college life was still based on the boarding school house model. Students were awakened by bells and took breakfast and lunch with the Roberts-Thomsons. A considerable element of formality lay over these meals. Students were rostered to sit at the top table with the Roberts-Thomsons, who took particular interest in the style and manners of students, regarding good etiquette as an essential skill in the pastorate. Ties were to be worn. (A rebellion which called for the recognition of cravats was soon quashed.)[12] In the evenings the Principal's family generally dined alone. On Sundays the convention was that students would be out of the college for as much of the day as practicable, to enable a bit more freedom for the Roberts-Thomsons.

Inevitable changes came about, however, due to the separate living quarters. The students now had much more unsupervised time. The North wing consisted of a lounge and communal bathroom, plus twenty single rooms which doubled as studies. These were on both sides of a long corridor. It was basic accommodation. The students had to fight for tea making facilities. In the late 1950s power restrictions led to a prohibition on the use of heaters.[13] Most of the residents were students of the college, although boarders (generally Baptist university students) were brought in if there were vacancies. On Saturday nights, students could invite girl friends and fiancés to dinner, after which they might visit in the North wing common room. Annual Fellowship Meetings with the Bible Training Institute (B.T.I) and Trinity Methodist continued as they had since the early years. In 1955 the B.T.I. meeting was planned early in the year but 'a suggestion that the girls be invited was not approved'.

A tradition of annual retreats emerged. These did not begin as especially 'spiritual' events but usually consisted of borrowing a bach and relaxing for a weekend of 'organised chaos'.[14] By 1960 they had become serious affairs, requiring a visiting speaker. With the arrival of the Deaconess trainees a dilemma presented itself. Could they come to the

---

[12] Students Minutes [SM] July 1957; 8 August 1957; 6 March 1958. NZBA B15A/3.
[13] SM 10 July 1958; 8 April; 4 June 1959. NZBA B15A/3.
[14] SM 1 July 1954. NZBA B15A/2.

retreat? In 1959 it was decided to invite them 'subject to the Principal's consent'. It wasn't granted.[15]

Although the college had never restricted its training to men, no women had been students since Thelma Gandy (1926-28) and it was the unspoken assumption that 'the ministry' was a male domain. However, a number of churches had established staff positions for Deaconesses who might have trained at the B.T.I. and who were employed to assist with pastoral visiting. In other denominations, notably the Presbyterians and Methodists, a trained order of Deaconesses had long been established. The Baptists took a while to follow their lead. Following a call at the 1952 Assembly to reconsider the role of women in ministry a Deaconesses training programme was instituted. In most ways this mirrored the men's course. It was governed by a Committee consisting of the College Board plus a number of women and there was an Auckland Administrative Committee consisting of the College Administrative Committee plus a smaller number of women. The academic programme was proposed to be a minimum of one year, though in content it was identical to that of the men. The only difference (in theory) was in practical experience, which was to be focused on pastoral care, women and children. There was no female faculty member and the Principal had the same responsibility for the Deaconesses as for the Ministry trainees.

The Deaconesses course was in some ways a strange programme. The New Zealand Baptist version was derived from local and overseas models. It provided a means of recognising professional ministry by women. In some cases work roles already filled were acknowledged through the new scheme. There was an early wave of interest. In August 1956 it looked as if there would be more applicants for the Deaconess course than for ministerial training.[16] That it gave a valuable lift in status and visibility is without question, as is the contribution which the women who became part of the scheme made to denominational life and mission. But it came late and was a half-way house that would eventually be overtaken by the question 'why not equal standing with men?' There seems to have been no clear philosophy behind it.

Nevertheless, the impact on the college was profound. The presence of women in the classroom, in some cases achieving the best marks and winning prizes, was a novelty. On average the Deaconesses were an older

---

[15] SM 8 April, 4 June 1959. NZBA B15A/3.
[16] Admin. CM 7 August 1956. NZBA B15/91.

group (by about five years) than the men. Those at the Methodist hostel were similarly older than the average Methodist students who stayed there. Their presence in the college required a certain lift in decorum, particularly with the very correct model of the Roberts-Thomsons always on display.

Other than the arrival of women, the most obvious example of change among the students across the fifties was the increase in numbers. The period was a time of almost constant growth. This was a sign of confidence in the college but it created headaches. Plans for extra accommodation were regular business items for the Administration Committee. Statistics and projections were pored over, in an effort to predict needs and demand.

Marriage continued to be a contested issue. The college did not pretend to be able to house or support families. Roberts-Thomson called for a review of the whole question of married students but this produced little change.[17] For unmarried students, getting engaged was not a problem, although it was expected that the matter would be discussed with the Principal. The College Board was very clear, however, that arrangements for marriage should not be made until a student was placed in a church at the conclusion of his study.[18] The board negotiated placements with churches and needed to be sure that appropriate accommodation for a married couple was available. The students chaffed at this level of control. The difficulties presented by having to wait for up to four years proved too much for some engagements. Approaches were made to the board to reconsider the policy. Again, there was no change.[19] A pattern emerged in which there was a batch of exit student marriages between December and February at the end of training.[20] In 1959 a suggestion by the Administration Committee that any future plans give consideration to married quarters was rejected. 'It is the firm opinion of the college that single students, living in is the ideal in training men for the ministry.'[21] The issue would not go away. In August 1960, with a shortage of trained ministers becoming evident, the Board noted that three married students had applied for entry in 1961.

By the late 1950s the student body was changing in other ways. They had to resolve among themselves how they would regulate smoking and

---

[17] Admin. CM 3 October 1955. NZBA B15/91.
[18] BM 3 November 1954, f. 160. NZBA B15/91.
[19] SM 3 March 1955. NZBA B15A/3.
[20] See e.g. Admin. CM 6 October 1958. NZBA B15/93.
[21] BM 26 October 1959. See 'Report of Property Sub-Committee', Admin CM 6 August 1957. NZBA B15.

gambling in the common room.²² A number became interested in emerging Pentecostal trends and some invited visitors to speak to students. On at least one occasion this was done without consultation with the faculty. Ayson Clifford felt that Roberts-Thomson dealt sensitively with the question. The students, however, were not so sure. A meeting on July 14 (Bastille Day) resolved that

> while we recognize the need and value of advice from those who are more mature and experienced, we deplore any denial of religious liberty through pressure applied to students to prevent them hearing, reading, being present or participating in that which they feel will be of personal spiritual profit, or for the better understanding of their ministry.²³

As the new decade progressed, the college faced a range of new demands and pressures as the students evolved into the baby boom generation. As in wider society, rapid and multifaceted change would have a profound impact on the Baptist training and ministry.

Roberts-Thomson gave notice of his resignation as Principal in 1960. It was, to most in Baptist circles, a surprise. His Principalship had been peaceful, whilst at the same time full of apparent change and expansion. Roberts-Thomson had been appointed for an initial five year term. Perhaps because things were going so well the usual practice of confirming reappointment a year ahead was not followed.²⁴ In May 1957 terms were proposed which offered an unlimited term. An important innovation was a recognition of the principle of a year's paid leave after eight years service (presumably for study purposes, although this was not specified). In addition to the salary, £200 was to be provided to assist with travel costs. However, after consultation with the full Board, the provision for travel costs was dropped.²⁵ This alteration may have rankled, but the fact remains that Roberts-Thomson had the full support of the denomination and that, further, he chose to conclude his Principalship at the very time that he would have been eligible for his study leave.

Other factors can be identified which may well have contributed to Roberts-Thomson's decision to resign. In December 1958 he proposed to that Board that the college purchase 3.5 acres of bare land adjoining the

---

[22] SM 7 November 1957; 1 May 1958; see also SM 5 October 1961 for an identical policy on smoking. NZBA B15A/3, 4.
[23] SM 41 July 1960. NZBA B15A/4.
[24] Admin. CM 30 October 1956, f. 181. NZBA B15/93.
[25] Admin. CM 5 May; 6 August 1957. NZBA B15/93.

college property. This had just become available and was lauded by Roberts-Thomson as 'our amazing opportunity.' The Board, however, took no action. This was deeply regretted by their Principal. In May 1959 he lamented 'it looks as if we have hesitated too long.'[26] It is clear that Roberts-Thomson had a big vision for the college. His earlier moves to align its title and practices with international conventions reflect that goal. That the board did not see itself able to grasp that vision as firmly as he wanted it to in 1959 was a disappointment.

Towards the end of 1959 the strain of the heavy work-load of the Principal began to exact a toll on both Dr and Mrs Roberts-Thomson. In March 1960 he was reporting to the board that medical advice suggested relief, either through extra staffing or through resignation. The Board, which had been considering the possibility of an additional tutor for some time, acted swiftly to adjust duties and provide leave as soon as possible. By July a decision had been made to appoint a third tutor and to provide a Principal's house to relieve Mrs Roberts-Thomson of domestic supervision. By then Roberts-Thomson had been nominated to the Principalship of the Baptist College in New South Wales.[27] His perception of what would be possible in Sydney was undoubtedly part of the 'pull' to the new position. There seems to have been little to 'push' him from the New Zealand college, other than perhaps a sense that the horizons were smaller, and that he may already have achieved there what he would. This, coupled with his health crisis, meant that Roberts-Thomson had run out of steam somewhat. As it transpired, the strong sense of call to Sydney he avowed would be cruelly knocked. Things may not have been easier, even if he had stayed in New Zealand. His time in Auckland had been immensely successful, but new challenges were coming and renewed energy and commitment would have been necessary had he stayed.

The Principalship now came at last to Ayson Clifford. It was a challenging time to take on such a role. The optimism of the 1950s initially carried forward into the next decade. Indeed New Zealand reached a peak in its standard of living. The baby boom was affecting many aspects of society, from housing to education. Cities continued to expand and to draw in rural populations. The bulge in numbers did not have a serious impact on employment until the later 1960s. Terms of trade were good, television

---

[26] Admin. CM 1 July; 1 September 1958; 2 February 1959 and Principal's Report 4 May 1959. NZBA B15/93.
[27] Admin. CM 7 March; 11 July 1960. NZBA 15/93. See also the report of a sub-committee on staffing Admin.. CM 4 May 1959. NZBA B15/92.

had arrived and more New Zealanders than ever gained access to tertiary education. Few foresaw that this heady combination of affluence and exposure to world trends and new ideas would lead to social revolution. Ayson Clifford certainly did not. His Principalship would be characterised by efforts to diversify the college's offerings and to analyse trends in the denomination. The college continued to receive support from *The N.Z. Baptist* magazine and the College Board became one of the premier committees, with healthy competition for election. Yet, like most others, Clifford did not anticipate the extent of change in society at large. Despite his best efforts, by the end of the decade the college was languishing.

Structural questions were often manifestations of other pressures. One of the first challenges facing Clifford was the reemergence of the Pentecostalism question. In 1961 a senior student returned from the summer enthusiastic for the movement and keen to promote it in the college. Revivalist meetings promoting speaking in tongues were being held in Dunedin. In connection with these, Eric Batts of the Hanover Street church heard of claims that 'ten of our College students have rec'd the baptism and spoken in tongues'. His letter recounting this caused Clifford concern, as he had misgivings about the way the issue was presented and did not want the churches to gain an incorrect impression of the college.[28]

As the decade progressed hard-line Pentecostalism translated into 'Neo-Pentecostalism' which in turn morphed into the charismatic movement in Baptist churches. Nervousness over the issue meant that, when the students made the Holy Spirit the theme of the *College Magazine* in 1968 the Board deputised Clifford and Union General Secretary Hugh Nees to discuss the contents with the editors before it was prepared for publication. Key substantive articles on the subject were ultimately contributed by Stan Edgar, Angus MacLeod and Ernest Payne of England. Student voices on the questions were outweighed. Clifford was a member of a commission of the Baptist Union in 1969 which concluded that there was little ongoing place for 'neo-Pentecostalism' in the corporate life of Baptist churches. This reflected Clifford's own position. He was never comfortable with the Pentecostal style and its implications for ecclesiology. Late in his Principalship he took time to warn students of what he saw as its dangers. By 1973 the issue was becoming a defining question. Students organised seminars by leaders in the charismatic movement, at one point asking for an alteration to the lecture schedule so as to accommodate these extra-

---

[28] Clifford Memoirs 3.58.

curricular sessions. In September 1973 *The N.Z. Baptist* published a sermon critiquing the movement by Gordon Hambly, who was associated with the college in a number of ways. Twelve of the college students, led by the Student's Association President for that year, Laurie Guy, responded with a letter calling for recognition of the strengths of the movement. The students' letter was moderate, seeking presentation of both sides of the picture. Nevertheless, it generated a rebuke from Ayson Clifford, who recalled that he was concerned in case 'only one side of the controversy should emerge from the college.' That Clifford reacted in this way reveals both his sensitivity to the issue and the distance between his position and that of a growing number of students and ministers.[29]

The steady growth of the 1950s was not continued in the new decade. The Deaconesses course failed to live up to its initial promise. Only five took the course in the 1960s and there were none after Diane Miller in 1968-9. Ministerial students plateaued. The expanded college started to look like a white elephant. Ayson Clifford was not about to wilt under the pressure of these trends. A series of new initiatives employed the college facilities better, but also added to the pressure on staff and increased the complexity of the college's life. Extra-mural programmes and a Social Services course were begun. More structure was given to the Ministers' course. These stricter procedures may in themselves have had an impact on student numbers. In 1972 Clifford pointed out that the total number of applicants for training in the 1960s was 141, exactly the same as it had been in the 1950s. However, of these applicants, only 74 (53%) had been accepted, as against 98 (70%) in the earlier decade. Clifford's conclusion was that 'either there was a drop in the standard of those applying, or the selection process is more severe'.[30] This may have been so, although underlying the decline was also the tardiness of the Board in making full provision for married students, thus limiting the pool of applicants. Whatever the reasons, it is clear that the growth in student numbers encountered in the 1950s was not continued in the 1960s.

The college had become a complex and busy organisation. The pressure on staff, especially on the Principal, was acute. The college had in a sense reached a point of institutional maturity. It had three full time staff who were its own graduates and whose combined qualifications were of the

---

[29] *NZB* (September 1973): 16-17; (November 1973): 7; Clifford Memoirs 4.94.
[30] See Clifford's Principal's Report, Admin. CM 2 October 1972. NZBA B15/97.

highest quality. Yet it was running on a near empty tank, scrambling to use its building to the fullest and to meet as many needs as possible.

The college's model was creaking and groaning under the pressure of growth and diversification. The Household approach had unraveled with the new location and expanded staff. The Principal and his wife were still, theoretically *in loco parentis*, but the students were no longer in the same building and some were living elsewhere. With the new appointments fresh strains were added. The Cliffords continued to live in their separate house. Bob and Shirley Thompson were offered a flat upstairs in the main building. The shaping forces were no longer overwhelmingly from Principal to students but increasingly included the influence of tutors and other students. The shared 'place' was still crucial - all staff and most students lived within sight of one another – but the sense of being one family faded. Students were formed in a matrix of relationships far more complex than that which had pertained in 1926 when J.J. and Cecelia North set up home with nine adopted 'sons'.

By 1970 Ayson Clifford was questioning the usefulness of retaining the vestiges of the Household model. The constant difficulty in finding domestic staff was wearing thin. Consideration was given to buying in TV Dinners and thereby doing away with the need for a cook. Clifford wondered if the rooms could be converted into self-catered units. 'With a much smaller number of students now resident the work should be a good deal lighter but we continue to keep it heavy by taking in more and more boarders.'[31] The form of the model was being sustained beyond the substance. It had become clear that the Driver House extension had been undertaken to meet a fading market. In 1971 the Board reported twelve married students, with only eight single students, supplemented by eleven boarders. This, in a college with capacity for thirty-six single students.

Many of the routines of the college continued along familiar lines, but the homogeneity generated by the vast majority of single male students 'living in' broke down as the community became more diversified. This was not true in all respects. The gender bias, for instance, remained. The few Deaconesses were supplemented by female missionary and independent students, but the student body remained overwhelmingly male. It was also increasingly sourced from the North Island. South Island applicants for the Ministerial course gradually fell from over 30% in the 1940s to less than

---

[31] See Admin CM 7 December 1970; 5 April 1971 (Principal's Report). NZBA B15/92.

20% in the 1960s. Nevertheless, where once the college had consisted of the 'Teddy Boys' plus an occasional married student, increasingly it was a mixed company. Single ministerial students gradually declined whilst married numbers, despite the barriers to entry, crept up. Independent students became more common as did boarders who, although they did not often take college courses, were in other respects full members of the residential community. A place was kept for a number of years for scholarship students from Asia.

At the beginning of the sixties a more or less formal stratification by year groups was accepted. This extended to the seating arrangements in lectures, with first years up the front, and fourth year students, some of whom had already by then completed the external requirements of the programme, taking up the back rows. The Senior Student would always be from the fourth year as, generally, would the *College Magazine* editor. This 'class structure' gradually eroded. Through the period the Students Association was constantly considering its rules and membership, with the status of boarders, Social Services students, independent students and student spouses regularly coming up. A more open constitution was adopted in 1970.

Retreats continued as a feature of college life. The speakers at Waiheke Island in 1965 were L.A. and Frances North, who 'brought their own pack of cards'. A notable feature of this gathering was the presence of women students for the first time.[32] Not all institutions survived. The 'Open Airs' which had been a joint venture with the B.T.I. when it was situated in Queen Street survived the shift of the B.T.I. to Henderson but by 1966 the negativity with which they had always been regarded caught up with the practice and they were dropped.[33] In 1973 the much lampooned 'Misogynists Club' (essentially an umbrella for those single men not yet engaged) was laid to rest and its records ritually burned.[34]

In 1971 the Students' Executive was pondering the 'deadness' of community life, which it associated with so many living off the site.[35] Neither were relationships with college authorities always warm. The faculty was respected and generally liked. Yet, it was sometimes felt that Clifford did not communicate with students as well as he might. He could be intransigent, even dictatorial. As one student President lamented:

---

[32] Students Association Annual Report 1965.
[33] SM 19 April and 16 June 1966. NZBA B15A/5.
[34] SM 8 August 1973. NZBA B15A/6.
[35] Students' Assn Executive Minutes 29 September 1971. NZBA B15/7.

'students have often disagreed as to whether we should go round Ayson or over his head in policy-making decisions, but all agree that it is still as hard as ever.'[36] In 1971 the Student Executive proposed appointing a 'go between' to mediate between Clifford and the students. A year later it lamented a 'lack of closeness' between lecturers and students. Again a better liaison was sought.[37] Relations with the College Board were even more problematic. The course structure by which students had to be readmitted after two years created a tension point if a student failed to progress. In 1966 the students complained at the Board's 'lack of initiative' in supporting married students. In 1968 matters had deteriorated further, with one student describing relations with the board as 'lousy'. A formal complaint over lack of communication was lodged at the full Board meeting in November that year. Little seems to have changed. Students continued to seek representation on the Board and to ask for faster, better information on matters which affected them.[38]

The biggest and most obvious shift was demographic. Married students were no longer an anomaly. They were fast becoming the norm and faced a number of hurdles. Ayson Clifford, reflecting in 1970 on the evolution of the college noted a key shift.

[The] increasing proportion of married men makes a community spirit more difficult to capture. Students are no longer here all the week. Extra-curricular activities become a Cinderella. Special thought is required to maintain community worship and group prayer. In the old days, it used to be said 'College life is good for a man. He gets his corners knocked off.' Today, unless this abrasive process is already done or is done by his wife, a man may go out into the ministry corners and all.[39]

Although the issue of married students' accommodation was raised a number of times in the late 1950s little had been done to address the growing need. The Board invested instead in the continued expansion of its current model, which assumed a steady growth in single students. Norm Reynolds recognised early that action would be needed. In 1962 he raised the matter with a proposal to move quickly to building new facilities or altering present ones. In 1963 he lodged a major report on the question of

---

[36] Students' Association Annual Report 1965.
[37] Students' Executive Minutes 28 September 1971; 27 June 1972; 11 July 1972. NZBA B15A/7.
[38] SM 28 July 1966; 11 & 26 June 1968; 10 August 1971. NZBA B15A/5,6.
[39] *College Magazine* 1970, 3.

married students. Concerned at 'our apparent lack of a systematic approach to the recruitment of married men' he noted a general trend to younger marriages and that some overseas colleges had already had to address the issue. He proposed that free accommodation be provided on the college site. Ayson Clifford responded with a memo cautioning the Board that an intentional shift towards married students might weaken the ethos of the existing training. He feared 'absenteeism and unpunctuality, reduction of cohesion of student body, disproportionate burden of student organisation on single men, resentment of single men at acceptance of married men of younger age, empty rooms.' Reynolds' proposals, blunted by Clifford's misgivings, resulted only in some loosening of entry provisions and a policy change to allow final year students 'having attained the age of 26 and doing a satisfactory course' to marry. No plan was made to supply married accommodation.[40]

The Anglican St John's College had had a similarly 'single-minded' history but it moved on the issue sooner. The first four flats for married students at St John's were opened in 1961, with another six built in 1966.[41] St John's had greater resources and more students overall but its willingness to anticipate the increasing demand from married students is a contrast to the slower progress at the Baptist college.

At the end of the decade the college had substantial property holdings. It occupied a large plot of land in a leafy suburb which included staff residences and single person's accommodation for nearly forty students. It had three flats near-by and an office building in the city. The value of the asset was impressive but its usefulness was low. Too much was held in the wrong classes of property. The college had plenty of bare land, a surfeit of hostel type accommodation and an investment property. What it needed was family housing and a new library.

By now Clifford had acknowledged the inevitability of the trends. In March 1970 he called for yet another look at the question of married students. The rules about current students marrying were relaxed significantly. Permission was still needed from the board but the option was opened to all students, not just to those in their final year.[42] Writing to E.P.Y. Simpson in April 1971 Clifford noted these developments with some ambivalence.

---

[40] See BM 29 October & 1 November 1963. NZBA B15.
[41] Allan K. Davidson *Selwyn's Legacy: The College of St John the Evangelist Te Waimate and Auckland 1843-1992* (Auckland: St Johns, 1993), 209-10, 218.
[42] BM 29 October 1969. NZBA B15A.

> With the continually increasing proportion of married men we are slowly getting around to providing accommodation....This is something students have been agitating for, for some time. Oddly enough, now that we have decided to do it, and have all the plans completed,... several students are now not in favour of building flats. They say the college should be decentralized and scattered throughout the community. You will recognise the point of view. However, it comes at an awkward time, since all this was discussed last year before we went ahead with the plans.[43]

Clifford was alluding to an 'Open Letter to the College Board' from third year student Ivan Howie, which was about to be published in *The N.Z. Baptist*. Howie objected to the further enforcement of the residential model, suggesting that far from the college 'knocking off corners' (as Clifford had celebrated) it should free its students from its 'pressure to conform' and release them to the multitude of settings in the wider community. Howie's voice, though prescient, was not necessarily representative. In the same issue, sixteen other students recorded support for the new accommodation.[44]

The constant pressure of building inadequacies, low student numbers and changing times had an inevitable effect on Ayson Clifford. In October 1970 he informed the Board that he did not intend to remain as Principal until his retirement.

> I believe that the time is close upon us when the College will need a younger man to guide the work into the future, a stronger man to meet the pressures that come upon us and a more learned man to set new standards of scholarship within the College.[45]

Clifford was running short of creative energy. In May 1972 he reviewed that situation of the college in a pessimistic 'Memo on College Development (or Decline)'. The most profound challenge he identified was 'Our Image in the Churches'.

> I am convinced that there are a large number of church people who are either ignorant of the College, or negative to it and whose conception is

---

[43] Letter, Ayson Clifford to E.P.Y. Simpson, 19 April 1971. NZBA Clifford Correspondence.
[44] *NZB* (May 1971): 24. See also subsequent correspondence *NZB* (July 1971): 6 & (September 1971): 7.
[45] Letter, Ayson Clifford to F.C. Mills, 19 October, 1970. NZBA Clifford Correspondence.

of a remote, over-academic, unspiritual, unbiblical, unpractical, affluent institution....in some churches, prospective candidates are actively discouraged from applying and those who do are threatened with the dire results of attendance here... We have watched with concern the decline of other denominational colleges.... It would be foolish to say this could not happen to us.'[46]

Perhaps the most telling part of the memo lies in what Clifford did not include. There was no hint of any radical answers to these challenges. Although he listed nine suggestions for action they amounted to little more than tinkering with the present system, trying to do better what was already being done. There were no new strategies.

By the end of 1973 the college still had no new library but it did have eight flats for married students. There was a considerable way to go if all married students were to be accommodated but a clear shift from a single 'Household' to a 'Community' model had now been accepted. Howie's letter to *The N.Z. Baptist*, however, raised a disturbing prospect. Had the college responded too slowly to one trend only to miss the next one as well? The Household model which had worked so well under J.J. North, only to have its limits exposed under Luke Jenkins, had been granted an extension in the optimistic climate of the 1950s. With hindsight it is clear that the Driver house addition of 1959 was a mistake. Instead of building yet more single persons' accommodation the college should have at that point pursued married quarters. The signs were already present that this was a growing need. Yet significant change in this direction had to wait nearly a decade and a half, by which time demand was already peaking, shortening the useful life of the new developments.

Clifford's observation about other denominational colleges is worth noting. The ranks had thinned among smaller denominations. The Baptist College had shown remarkable resilience, even staying open with miniscule numbers during World War II. It had bounced back confidently after the paralyzing tensions of the Jenkins era. The 1950s, however, was an 'Indian Summer' for the church in New Zealand, including the Baptists and their college in particular. The need to evolve, though recognized by some, was inadequately addressed in practice and policy. The college reached the fragmented 1970s with its traditions strong but its future uncertain.

---

[46] Clifford, 'Memo on College Development (or Decline)' see Admin. CM, 29 May 1972.

The college had not adapted well. Ayson Clifford was a safe pair of hands but he had probably come to the job and concluded it five years later than would have been ideal. His assumptions and expectations were not flexible enough to manage the changes in both church and society in the later 1960s. Little lead was given on how to grapple with the moral and theological change of the time. His reluctance to move on married accommodation and his lack of sympathy with the emerging charismatic movement meant that the college did not respond early enough to those major shifts. He was not alone, of course - Baptist leadership as a whole struggled to contain the rapid diversification of the denomination – but the conservative approach constricted the college's development and sowed seeds for later tension with the churches. The college was no longer generating the core of the denomination's ethos. It would increasingly be seen to be at odds with it.

The college had been one of the key drivers of the tighter, more self-assured sense of Baptist identity which emerged mid-century. In the 1970s, struggling to find its own way, it would play that wider role less and less. Baptists, it seems, were seeking something else, something their institutions could not provide.

Chapter Fourteen: from confidence to confusion

In the first decade of the twentieth century a new generation of Baptist leaders came to the fore with assertive, even aggressive, ideas to reform and redirect the denomination. One of the key activists of 1901, Harold Peters, would succumb to tuberculosis before being able to make his true contribution. M.W.P. Lascelles, R.S Gray and Joseph Kemp died with aspects of their grand designs unfulfilled. J.J. North would stay the course and, through his energy, communication skills and integrity, would dominate the life of the denomination. In a remarkable way North would see his visions through their natural cycle of rise and decline. In the 1950s and again in the 1980s leadership would again pass to a new generation. Their challenges and ambitions were inevitably and rightly different from those of J.J. North; their successes are less easy to measure.

The family album

J.J. North retired from the editorship of *The N.Z. Baptist* in failing health in 1948. The last few of the issues nominally under his care were in fact put together by J.T. Crozier. N.R. Wood became the next editor. Wood had trained as an early student of North at the Baptist College. He declared himself determined to carry forward the Baptist witness of the newspaper.

> To the church, in its various branches, the people called Baptists bear their witness to the true nature of the church of Christ, to the competency of the individual soul in all matters of religion and to the true nature of baptism. The fact that the barriers separating the churches are being broken down does not make any less urgent the obligation upon Baptists to bear their testimony.[1]

For all this, Wood's would be a softer sectarianism than North's had been. In keeping with the spirit of post-war New Zealand, the tone was organizational and institutional, with major denominational initiatives often the natural focus of the content. Finances were difficult. In 1951-2 the issue size was reduced to 24 pages and the subscription rate increased from 6s to 7s 6d. The trend to make more of the covers (begun in 1944)

---

[1] *NZB* (February 1949): 29.

continued, with large images on the front displacing advertising, which was soon eliminated from the body of the paper altogether, reducing available space to just three pages of the cover. Subscriptions hovered around 3300, never threatening the hoped-for 4000 which was the focus of a familiar sounding campaign to get "The Baptist' in every Baptist home'.

There were other trends. The reports from churches grew in profile, at times taking up 40% of each number. The financial responsibility began a shift towards the denomination and away from subscription. By 1955 a substantial annual subsidy was embedded in the accounts. The 1950s was a decade of confidence and expansion for New Zealand Baptists and the paper reflected that mood. Wood had been an activist and self-identified moderate pacifist in earlier years. His stance seems to have shifted by the time he became editor.

After the First World War the church rediscovered the social gospel. It was an attempt to help a bewildered society find a new foundation. Pacifism and socialism appeared to many as certain doors into the Kingdom of God. The events of the fourth decade have shattered these rosy dreams. The challenge to religion is now largely from the economic angle. The souls of men are being drugged by social security. Their outlook may not altogether unfairly be described as that of 'beer and bread; races and sex.'[2]

A search of the pages of the first seven years of Wood's editorship reveals no significant editorial reflection on the Korean conflict or on pacifism. On the other hand there was much which signaled loyalty - that is: national and imperial loyalty. Queen Elizabeth II featured on three covers in less than two years. In April 1955 the cover was given over to the ship which would take the New Zealand delegates to the B.W.A. Congress in London. Three months later the British Houses of Parliament were shown with the by-line 'The Heart of Empire: Home of the Baptist Congress'.[3]

The magazine continued through its ninth decade as a key element in Baptist identity. An important shift had, however, begun. Under North's early editorship, its messages vigorously attempted to build, shape and strengthen Baptists' view of themselves. The impression one gets of the magazine in the 1950s is more that it reflected, rather than drove its

---

[2] *NZB* (January 1950): 2.
[3] See the covers of the *NZB* March 1952; June 1953; January 1954; April 1955; July 1955.

community. This decade saw the largest percentage growth (45%) of Baptist members and an even bigger increase in the take-up of *The N.Z. Baptist* (66%).[4] There is a likely link between these factors. The newly confident denomination was more comfortable with its place in New Zealand church life. It had less need for a paper which aggressively staked out new ground. Rather, what it wanted was to see its image in the pages of a family album. By the end of the 1950s that was the principal role of *The N.Z. Baptist*.

The very survival of *The N.Z. Baptist* is a testimony to its importance in the story of the denomination in New Zealand. Larger bodies were unable to maintain continuous publication of their periodical. Whatever the reasons for the demise of other titles (some of them positive, such as attempts at unity in the joint publication of the *Outlook*), for thinly spread Baptists the newspaper enabled communication and the gradual shaping of identity. J.J. North's strong advocacy of Baptist principles contributed to the emergence of a confident post-WWII denomination. Ironically, North may have overdone it. With confidence came a fascination with themselves, reflected in the 'family magazine', which made New Zealand Baptists ill-prepared to face the challenges of the radical sixties.

This is not so counter intuitive as it might appear. The notion that self-confidence can lead to a fall is hardly a new idea. Baptists worked hard to respond well to their context. They had talented leaders of great integrity, but the nature of 1950s New Zealand, with its increasing prosperity and secure international links, encouraged a false sense of progress when there was in reality a developing lassitude. Baptists became victims of their own success at a time when they might have gained from a more naturally Baptist self-questioning and provisionality. *The N.Z. Baptist* reflected this softening of the edges, as did the outstanding leader of the period, from the third generation of Norths.

L.A. North

L.A. North was a grandson of Alfred and nephew of J.J. North. He was a prodigy by New Zealand Baptist standards. Virtually without apprenticeship he commenced his ministry in one of the four 'flag-ship' central-city churches. Also unusually for Baptists, L.A. North was one of the leaders of the ecumenical movement in New Zealand. In 1937 he was on the steering committee for the newly-formed National Council of

---

[4] Figures taken from the Baptist Union *Annual Reports*.

Churches. When the next year he moved to Wellington, he continued this involvement and in addition gained access to many leading politicians and public servants. He was an accomplished singer and during World War II his rhetorical abilities were employed by the Government Broadcasting service for radio news reports. North embodied the mid-century Baptist move to mainstream acceptance.

In 1955 L.A. North was appointed General Secretary of the denomination.[5] Until his retirement in 1968 he held together a sometimes disparate group of churches and saw the denomination through a period of considerable growth and increasing change. His precise administrative skills established a modern pattern of leadership. On his retirement his approach was encapsulated in the booklet *Baptist Church Life and Administration*[6] which became the standard manual for Baptist churches. Throughout his secretaryship North was a figure of stature in the international community of Baptists and his ongoing commitment to ecumenism saw him serving the National Council of Churches in a range of capacities, notably as President 1959-60.[7]

Order, efficiency, mainstreaming: L.A. North sought a profile for Baptists which avoided them being dismissed as fringe sectarians. In this he only partially succeeded. Although he had influential allies in denominational leadership, there remained a deep stream of Baptist life, often shaped at Kemp's Bible Training Institute and influenced by more conservative ministers, for whom biblical purity was paramount and who put a greater premium on heart religion than on mainstream acceptability. Though largely outside denominational structures, such Baptists had not been silent. As we have seen, a sustained campaign against ecumenical entanglement was waged in the late 1940s and conservative disquiet did much to undermine the Principalship of Luke Jenkins.

The centripetal approach in this middle period of the century was a genuine, if unstated, attempt to construct a new Baptist identity in New Zealand. Baptists continued to champion evangelical enthusiasm and

---

[5] This was the second time he had been appointed to this role. The move to Wellington in 1938 had been to take up the secretaryship at the young age of 34. North lasted less than a year, after which he accepted appointment to Boulcott Street, the central church in Wellington.

[6] L.A. North, *Baptist Church Life and Administration* (Wellington: N.Z. Baptist Union and Missionary Society, 1968).

[7] See entry for L.A. North in *The Dictionary of New Zealand Biography*, 4 (Auckland: Auckland University Press, 2000).

freedom of conscience but it was hoped to achieve this in a way which did not alienate other denominations. Baptists too could be regarded as pillars of the Christian establishment. This aspiration was not unique – indeed it mirrored aspects of the British story – but it was intentional and it was remarkably successful.

The 1950s were a period of considerable growth. Membership increased by over 45%. Members as proportion of the population were also growing even though total adherents were stable. Though by no means conclusive, this closing of the gap between membership and adherence is interesting. We must be careful not to read too much into this, but, the relative willingness of nominal Baptists to be committed to baptism and membership might be cited as an indicator of denominational loyalty and a crude guide to the strength of Baptist identity. If so, then the mainstreaming period did not apparently weaken the Baptists' sense of themselves. With leaders like L.A. North and others prominent in wider affairs, a sense of confidence seems to have accrued to denominational life.

In his report of 1960 L.A. North was able to celebrate growth and the religious enthusiasm which lay behind it.

The work has continued to develop.... This is in line with the forward movement that has been witnessed in recent years....The spirit of evangelism has been fanned into flame again in many of the churches, as has the desire for increased Bible knowledge through the All-age Sunday School movement.

Just as crucial, however, was stability.

We are a united people and for this we give thanks....From time to time we are conscious of external influences and pressures which, if heeded, would lead to suspicions and divisions. Such things are, unhappily, to be seen among our people in certain other lands. The spirit of our Denomination in New Zealand is against such things. We do not all think precisely alike, nor do we all express ourselves in exactly the same terms; but we serve the one Lord and we treasure the spirit of mutual respect and love among us.[8]

This unity was maintained at a cost. Laurie Guy has shown that a proposed Baptist response to the Vietnam War was silenced by the Union Council in 1965. A strong official stance would have been divisive. In 1970, dissatisfaction over a Public Questions Committee report on

---

[8] *Baptist Union Year Book 1960-1961* (Wellington: Baptist Union of New Zealand, 1960) 19.

abortion (though it had been adopted by Assembly) revealed divisions over this issue too. Unlike other denominations Baptists chose not to make a submission to the subsequent Royal Commission. Once again concern over possible division is the most likely reason. 'Increasingly, it seems, Baptists as a whole were failing to reflect on public issues of the day and were opting to have church horizons limited to matters of evangelism, piety and church life.'[9]

Even these in-house matters could produce conflict. When L.A. North referred to 'external influences and pressures' he was almost certainly speaking of aggressive fundamentalisms which could be observed overseas and which had occasionally entered the New Zealand debate. The peace, however, was to be challenged by another, unexpected, 'external influence' - one which soon found its way to the heart of Baptist life.

As L.A. North approached retirement a growing unease was evident. In 1964 he acknowledged 'disturbing questions concerning the life of our Denomination, our objectives and the results being achieved.'[10] It was around this time that the charismatic movement began its course. In New Zealand, unlike the situation in some other countries, the greatest effect of what was first termed 'neo-pentecostalism' has been within existing denominational structures. Independent churches were formed and small Pentecostal denominations emerged, but otherwise 'mainstream' bodies have been greatly influenced by renewal. This is certainly the case among Baptists. However, through the sixties the fledgling charismatic movement was viewed with great suspicion by Baptist leaders, who regarded it as anarchic and divisive. In another part of his 1964 report North warned of

> cases in which a minority has refused to accept the leading given through the judgement and vote of the majority and has proceeded to disturb the life of the church to the frustration of the work of the Holy Spirit. The claim that the majority must submit to the minority is a denial of true democracy and of our doctrine of the church.[11]

This negative response to charismatic stirrings was hardly unusual from senior figures across the denominations. However, North highlighted a key issue in Baptist life, the locus of authority. For him, religious authority

---

[9] Laurie Guy, *Shaping Godzone: Public Issues and church Voices in New Zealand 1840-2000* (Wellington: VUP, 2011), 271-2; 405-7.
[10] *Baptist Union Year Book 1964-1965* (Wellington: Baptist Union of New Zealand, 1964) 17.
[11] *Baptist Union Year Book 1964-1965*, 28.

must rest with the informed individual conscience, exercised within agreed structures. The 'work of the Holy Spirit' was to be found primarily in the ordered democracy of the church meeting. The notion that the Spirit spoke exclusively or uniquely to some was anathema.

For two decades there were attempts to check the spread of charismatic styles and practices. In 1969 a report on the movement concluded that it could be tolerated within current structures, but that leaders

> have a responsibility to graciously but firmly request any member, adherent, or group, who holds convictions differing from the main stream of doctrine and practice among Baptists to refrain from any form of propagation or influence of others.[12]

Any who sought to 'propagate or influence' should leave the denomination. The movement was a challenge to order and, what's more, threatened to relegate Baptists once more to the fringe.

Devolving the centre

Despite these misgivings, the charismatic movement continued to make ground among New Zealand Baptists. Its characteristic passion and emotional commitment fitted naturally with the sectarian enthusiasm of earlier groups. Indeed among Baptists the renewal movement combined with the Spurgeon/Kemp stream of Biblical conservatism to create a powerful new force which, by the 1980s, had come to dominate Baptist life. There were inevitable consequences for denominational organisation. By North's retirement the momentum of Baptist life was already swinging back to a centrifugal model. Society was changing rapidly and Baptists, like many others, were beginning to feel threatened. In 1969 a committee was set up to address a sense of 'statistical disappointment and financial crisis'. In 1970 North's successor conceded the top-heavy nature of the administration and signalled a new mood.

> At the present time the organisation is too large for the actual amount of productive work done for the local congregations. The original statement of the Research Committee that was reaffirmed at all levels was 'It is the Committee's belief that the strength and growth of the Denomination is a spiritual matter related to the individual lives of our

---

[12] *Baptist Union Year Book 1969-1970* (Wellington: Baptist Union of New Zealand, 1969), 178-79.

people and it will be the quality of their lives which in the ultimate will determine our effectiveness as a Denomination.'[13]

The result was the first in a series of 'restructurings' which would gather pace in the 1980s. By the 1980s many aspects of New Zealand society were about to change dramatically. Baptists would follow, indeed almost mirror some of these changes. Not immune from the trends of the times, Baptists came to shape themselves in ways which were designed to reflect the needs of mission. Leadership patterns in particular have undergone a profound transformation.

The mid 1980s saw another significant transfer of senior leadership in the denomination. The General Superintendent, Stan Edgar, and the Principal of the College, Bob Thompson, both stepped down in 1984. Edgar and Thompson were of the last group to have been directly influenced by J.J. North. Their replacements were from the next generation. Brian Smith who became College Principal was trained in the 1950s and Gerard Marks, Edgar's successor, in the 1960s. Smith recognised the college's unique role in maintaining relational cohesion among ministers and became himself a key respected figure in the denomination. Yet, despite a radical attempt at missional restructuring in the 1990s, he was unable to shake the theological suspicion which attached to the college. Marks, with a wider brief, is particularly significant. He was sympathetic to the renewal movement and personally drawn to the need to read the signs of the times. In the New Zealand of the mid 1980s there were many such signs to read.

In 1984 the country saw the election of the fourth Labour Government, headed by David Lange. This, one of the most activist ministries of post-World-War-II New Zealand history, radically altered the political, economic and social landscape of the country. After the restrictions of Robert Muldoon's policies there was an eagerness for change in the nation. This appetite was found too among Baptist leaders, who faced challenges similar to those of the Government. After years of decline in terms of trade and competitiveness the New Zealand economy was in a serious state in 1984. The first crisis faced by the new Government was a run on the currency, leading to a massive devaluation and, later, the floating of the dollar. Baptists too faced a financial squeeze, with a substantial deficit in

---

[13] *Baptist Union Year Book 1970-1971* (Wellington: Baptist Union of New Zealand, 1970), 14.

1984 and a worse shortfall predicted for the coming year.[14] In large part this was caused by the problems in the economy, but denominational leaders suspected a deeper malaise. In a move which copied the Government's tactic, a series of regional meetings, 'opening the books', was held to identify the difficulties and to reconsider the core roles of the denomination.

In this process Gerard Marks' convictions were key. In his first report in 1984 he sounded two themes which would have a major influence on later developments. The first was decentralisation. This had been a factor in Baptist debate since the late 1960s but Marks placed it at the core of his leadership.

> What I believe is that at the heart of Baptist church life, is the principle of de-centralisation. This means that all along the line, we free the local church and the local church in turn frees its members, to grow and serve Christ with all the rich variety that we ought to see in the body of Christ.[15]

Yet, alongside this general drive for devolution lay another observation which sat in uneasy relationship with the ideal of releasing all levels into freedom. A large congregation, at Hokowhitu near Palmerston North, had decided to leave the denomination. This event, taking place as it did in his first year, had an impression on Marks.

> One of the lessons to be learned…is that leadership has almost total control over the ultimate direction that a church takes. It is the leadership that determines who will minister in the pulpit and what wider work is promoted and whose support is encouraged. It is leadership that by and large determines the associations that the church will have.[16]

Subsequent developments reflect the interaction between these two themes: devolution and leadership. The first became the slogan of the next decade and a half, but it would be the second, leadership, which would be dominant by the end of the century.

True devolution is harder to achieve than to propose. However well-intentioned or ecclesiologically authentic it is a difficult policy to implement in reality. Through the 1980s there was certainly considerable restructuring in the New Zealand Baptist denomination, but it is not

---

[14] *Yearbook* 1984, 31.
[15] *Yearbook* 1984, 16.
[16] *Yearbook* 1984, 17.

always easy to understand those developments in terms of devolution. The Union and the Missionary Society were brought more closely together, governing bodies were made smaller (and inevitably less representative, more clericalised). The combined expenditure of the Union and Missionary Society grew (admittedly amidst high inflation in some years) by more than 80% between 1984 and 1991. The Head Office of the Union was moved to Auckland from Wellington. Whilst having the obvious advantage of moving the office closer to the largest concentration of churches, this was not a decision which looked to the regions like decentralisation.[17]

In 1991 a new level of leadership, Regional Superintendents, was introduced. On the face of it, this was clearly devolution. Now significant senior figures would be available to encourage and to coordinate local efforts. The national leadership, nevertheless, remained in place. Superintendents were an additional layer, partly funded from the centre. Most importantly, their role evolved. Initially presented as a means of providing pastoral care to local pastors and church leaderships their focus soon became mission leadership. Ian Brown, who succeeded Marks in 1991, identified a further role. 'The Superintendents will certainly give pastoral care and direction to churches and pastors but equally important will be their apostolic role.'[18]

In talking of an 'apostolic role' Ian Brown was looking to a responsibility of care to provide overview and cohesion, rather than an authoritative office in a Pentecostal sense. Yet a shift in approach had been taking place over the previous two decades in which some churches and leaders moved towards charismatic styles and models. This sat in inevitable tension with the continued desire for decentralisation which was as characteristic of Ian Brown's leadership as it had been of Gerard Marks' approach.

Gerard Marks had taken the title 'General Superintendent'. Ian Brown, by contrast, was given the designation 'Executive Secretary'. This reflected an expectation from some that a key task would be to restructure the administrative functions of the Union. In keeping with his own commitment to devolution, Brown addressed the 1992 Assembly on the theme 'absolutely, positively Baptist'. He warned that 'our sense of identity and our reason for existence as Baptist congregations – communities of faith – is in danger of disappearing.' To reverse this, Baptists must

---

[17] See the summary of restructurings in *NZB* (December 1991): 8.
[18] *Yearbook* 1992, 38.

recapture the informal, non-institutional nature of the Baptist way. It was crucial, he asserted, that Baptists speak of themselves as a 'movement' rather than a 'denomination', with all the structural and institutional baggage which had attached to the latter term.[19] This call has been immensely influential. Brown captured the mood of the decade with poignant accuracy. A year later the 1993 Assembly was galvanised by a similar address, by leading Pastor Murray Robertson, with the notion that 'the age of the institutional church is over, and the day of the relational community has begun.'[20]

Restructuring leadership

These forces – devolution/deinstitutionalisation and apostolic leadership – are clearly not perfectly congruent. This incongruity led inevitably to mixed signals, a confusion of messages as to the way forward. In 1997, for instance, a new statement of the role of superintendents was adopted. In this the emphasis shifted slightly, with the key aspects of the role defined as:

1. Provide spiritual leadership to local church leaders.
2. Ensure ministry staff receive effective pastoral care.
3. Promote healthy churches.

In the same year, perceiving a continued drift in denominational life, the new leadership core of Ian Brown and the Regional Superintendents called Assembly to 'New Directions', an effort to refocus the 'movement' around mission and evangelism. This proposal was strong on organisational theory and sentiment but relatively short on concrete proposals. Though it was adopted by Assembly, Brown conceded that it 'did not receive the acceptance we believed it would'. Very little change resulted.[21]

This was a major disappointment to the leadership. Their efforts seemed to have fallen flat. Yet another start on the issues was made in 1999. At the November Assembly Ian Brown was commissioned to bring together a process of reflection on the nature and mission of New Zealand Baptists in the 21st Century and the structures and leadership models required.[22] It was expected that documents for discussion would be ready

---

[19] *NZB* (December 1992): 3.
[20] Rev. Murray Robertson, reported in *NZB* (December 1993): 20.
[21] Ian Brown, 'Annual Report' *NZB* (November 2000): 1.
[22] See Ian Brown 'Towards Bethlehem 2000' *NZB* (December 1999): 5.

by February 2000. This timeline had to be abandoned, as events took an unexpected turn. The previous contact of some leaders with American Baptist Leader Paul Borden set up a fact-finding visit of a group led by Ian Brown to the American Baptist Churches of the West (ABCW) in Northern California during February 2000. The visit had a profound impact. The visiting group was struck by the 'Growing Healthy Churches' emphasis in the ABCW. On its return this became the focus of reflection on the New Zealand scene. More startling for the churches was Ian Brown's decision, communicated soon after his return from California, to conclude as Executive Secretary a year before the expiry of his term. What was needed, he explained, was 'a new style and age of leadership'.[23]

Events moved quickly thereafter. A taskforce 'to resource Assembly Council' was set up. Draft proposals were ready by May, 2000, with a revised version presented to the churches in August.[24] After identifying a number of concerns at the apparent lack of conversion growth in the denomination over the preceding decade and a half, the report signalled radical change. The thrust of the proposals was that the National Centre be reshaped 'to ensure all national ministry resources are focused on our core task, *Growing Healthy churches*.'[25] The Executive Secretary would be replaced by a 'National Leader' with, in addition, a 'National church Health and Growth Advisor' (later amended to 'National Consultant'). Superintendency was to be done away with and replaced with Regional Consultants who would assist churches to implement the Growing Healthy churches model, using diagnostic tools developed in the United States. This vision was communicated in meetings around the country and adopted at the Assembly in November.

Not everyone was happy with all the changes. Ian Brown, for instance, lamented the sudden abandonment of the regional superintendent model. This decision had been propelled by the choice by the superintendents themselves to do away with their office. All of them resigned, in the apparent conviction that a new model was needed. Perhaps no clearer demonstration of end-of-century confusion over direction can be found. A mere three years after the confirmation of a detailed definition of

---

[23] *NZB* (April 2000): 5.
[24] *NZB* (June 2000): 5.
[25] *NZB* (August 2000): 6 (emphasis original).

superintendency, the scheme itself was abrogated. In Brown's view it had 'been credited with too little.'[26]

In 2001 Paul Borden and John Kaisar from ABCW came to New Zealand to work with the re-focused Union, conducting training sessions and church consultations. In this year also, the key appointments of National Consultant and National Leader were made. Lindsay Jones was nominated and appointed without controversy to the first role. Moves to appoint to the second position encountered much heavier going. In December 2000, Assembly Council (the executive body between Assemblies) agreed that the position demanded a 'practitioner leader' - 'i.e. the new national leader would not only be a person with a proven track record in growing healthy churches but also lead the denomination while continuing in their present church-based leadership role.'[27] This was a new concept to many and generated considerable disquiet among the churches. It was thus decided to appoint an interim leader through to Assembly 2002, with the model of leadership to be debated at the upcoming 2001 Assembly.[28]

Brian Winslade was appointed to this role. In keeping with Assembly Council's model, he continued as Senior Pastor of the largest Auckland Baptist church, Windsor Park. Writing of the challenges he suggested a new version of denominational existence.

> Like a coach on the sidelines we will work with and train those willing to address issues of growth and health in their unique context. Or, as Paul Borden expressed it, the role of the denomination in the 21st century is less like a 'family of churches' and more akin to a true 'para-church' agency working alongside those with vision and commitment to be the people God calls us to be.[29]

The model of practitioner-leader was approved by the 2001 Assembly and Winslade was subsequently confirmed to continue as National Leader.

A final aspect of the shift in emphasis among New Zealand Baptists was the adoption of a prescriptive element in the Growing Healthy Churches model. More than a diagnostic tool, the consultations with

---

[26] Ian Brown, 'Annual Report' *NZB* (November 2000): 1.
[27] Brian Kenning, 'Council Comment' *NZB* (April 2001): 5.
[28] Brian Kenning, 'Council Comment' *NZB* (June 2001): 5. See the debate in the pages of *NZB* (June 2001): 16-17; (July 2001): 8
[29] Brian Winslade 'A New Saddle, a New Rider and a New Horse!' *NZB* (September 2001): 5.

congregations encouraged what was presented as a 'staff-led model', although this was later softened to a 'ministry-led model'. In theory the aim of this was to shift 'the emphasis of ministry from the pastors to the people'. The concept hinged on empowering those who are actively engaged with ministries with the requisite authority to operate within their sphere. The congregation was to be accorded the status of 'permission-givers' with governance in the hands of elders.[30] Some concern was raised over the place of the members. In practice the decision-making functions of the members' meeting were often reduced to appointments and global budgets at an Annual General Meeting. Gatherings between annual meetings are more likely to be for information, inspiration and celebration, than decision.

Throughout this period, Baptists have been united in a commitment to shaping for effective mission. There have been different opinions as to what that might mean for leadership and denominational structures. One effect of the restructurings of the final decades of the twentieth century is that Baptists have given tacit endorsement to more apostolic approaches to leadership. This is true at local level, with the promotion of the staff-led model and inevitable relegation of the members' meeting. It is even more evident at national level. The result has been a significant shift in ecclesiological practice.

Baptists were not alone in this of course. A general apathy with regard to denominational structures in New Zealand has led to numerous realignments and the demise of hitherto key bodies. Nevertheless the effect on Baptists has been particularly profound. The charismatic emphasis has in places led to stunning evangelistic successes. Some very large churches by New Zealand standards have emerged – almost all associated at some point with the renewal movement. The charismatic stress on experience has brought with it a suspicion of theology and a playing down of traditional Baptist distinctives. The impact on the denomination's sense of identity has been immense. Denominational mobility in New Zealand is very high and there are many within Baptist congregations who are there for the style of the service and the generally evangelical approach rather than because of the historical principles espoused.

---

[30] Lindsay Jones 'Staff-led Model puts focus on mission as main task', *NZB* (August 2002): 7. Because of the professional overtones the preferred name of the model has morphed into 'Ministry-led Model'. See *NZB* (November 2003): 13.

It was not just new adherents who were wondering what it all meant. In the 1994 Assembly Council report it was notified that the Council had begun asking such fundamental questions as 'Why are we Baptists at all?' and 'What do Baptists believe? suggesting that 'the basic beliefs set out in the Baptist Union [Act of Incorporation]...leave a great deal to be desired.'[31] Questions of this type, at the highest level of the denomination suggested a profound malaise and confusion. Indeed, by the final years of the century, the effect of this drift could be measured.

In the 1996 *Census* there was a startling 23.6% drop in those identifying themselves as Baptists. The figures mask a less brutal, but no less profound reality. The 1996 figure was in fact a return to normality from what had been aberrant figures in 1986 and 1991. The increase in those years and the drop in 1996 are almost entirely attributable to changes in the wording of the religious affiliation question. Before 1986 Baptist individuals had to nominate their affiliation by writing it in a blank box. In 1986 and 1991 the series of options provided included 'Baptist', meaning the respondents had only to tick their preferred category. The Baptist figures immediately went up by 30%. In 1996 the religious affiliation question reverted to the earlier form and the Baptist response declined correspondingly to earlier levels.[32] For a denomination (or movement) floundering over its sense of identity this was a deeply disturbing sign. The sense of being 'Baptist' was clearly weakly held. When forced to nominate an affiliation many Baptist adherents chose a non-specific label.[33]

The shallowness of the Baptist sense of identity was further confirmed in an extensive inter-denominational 'Church Life Survey' conducted in over 1200 N.Z. congregations in 1997. In response to a question on the importance of their denomination as a framework for faith a mere 13% of Baptists rated it as a 'Primary Framework'. This was the lowest of all denominations participating and compared with 17% for Co-operating Parishes (generally Methodist/Presbyterian), 21% for the Pentecostal Elim churches and an average of 27% overall. Interestingly the other area in which Baptist results stood out was in the 'Most helpful style of music'.

---

[31] *Baptist Union Annual Reports 1994*, Assembly Council Report, 39.
[32] The same pattern has been identified the 1991 Australian Census – Hughes, *The Baptists in Australia*, 39-40.
[33] In 1991 the Baptist figure was 70 155 (2.1% of responses), in 1996 it had fallen to 53 613 (1.6%). Smaller declines were recorded for Anglicans (-13.7%), Catholics (-5.1%), Presbyterians (-15.3%) and Methodists (-12.8%). Source: *New Zealand Official Yearbook* (Wellington: GP Print, 1998), 121.

'Contemporary Songs' were rated highest by 62% of Baptists, compared to 30% overall, suggesting that the principal distinctive of New Zealand Baptists now lay in what they sang.

By 1999 New Zealand Baptists were headed for their first ever decadal decline in actual membership and a significant fall in membership as a proportion of the population. The trend continued into the new century.

What, then, of a Baptist identity? The 1997 *Church Life Survey* revealed that Baptists were committed to biblical truth and evangelism and most were open to the exercise of charismatic gifts. They maintained the ideal of adult baptism, although many have open membership and some no real system of membership at all. They had not totally abandoned congregational government, although hierarchical models of leadership and governance were increasingly popular. They retain a healthy Baptist suspicion of outside authority, although there were periodically suggestions that the Union should be able to close down causes deemed to be struggling. Few congregations are willing to defend, much less incorporate, a thoroughgoing freedom of conscience. The clarity which J.J. North celebrated and L.A. North enjoyed has plainly faded.

A decade into the twenty-first century Baptists in New Zealand are evidently a shrinking group with an almost resigned air. In contrast to the Anglo-centric sectarianism of the nineteenth century, the vigorous anti-Catholicism of the early twentieth century and the confident mainstreaming of mid-century they appear hesitant, unsure of themselves, unclear that they have anything unique to offer the wider church or society at large. It remains to be seen whether a new identity will emerge.

Concluding Unhistorical Postscript

The New Zealand experience forced Baptists to adapt. There is no one way to be church. The shape of Baptist life shifted - at times creatively and fruitfully, at other times reluctantly or in confusion. This should be to our present encouragement – and challenge. It is clear that without profound change the church will not easily find its place in the 21st century. Whilst there are aspects of our context which are unique to New Zealand, the case can no longer be made that local issues alone determine the constraints and opportunities of Christian witness. Though with markedly different details, we, like the settlers, remain held in the tension between there and here – reflecting on our shores both a world beyond and the specific realities of the local context. J.J. North and his contemporaries called for solutions which reflected the immediate challenges of an emerging, isolated society. The answers must be 'racy of our soil.'[1] That remains true - New Zealand's history, bicultural challenges and Pacific setting make it unlike any other place – but global forces are just as powerful. They surge relentlessly around our questions and aspirations. The predicament New Zealand Baptists face echoes denominational angst the world over. None of us is the same as our Victorian English forerunners. Is it not possible that historical Baptist distinctives, forged amid old-world repression, are of limited value in the new? Maybe Baptist identity has simply had its day.

Maybe - but only if that identity is understood in terms of a set of doctrines or practices handed on from generation to generation. I have suggested that this is the wrong way to understand the Baptist vision. It is instead a way of moving, a dynamic seeking for the most authentic way to reflect the world to come in the world that is.

Which brings us back to the big themes of this book. New Zealand Baptists have consistently sought authentic means of connection. The remarkable persistence of individual congregations and the Union itself is testimony to the power of this impulse. In theological terms this is an instinctive expression of the thoroughgoing reconciliation promised in the Kingdom of God. Connection, covenant, commitment – these are reflections of the world to come. But Baptists live unembarrassedly in the

---

[1] *NZB* (August 1924): 170. See chapter seven.

world that is – a world of conflict. The calling of the church is to live as citizens of heaven in the flesh and blood world of real people, in real places.

A robust understanding of the mission of the church removes any need to impose or fabricate a false unity, an easy peace. The church is called as first fruit of the Kingdom. Its role is to demonstrate the mission of God. It is a mistake, however, to over-realise this eschatological vision. The church reflects the world to come in the world that *is*. The realities of the here and now are themselves integral to the mission. The church displays God's vibrant action, not some static end-point. There can be no imperative to exhibit perfect peace as if there is no process for getting there. Rather, the church is a site on which the reconciling power of the Spirit of God is worked out - in real time, among real people – through conflict and connection.

A congregational polity precludes the illusion that one can be connected to the church in general, without being part of one community in particular. This means that the treasure of connection has to be strived for in the messiness of real life. Conflict, if not exactly desirable, is certainly inevitable. Because there is no external human agency to which churches might appeal for resolution, divisive issues must be addressed at the local level. There is no place to hide, nobody else to hide behind. This is an inconvenient truth. It can make Baptists unattractive, hard to explain to more hierarchical groups. When there is anxiety over this image problem, a crushing conformity can be imposed, in an attempt to suppress open conflict. The temptation is to deny the division, or starve it of oxygen, or construct structures which arrogate decisions to themselves in the name of 'leadership'.

Yet the cases studied in this book have consistently revealed the resilience of Baptist communities. To be sure, churches do get damaged by severe conflict - but they rarely fail from it. Baptist congregations are more likely to die out of quiet indifference. The desire for connection is as strangely powerful at denominational level. It is impossible to specify quite what it is which holds Baptists together, other than the fact that they seem to prefer it that way.

Colonial Baptists did not arrive in an ordered fashion. In many cases churches, once formed, found that the effects of varying backgrounds and different assumptions led to profound stresses, often exacerbated by unpredictable or poorly equipped ministers. Conflict, sometimes severe conflict, flashed easily in such environments. It can't have been fun, but the gradual refinement of the Baptist vision could not have taken place without it. A clearer, confident and fruitful vision did appear after World War One, leading eventually (though with some pain) to a more homogenous group by the 1950s. Today, the sheer diversity of the denomination makes it, in that respect at least, more like the colonial churches than those of the mid-twentieth century. Do we risk a return to such frontier turmoil? We can do without the excesses of James Thornton. We have come to accept regional variation and have found ways to hear and respect the concerns of prickly radicals such as William Birch. Nonetheless we must still expect that change and development – life - will emerge out of the contest of ideas and practices, visions and dreams.

Maybe, then, it is time to put in a good word for conflict, gently conducted. In this we are fortunate in that our history provides an outstanding example in the relationship between J.J. North and Joseph Kemp. These two unlikely allies disagreed on many fronts, sometimes publically, but their ability to do so whilst valuing the other is surely a model. Contrast the destructive raging of Forde Carlisle. On the other hand, when, out of shame or a concern for propriety, New Zealand Baptists denied the pain in their history they began to live out of an illusion. When we today are embarrassed by vigorous argument we do the same. Movement, denomination or church, we become lifeless - as J.K. Archer, quoting Tennyson, put it: 'faultily faultless, icily regular, splendidly null, dead perfection, no more.'

A fruitful sense of identity can emerge, if energy can be given to it and space is made to wrestle with ideas and difference. We remain, however, caught in the atrophy of mid-century. The drift to more hierarchical leadership in recent decades has muted debate and dissension. In a desire to avoid conflict we risk preventing real change. That is fatal, as Baptists, by nature, must reinvent themselves constantly. Such reconversion does not emerge out of an imposed uniformity – nor, conversely, from an unchallenged diversity. Troublesome questions cannot be ignored, but neither should we endeavour artificially to find 'one voice'. Unity, it seems, cannot be forged, it can only be grown.

Index

Adams, A.S. (1861-1937), 91, 92, 93, 112, 122, 171
Adams, T.W. (1842-1919), 23
Adelaide (North) Baptist Church, 169
Albertland/ Minniesdale, 9, 10, 19, 23
Aldridge, George 67
Ambury, Ray (d.1918), 148
Anglican/Church of England, 1, 7, 8, 10, 20, 83, 84, 105, 109, 127, 136, 142, 149, 163, 183, 231
Archer, John Kendrick (1865-1949), xxiii, 13, 62, 82, 89, 90, 92, 94, 95-112, 115, 116, 151, 161, 167, 172, 189, 253
Armstrong, H.T. 104
Arnold, Rollo, 5
Auckland Baptist Church/ Tabernacle, 12-13, 23, 24, 27, 33-47 *passim*, 48-62 *passim*, 64, 71, 73-75, 78, 120, 139, 149, 151-154, 157, 169, 182, 194, 196-200, 201, 209
Auxiliaries of the Baptist Union of N.Z., 147
- Auckland, 149, 184
- Otago & Southland, 30, 118
- Canterbury, 30, 32
- Central Districts, 30, 184, 185, 188
Averill, Bishop Alfred Walter (1865-1957) 142, 143, 201

Bacon, Annie (d. 1946), 173
Baptism, 11, 66, 118, 133, 144, 145
Baptist identity, ix, xxi, 14, 32, 62, 82, 116, 120, 131, 132, 143, 150, 234, 236, 238, 239, 248-250, 251-253 and *passim*
Baptist Magazine, 6, 8, 9, 12, 19, 20
Baptist Ministers Wives' Union (B.M.W.U.), 123-124.
Baptist Union of New Zealand, xvii, xx, 10-14, 19, 23, 24, 27-33, 36, 40, 45, 53, 58, 60, 61, 63-80 *passim*, 82, 85, 86, 90, 92, 105, 108, 110, 115-145 *passim*, 146, 147, 163, 167, 168, 171, 172, 174, 176, 178, 180-194 *passim*, 195-216 *passim*, 219, 226, 237-244, 247, 250-251
Baptist Women's League (B.W.L.), 124, 131
Baptist Women's Missionary Union (B.W.M.U.), 123, 125, 126, 127, 128, 130, 131
Barnett, E., 44
Barry, Samuel (d.1963), 198
Barry, Walter (1871-1953), 173-175, 177
Battley, Frederick (d. 1904), 42, 44
Batts, E.W. 117, 157, 226
Batts, Miss Vera,124
Batts, Mrs T., 57
Bebbington, David, 81, 109
Beckingsale, Emma (1870-1955), 127
Beilby, George T., xxiii, 108, 117, 123, 172, 177, 178
Belich, James, 1, 3, 14, 45, 88, 178, 179
Bennett, Mrs S.B., 125, 126, 128, 130
Bible Class, 126, 127, 162
Bible in Schools, 82-93 *passim*
Bible Standard, 67, 68, 72, 73, 74
Bible Training Institute (B.T.I.), 81, 120, 149, 150, 153, 157, 159, 163, 221, 222, 229, 238
Birch, William (d. 1900), 13, 48, 52-62, 65, 78, 146, 167, 253
Blaikie, James, 86
Blaiklock, E.M. (1903-1983), 142, 143, 198, 209
Blair, Justice, 192, 193
Borden, Paul, 246, 247
Boreham, F.W. (1871-1959), 137-139
Brainsby, A.T. 168-172, 174, 178

Brash, Alan, 206
Bray, Thomas (d. 1900) 35, 71
Brethren (Plymouth), 23, 54, 56, 117, 143, 154, 203, 218
Brethrenism, 14, 143, 213
Breward, Ian, 83, 84, 85, 87, 90
Bright, Charles 134
Bristol, 218
Brookes family, 10
Brown, Charles Crisp (c1849-1926), 13, 30, 60, 63-80 *passim*, 116, 134,
Brown, Ian, 244-246, 247
Browning, Robert, 101
Brunswick Baptist Church (Melbourne), 218

Church Missionary Society (C.M.S.), 7, 8
Cambridge Baptist Church, 12, 14, 24, 33-47*passim*, 48, 52, 65
Campbell, R.J., 97
Canterbury, xx, 13, 19-32 *passim*,, 33, 44, 46, 48, 60, 65, 68, 75, 76, 77, 79, 82, 95, 96, 102, 103, 116, 123, 124, 132, 133, 134, 143, 167, 174, 176, 177
Canterbury Association, 20, 26, 28, 30, 31, 32, 48, 167
Canterbury Baptist, 13, 20, 25, 26, 27, 28, 30, 32, 65, 95, 103, 132, 133, 134
Canterbury Evangelist, 26, 28, 133
Carey, W. 185, 200,
Carlisle, B.F. (1881-1962), 202-207, 253
Carter, Charles (1828-1914) 35, 67, 175
Catholic Church, 1, 83, 109, 117, 118, 144, 206
Caversham Baptist Church, 24, 118
Census of Population, 249
Central Mission (Christchurch), 61-62
Chandler, A.V.G., 118
Christian Order, 142
Churches of Christ, 67, 72, 77, 143, 201

Clifford, Ayson (1912-1999), xxiii, 39-40, 42, 53, 58, 139, 159-160, 207, 209, 210, 212, 217, 218 219, 224, 225-234
Clifford, John (1836-1923) , 89, 97, 98, 99, 101, 102, 104, 105, 108, 109,
Coates, Dandeson 7, 8
Colenso, William, 7
College, 13, 14, 119, 120, 123, 141, 146-64 *passim*,, 195, 196, 201, 202, 207-213, 217-234 *passim*, 235, 242
Collins, A H. (1853-1930) 62, 85-92
Commission of Enquiry, Union (Napier), 180-193 (Tabernacle) 198-200
Congregationalism, 31, 65, 85, 118, 119, 145
Congregationalist, 7, 10, 65, 87
Cornford, P.H. (1818-1901) 24, 26, 50, 67
Crickett, Samuel, 43, 44, 47
Crosby, H.J.F. 104, 105
Crozier, J.T. 141, 157, 211, 235

Dallaston, Charles (1852-1934), 28, 32, 60, 133, 134
Daniell, Henry Cooper (1817-1895), 10, 11
Davis, James Upton (c1837-1915), 12, 133
Deaconesses, 124, 128, 131, 222, 227, 228
Dewdney, Arthur (1864-1915), 28, 29, 135-9
Diaspora, understandings of 2-6
Dick, Thomas (1823-1900), 95, 112
Dissent, Nonconformity, Free Churches, 9, 13, 25, 72, 81, 84, 89, 94, 108, 109, 111, 112, 116, 167, 200
Doke, J.J., (1861-1913), 62
Dolamore, Decimus (1819-1912) 10-12, 30, 48
Down-grade Controversy (England), 70-72
Drew, W. 92

Driver, Annie (d.1943), 125, 131
Driver, Harry Herbert ('H.H.') (1858-1943) 86-87, 91-93, 125, 138-139, 141, 144, 175, 177, 228, 233
Duncumb, C.W., 190-192
Dunedin, 22-25

Eade, B.N. (1901-1988), 156, 162
Edgar, S.L. xxiii, 70, 207, 226, 242
Edger, Samuel (1823-1882), 9, 10
Education Acts, 80, 83, 105, 109
Elliot, Howard Leslie (1877-1956), 95, 109, 116, 117
England, xx, 2, 3, 4, 5, 6, 7, 8, 9, 10, 11, 12, 19, 20, 22, 25, 26, 28, 35, 54, 55, 59, 64, 65, 72, 79, 81, 89, 92, 96, 99, 100, 102, 104, 108, 109, 118, 132, 148, 169, 197, 205, 207, 218, 219, 226
Englishness, 4, 5
Epsom Baptist Church, 126, 129
Ethnicity, 4
Evangelicalism, 81, 144
Evangelism, 120
Ewen, Keith, 190

Fairburn, Miles, 45, 46
Fraser, J.G., 89, 92
Fraser, T.E., 138
Free Church, Dissent, Nonconformity, 9, 13, 25, 72, 81, 84, 89, 94, 108, 109, 111, 112, 116, 167, 200
Fundamentalism, 157
Fursdon, R.L., 157
Gainsford, Emily (d.1965), 127, 131
Gandy, Thelma, 156, 162, 222
Gerrish, T.J., 42
Gibbs, W.J., 141
Gray, R.S. (1863-1922), 86, 87, 91, 92, 122, 138, 167, 171, 174, 235
Greendale Baptist Church, 23, 25, 26, 28, 35, 44, 68, 176
Griffiths, G.O., 28, 29, 36-44 *passim*
Grigg, E.W., 156, 160
Grimsby, 96, 97, 99, 104, 105, 106, 109

'Growing Healthy Churches', 246, 247
Gustafson, Barry, 95, 96, 97, 98, 102, 110, 117
Guy, Laurie, xxii, xxiii, 62, 227, 239, 240

Hambly, Gordon, 227
Harris, John & James, 37
Harrison, E. (Grimsby), 96, 98, 99, 105, 106
Harry, F.E., (d. 1930), 149, 161
Hereford St Baptist Church, 27, 133
Hiddlestone, John, 149
Hill, Phillip (d. 1876), 25, 26
Hill, T.F., 53, 58
Hinton, W.H., 140
Hobart Baptist Church, 8, 138
Hodge, A.J., 120, 194, 197-199, 200, 201, 208, 213
Hokowhitu Baptist Church, 243
Holland, H.E., 97
Holland, S.G., 103, 107
Home Mission, 28, 29, 30, 32, 44, 128, 147, 148, 181
Home Missionaries, 147, 148
Horn, - (Nelson), 10
Houghton, J. 36, 38, 40, 41, 42, 43
Howie, Ivan, 232-233
Hughes, H.B. 148
Hughes, George (d.1957), 172-174, 177
Hyde & ors vs Baptist Union, 142-143

InterVarsity Fellowship (I.V.F)., 208
Incorporation, Act of, 13, 121, 122, 182, 192
Ingold, S.R., (c1858-1928), 30, 76
Ings, John, 173-175, 180-188 *passim*
Invercargill, 99, 102, 109, 110, 157
Isit, L.M., 95
James Guy, 85
Jenkin, Stanley, 140
Jenkins, Luke Hampden (1908-1988), 120, 201, 202, 207-213, 217, 218, 219, 220, 233, 238
Johnson Miss, 37
Johnston, George, 28, 29

Jones, C.D. 128
Jones, J. Farquarson,147
Jones, Lindsay, 247, 248

Kemp, Joseph (1872-1933), 81, 120, 149, 150-153, 157-159, 164, 181, 196, 197, 209, 235, 238, 241, 253
Kirk, Thomas 29, 112
Knox Theological Hall, 147, 160

Labour, 93, 96, 97, 102, 106, 109, 110, 115, 242
Labour Party, 96, 102, 106
Lange, David, 242
Lanyon, Percy (1890-1955), 14, 176, 177, 200, 211, 213
Larrington, W., 184, 185
Larsen, Timothy, 81-92 *passim*
Lascelles, Florence, 123
Lascelles, M.W.P. (1864-1939) 122, 123, 131, 180-194 *passim*, 202, 235
Leadership Models, 242-248
Legislative Council, 89, 96, 97, 98, 99, 100, 101, 102, 104, 106, 107, 111
Lincoln Road Baptist Church, 26, 27
Linwood Baptist Church, 32, 161
Litchfield, 36
Livingstone, Margaret (d. 1976), 156

Macgeorge, Rosalie (c1859-1891) 172
Machattie, O.G. (1884-1968) 13, 142, 147, 180-194 *passim*, 200
MacLeod, A.H., 27, 28, 32, 49, 50, 51, 61, 117, 226
Malvern Hills, 21
Maori, 2, 51, 84, 91, 127, 128
Marks, Gerard, 242-244
Matthews, Seering H. (1840-1924) 36, 41, 43, 47, 53, 54
Mazengarb, O.C., 178
Mazzini, Giuseppi (1805-1872) 100-102
McCarthy, Angela, 2, 3
McIntyre, Carl, 205-206
McKenzie, James, 83, 84
McKinnon, Alex., 37, 38
McLaren, Alexander, 53, 58

Methodism, 25, 26, 27, 118
Methodism/Methodists, 1, 10, 25, 26, 27, 28, 84, 88, 118 137, 154, 163, 221, 223, 249
Miller, Diane, 227
Milner, H.W.,182, 184, 185
Ministry, 7, 13, 93, 128, 142, 157, 187, 222, 248
Modernism, 157, 206
Morris, Samuel, 140
Morton, Robert, 52, 60, 133, 146, 167-169
Mt Eden Baptist Church, 35, 71, 73, 74, 95
Muirhead, John, 89
Muldoon, Robert, 242
Mullins, E.Y. 205

Napier Baptist Church, 13, 89, 99, 106, 109, 122, 142, 180-194 *passim*, 197, 200
Nash, Walter, 103
National Council of Churches (N.C.C.), 142, 143, 201, 202, 206
Nelson Baptist Church, 10-12, 129, 135, 143
'Nelson System', 83, 86, 87
Nettles, Tom. xix
'New Theology', 97
New Zealand Baptist Missionary Society (N.Z.B.M.S.), 14, 115, 116, 125, 127, 128, 129, 134, 135, 139, 151, 172-178, 180, 244
Nonconformity/Nonconformists, 9, 13, 25, 72, 81, 84, 89, 94, 108, 109, 111, 112, 116, 167, 200
North, Alfred (1846-1924), 70, 71 74, 75, 86, 95, 115-119, 134, 147, 149-152, 173-178
North, Charles 174
North, John James (J.J.) (1871-1960), xxiii, 14, 92, 93, 109, 112, 115-121, 122, 131, 132, 139-145, 146-164 *passim*, 167, 169, 170, 171, 172, 174, 177, 179, 192, 193, 194, 195, 197, 199, 200, 201, 202, 207,

209, 217, 219, 228, 233, 235, 236, 237, 242, 250, 251, 253
North, Lawrence Alfred (L.A.) (1903-1980), 211, 212, 213, 229, 237-241, 250
North-East Valley Baptist Church, 126

Oamaru, 118
Otago, 19, 23, 24, 30, 31, 51
Outlook, 84, 90, 137, 138, 169, 237
Oxford Terrace/Christchurch Baptist Church, 10, 11, 12, 13, 27, 32, 48-62 *passim*, 66, 86, 133, 138, 139, 167-169, 196, 200.

Pacifism, 236
Parsons J.L., 12, 24
Payne, Ernest, 63, 205, 226
Pentecostalism, 226
Peters, Harold (c1869-1902), 119, 137, 138, 147, 235
Pillow, Hopestill (1857-1895), 172
Pole, William (1814-1879), 26-28, 133
Ponsonby Baptist Church, 85, 91, 161
Presbyterian Church/Polity/People, 10, 23, 83, 84, 88, 118, 142, 147, 154, 168, 206, 212, 213, 249
Primitive Methodist, 23, 25, 26, 27, 82, 84, 85
Protestant Political Association, 95, 116

Radford, F.H. (d.1933), 126
'Rambler', 126
Randall, Ameila Mary (1844-1930), 181-184, 219
Rangiora Baptist Church, 11, 32
Rawdon College, 115, 134
Reeves, William Pember, 1
Regents Park College, 207
Regional Superintendents, 244, 245
Reynolds, Norman, 230
Rice, Frank, 181, 184, 185, 191, 192
Richmond Baptist Church (Auckland), 126, 147

Robertson, Murray, 245
Roberts-Thomson, Gwen, 218
Roberts-Thomson, Edward (1909-1987) 213, 217-225 *passim*
Rollings, W.S., (1871-1944), 140, 175, 176
Ruskin, John (1819-1900), 99, 100, 102

Student Christian Movement (S.C.M.), 208-209
Salvation Army, 41, 42, 43, 44
Sargeson, Frank, 179
Saunders, John (1806-1859), 7
Saunders, W. 87
Sawle, James (1835-1920), 26-28, 95, 133
Scott, Manford, 37
Scroggie, W. Graham, 197
Selwyn, Bishop George (1809-1878), 2
Selwyn County, 21, 22
Shackleford, Lewis, 68, 69, 70, 72, 74, 78, 134, 135
Shalders, Richard (1824-1914) 56-62
Sheffield, 21, 26
Silcock, A.L., 198, 200, 210
Simpson, E.P.Y., 174, 176, 177, 231, 232, 231, 232
Simpson, J.E. (Ewen) (1906-1992), 157, 161, 163, 200, 201, 202, 209, 212
Smith, Brian 22, 242
Smith, L.B.J. 140, 199
Smyth, T.W., 28
South Malvern Baptist Church, 26, 29
Southland, 30, 99
Spedding, Belle (d. 1931). 128, 129
Spencer, William, 134
Spurgeon, Thomas (1856-1917), xxiii, 24, 34, 35, 36, 42, 52, 53, 59, 60, 64, 66, 67, 71, 73, 74, 75, 78, 79, 120, 196, 241
Spurgeon, Charles (1834-1892), 13, 53, 54, 55, 57, 58, 59, 60, 63, 64, 67, 68, 69, 70, 71, 73, 74, 75, 78, 118, 133, 135, 196, 197

St John's College, 231
Stenhouse, John, 2
Stepney College, 9, 24
Stevens, H.T., 198
Stewart, D.H.. 160
Strong, Augustus Hopkins (1836-1921), 160, 203-205
Students Committee, 147-163 *passim*
Church Life Survey, 249-250
Sydenham Baptist Church, 110, 111, 161, 189.

Takle, John (1872-1939), 125, 129
Thames Baptist Church, 79, 86, 134, 137
Thompson, R.J. (1924-2000), 156, 228, 242
Thompson, Shirley, 228
Thornton, James, 12, 13, 48-62, 65, 146, 167, 190, 253
Timaru Baptist Church, 19, 30, 65-79 *passim*, 162, 180, 181, 185, 187, 190
Took, Eliza, 37
Trewhellan, T. 38, 41
Troeltsch, Ernst, 89
Turner, H.R.,140
United Labour Leader, 110

Varley, Henry, 54-56
Vivian St Baptist Church, 109, 168-172, 196, 200

Waddell, Rutherford, 90
Wade, William (1802-1891), 7, 8, 19
Waikato, 33, 34, 44
Walker, F.W., 135
Walker, John, 169
Wanganui Baptist Church, 68, 209
Wayland, Francis 205
Webb, A.W. (1839-1902), 24, 34, 134
Wellesley St Baptist Church, 33-35, 48, 50
Wellington, 19, 21, 22, 24, 25, 26, 29, 32, 77, 107, 123, 143, 149, 150, 200, 208, 209, 244
Wesleyans, 23, 25, 61, 81, 84, 87
White, Edward, 65
Whytock, David, 34, 35, 40
Williams, John, 12, 24
Williams, T.A. 86-92
Wilson, J.G., 36, 37, 38
Wilson, B.M., 157
Winslade, Brian, 247
Wood, N.R. (1907-1979) 96, 103, 142, 161, 200, 201, 202, 203, 204, 207, 208, 209, 210, 211, 235
Woolley, W.R. (1850-1923), 30, 41, 44
World Council of Churches (W.C.C.), 201-206
'Wrox', 125, 173

Young, Robert J.C., 3-5

Earlier versions of some of the studies in this book may be found in the following articles. My thanks to the editors of these journals for permission to revise and incorporate previously published material.

'Pulpit or Podium? J.K. Archer and the Dilemma of Christian Politics in New Zealand', *NZJBR* 1 (October 1996): 26-46; '"Down-grade with a vengeance": New Light on a Tabernacle Controversy', *NZJBR* 2 (October 1997): 79-96; 'Downgrade Down Under: Conflict and Cohesion among New Zealand Baptists', *Baptist Quarterly*, XXXVII/7 (July 1998): 351-363; 'Cohesion and Conflict in 1880s Cambridge', *NZJBR* 4 (October 1999): 3-21; 'A Baptist in the Nest: William Wade and the C.M.S. in New Zealand', *NZJBR* 5 (October 2000): 67-83; 'The Basis of Union: New Zealand Baptists forge a Denomination in the 1940s,' *Journal of Religious History* 27/1 (February 2003): 67-82. 'Joseph Kemp and the N.Z. Baptist College' *NZJBR*, Vol. 8, Oct. 2003: 32-51; '"Better to Ignore the Past:" New Zealand Baptists and Historical Memory,' *Fides et Historia* 36 (2004): 41-52; 'Baptist Development in Colonial New Zealand,' *NZJBR* 9 (October 2004): 3-22; 'Free Church Ecclesiology and Public Policy in New Zealand 1890-1914,' *PJBR* 1/1 (October 2005); 'The *NZ Baptist* as an Agent of Denominational Identity 1874-1960,' *PJBR* 3/1 (April 2007): 23-39; 'Hesitating too long: the New Zealand Baptist College, 1952-1974,' *PJBR* 6/2 (October 2010): 31-66.

www.ingramcontent.com/pod-product-compliance
Lightning Source LLC
Chambersburg PA
CBHW030414100426
42812CB00028B/2960/J